ESOTERIC
FREEMASONRY

© Patricia Bourin

About the Author

Jean-Louis de Biasi is an author, lecturer, and philosopher who has studied various topics of spirituality since the 1970s and has been initiated into the highest degrees of several Western initiatic traditions. Introduced very early into the Ordo Aurum Solis, de Biasi became the tenth Lifetime Grand Master in 2003.

De Biasi's philosophical and spiritual tradition is rooted in Neoplatonic and Hermetic affiliations, and includes masters of the tradition such as Plato, Proclus, Iamblicus, the Emperor Julian, Pletho, and Ficino, to name a few. He is also the head of the Ordre Kabbalistique de la Rose-Croix (the Kabbalistic Order of the Rose-Cross, O.K.R.C.).

He was initiated into Freemasonry and raised in 1992. He is a 32° Scottish Rite Freemason (Southern Jurisdiction, US) and Royal Arch Mason. Before joining American Freemasonry, he received the highest degrees in Freemasonry in Europe, including the degrees of Egyptian Freemasonry (33°–95°-AA). He specializes in esoteric Freemasonry and rituals. He is also reorganizing ancient rare Masonic systems of high degrees.

De Biasi is invited regularly to various countries where he gives lectures and workshops. He is the author of several books in French. He has been writing in English for Llewellyn since 2010, and his books have been translated into several languages.

To read more about Jean-Louis de Biasi, please visit him online at www.debiasi.org and www.facebook.com/jeanlouis.debiasi.

ESOTERIC FREEMASONRY

RITUALS & PRACTICES FOR A DEEPER UNDERSTANDING

JEAN-LOUIS DE BIASI

Llewellyn Publications
Woodbury, Minnesota

First Edition
Second Printing, 2022

Cover design by Kevin R. Brown
Interior illustrations by Jean-Louis de Biasi
Interior photos credited per photo

Llewellyn Publications is a registered trademark of Llewellyn Worldwide Ltd.

Library of Congress Cataloging-in-Publication Data

Names: Biasi, Jean-Louis de, author.
Title: Esoteric freemasonry : rituals & practices for a deeper understanding
 / by Jean-Louis de Biasi.
Description: First edition. | Woodbury, Minnesota : Llewellyn Worldwide,
 [2018] | Includes bibliographical references.
Identifiers: LCCN 2018005406 (print) | LCCN 2018003121 (ebook) | ISBN
 9780738752907 (ebook) | ISBN 9780738748481 (alk. paper)
Subjects: LCSH: Freemasonry—History. | Freemasonry—Rituals.
Classification: LCC HS403 (print) | LCC HS403 .B45 2018 (ebook) | DDC
 366/.12—dc23
LC record available at https://lccn.loc.gov/2018005406

Llewellyn Worldwide Ltd. does not participate in, endorse, or have any authority or responsibility concerning private business transactions between our authors and the public.

All mail addressed to the author is forwarded, but the publisher cannot, unless specifically instructed by the author, give out an address or phone number.

Any internet references contained in this work are current at publication time, but the publisher cannot guarantee that a specific location will continue to be maintained. Please refer to the publisher's website for links to authors' websites and other sources.

Llewellyn Publications
A Division of Llewellyn Worldwide Ltd.
2143 Wooddale Drive
Woodbury, MN 55125-2989
www.llewellyn.com

Printed in the United States of America

Other Books by Jean-Louis de Biasi

Secrets and Practices of the Freemasons
(Llewellyn, 2011)

The Divine Arcana of the Aurum Solis
(Llewellyn, 2011)

Rediscover the Magick of the Gods and Goddesses
(Llewellyn, 2014)

The Magical Use of Prayer Beads
(Llewellyn, 2016)

Hidden Mandala Coloring Book
(Llewellyn, 2017)

Acknowledgments

The writing of a book is often a solitary activity. However, it cannot be done without the help and support of several people.

First, I would like to thank my wife, Patricia, for helping me in various research developed in this book.

I would like to offer my grateful thanks to Pierre Mollier, specialist in Freemasonry, director of the library of the Grand Orient de France, and curator of the Museum of Freemasonry in Paris.

I would also like to thank Darius A. Spieth, author of the book *Napoleon's Sorcerers*, for the discussions we had about the subject of his book.

I also thank Florence Mothe, owner of Château de Mongenan (France) and curator of a fascinating Masonic collection, for her warm welcome during the research for this book.

Finally, I want to thank my publisher, Bill Krause, and the team of professionals at Llewellyn Publications. Without them, nothing would be possible.

Contents

Figures

Chapter 12: The Masonic Regalia

Chapter 14: Rituals and Practices of the Three Degrees

Chapter 15: The High Degrees of Egyptian Freemasonry

Chapter 17: Consecration of the Lodge

Chapter 18: Cagliostro and the Mysteries of the Prophetess

Foreword
by Chic Cicero and Sandra Tabatha Cicero

The roots of Freemasonry are swathed in mystery and speculation. Over the last three centuries, Masonic authors have advanced numerous conjectures into Masonry's beginnings, suggesting that the answer lies in ancient Egypt, Rome, the Knights Templar, and Solomon's Temple. Contemporary literature overflows with Masonic intrigue, conspiracy theories, and whodunits. Current research indicates that the origins of Freemasonry are likely to be found among the medieval stonemason's guilds of Scotland and England. Nevertheless, Freemasonry has substantial historical ties with esotericism, providing the basic structure for most of the occult groups that followed it. The entire lodge framework, officers, degree system, ceremonial patterning and floor work, symbolism, secret passwords and handshakes, signs and knocks, grade initiations, ritual drama reenactment, and sometimes even the exact wording of certain speeches in Freemasonry have all been adopted by esoteric and occult groups of the modern era.

Due to increased interest in all things Masonic, many new lodges formed during the latter part of the 1800s. According to Masonic historian S. Brent Morris, more than 150 new fraternal organizations were formed in the USA from 1885 to 1900, and by 1920 half of America's adult population—thirty million people—were members of a least one of the 800 or so "secret" fraternities that were embedded in the fabric of the country's social life.

Outside of a brief resurgence here and there, membership in most American Masonic groups began a slow drop after 1930, a decline that continues to this day. The "graying" of the lodge membership is an inescapable fact not lost on those who love Freemasonry. Masonic newsletters are full of essays decrying the wane in membership and giving ideas on how to get young people, particularly young men, interested in Masonry again. Many of these articles bemoan the current times we live in, wherein young men have far too many modern distractions and time-intensive responsibilities that keep them from joining the lodge. The usual remedies proposed in these essays stress that Masonic meetings should be made more interesting, more family events and dinners should be planned, networking and communications between the brothers should be encouraged, and more attempts at community outreach should be proffered. While such efforts may bring in a few more members, they do not begin to address what we feel is the primary problem: many young men (and women!) who seek out Freemasonry today do so because they are interested in the *esoteric* side of Masonry.

We've heard the same story so many times we've lost count: an eager young man asks about joining the Freemasons because he wants to learn about esotericism, only to be discouraged by an older Mason to such an extent that the light of enthusiasm slowly but clearly drains out of his eyes and he never returns to the lodge. Once even *we* were told by a high-ranking Mason to "stay away from that Qabalah stuff." While philanthropy and social improvement are unquestionably worthy goals for many Masons, others yearn for something more; they seek further Light in the form of the ancient mysteries, theurgy, hermetic knowledge, and an increase in psychic awareness. Luckily, a few Masonic lodges here and there are returning to their arcane roots and making the lodge a welcoming place for esoteric thought and practice. As a result, some of those eager young men are staying in lodges that are more accommodating to the mystical Mason.

Jean-Louis de Biasi's book *Esoteric Freemasonry: Rituals & Practices for a Deeper Understanding* could not have come at a better time. The focus of this text is on an individual approach to the practice of Freemasonry. There is nothing inherently gender-specific about ancient wisdom teachings; their knowledge is open to all with eyes to see and ears to hear. As the author explains, "The purpose of esoteric Freemasonry is to unveil to the initiate the mysteries of life and death through initiations and efficient individual practices." This more mystical type of Masonry seeks to move beyond the mere theatrical form and ritualized reenactment that often characterizes its exoteric cousin. Additionally, esoteric Masons are more inclined to have a personal lodge space in their home for their own private use. This book offers men and women the opportunity to study and experience esoteric Masonic Light in a solo fashion, outside of the lodge setting where members of different groups and jurisdictions may not have the ability to work together.

One of the primary forms of esoteric Masonry covered is Egyptian Freemasonry. De Biasi provides readers with all the tools necessary to begin their own regimen of Egyptian

Masonic practice, including regalia and other items for the lodge space. Simple yet effective rites for self-initiation are paired with equally efficient meditations, rituals, and exercises designed to facilitate the practitioner's work.

Masonic author Carl H. Claudy once wrote, "It is not only with the brain and with the mind that the initiate must take Freemasonry but also with the heart." This is certainly true of esoteric Masonry and especially true for any solo Masonic practice. Jean-Louis de Biasi has done a great service to the reader by providing the practical keys to unlock these timeless truths for the individual enthusiast.

—*Chic Cicero and Sandra Tabatha Cicero*

Introduction

This book is about esoteric Freemasonry and, more precisely, Egyptian Freemasonry. I am sure that you have already heard this expression. Maybe you have even heard or read about what is presented here as an aspect of Freemasonry. As a matter of fact, Freemasonry today often talks about esotericism being a part of this tradition, or even a marginal section of it. It is true that esoteric Freemasonry is not all Freemasonry. Although your heart is not your whole body, it is the essential organ that keeps you alive. Esotericism is the heart and the essence of Freemasonry. Without it, life will disappear and this organization will become a body without a soul.

To keep this essence alive and in good health, we have to be aware of its existence and its function. The consequences of not taking care of it, or denying its importance, could be huge for the tradition itself and its initiates. I am always surprised to see how often Grand Officers or officers know so little about esotericism and its role in an initiatic tradition. We may be surprised to realize that this aspect of Freemasonry has been minimized or hidden by the main Masonic organizations.

I am not saying that Masonic organizations do not mention the esoteric aspect of their tradition or the other branches of Freemasonry. I am saying that most of the time they do not really know what they are talking about. It is easy to understand the main misconception. *Esotericism* in Freemasonry is usually taken literally. This word is understood as a synonym for the term *symbol*. The latter is seen as something hidden, veiled by the visible aspect of a representation. For example, a Masonic tool such as a square will be associated with the meaning of rectitude. Consequently, the square becomes the symbol of this virtue. From this simple understanding, it could be easy to deduce that esoteric Freemasonry is the learning of the symbols allowing the initiate to find the hidden secret. Obviously, this is what most of the Grand Officers are teaching very seriously. If such assumption is correct, a simple dictionary should suffice. Masonic books, rituals, and initiations would be useless.

As a matter of fact, this is not the case, because esotericism cannot be marginalized in such a way. Esoteric Freemasonry has been a very powerful part of Freemasonry from the beginning of its history. As you may have noticed, I used the expression *esoteric Freemasonry* instead of just *esotericism*. The reason is simple but should be highlighted. When *esoteric* and *Freemasonry* are associated, that means we are talking about a specific branch that is still part of mainstream Freemasonry. That has been the case from the beginning of this tradition. Several lineages can be found in esoteric Freemasonry. They all have specific rituals that have been developed to maintain occult traditions from a time before the official birth of Freemasonry. Some of them are more focused on Qabalah, whereas the main and more original part is known as Egyptian Freemasonry. If, as I wrote before, esotericism in its full meaning is the heart of this tradition, then this branch should be the place where the secret keys can be found. It should be the Holy of Holies, the secret Naos that every Mason is looking for. But before approaching this sacred sanctuary, rituals and practices should be used to purify and train the initiate. This is the real essence of what can be called an initiatic tradition. This is what the founders of esoteric and Egyptian Freemasonry intended to do. However, this is not what you can find in most of the Masonic lodges around the world.

Over the years, Freemasonry has become something else. At best, this organization has developed into a philanthropic organization using a ritual inspired by the Bible. At worst, it has become an organized power aiming to eradicate or at least control the esoteric branches of Freemasonry. In some countries, such as the United States of America, the main opponent to defeat at all costs is Egyptian Freemasonry. It will be very important to explain in detail the reasons behind this obsession and to highlight the good and bad of this specific branch of Freemasonry. But at this point you may think that I am introducing here another conspiracy theory, this time one inside Freemasonry itself. This is why I want to give you only one example among many. I will come back to all that with more detail later in this book.

The rites called *Memphis* and *Misraim* have been an important part of Egyptian Freemasonry. They are present almost everywhere on the planet in various forms. In the United States the rite of Memphis was introduced in 1856. Then associated with Misraim as *Memphis-Misraim*, it became active in 1861 and continued to work until the First World War.

Then in 1932 one of the Grand Officers of the Egyptian Masonic Rite of Memphis (96°) invested some of his friends to the high degree (95°) and reactivated a Sovereign Sanctuary of the Egyptian Masonic Rite of Memphis.

Then the Sovereign Sanctuary held a meeting to surrender the Sovereignty of its Rites for the purpose of being absorbed by an organization called the *Grand College of Rites for the United States of America* about to be formed. Officially, this new structure was presented as "a regular Masonic body, dedicated to preserving the history and rituals of defunct and inactive Masonic orders." But the second article of three is "the elimination of sporadic efforts to resuscitate or perpetuate Rites, Systems and Orders of Freemasonry in the United States, except to bring them under control of the Grand College of Rites." Of course, one of the main targets was every esoteric Masonic organization and, more precisely, Egyptian Freemasonry. This is one of the main reasons that this essential part of Freemasonry is so unknown by most people and even Masons. When you have such a monopoly and what seems to be a conspiracy, it is difficult to compete and tell the truth.

As I said previously, this is only one example among others. When I discovered such major objects of this important and well-established Masonic organization, I was stunned! As a Freemason myself, initiated in several rites, having received the highest degree of Egyptian Freemasonry when I lived in France, I knew that Masonic principles are different from that. Freemasonry should be an institution of tolerance, working to improve our virtues and helping all men to become better men. Everyone is free and freedom of speech is a right in most democratic countries. We can expect Masons to have the same rights. If Egyptian Freemasonry and other esoteric rites are the subject of such strong opposition, it is important to know why! Nobody implements and maintains such power without a clear motive. Esoteric Masonic rituals and organizations seem to have something that make them very dangerous for mainstream Freemasonry. They seem to appear to the latter as a threat against which every effort must be maintained.

Like me, you can sincerely ask yourself the important question, what it is? What could be so controversial and threatening in the esoteric part of Freemasonry? Are there particular teachings, practices, or rituals that we cannot find in classic Freemasonry?

The answer is *yes* to all that!

Yes, Egyptian Freemasonry represents an original part of this tradition as old as the mainstream organizations that are wealthy and well established.

Yes, Egyptian Freemasonry contains authentic teachings coming from the Ancient Schools of Mysteries.

Yes, Egyptian Freemasonry teaches inner practices that should be used individually and in groups.

Yes, Egyptian Freemasonry and esotericism are capable of providing a curriculum that allows you to know yourself and ascend to spiritual planes.

Yes, Egyptian Freemasonry is a branch of what we can call esoteric Freemasonry.

Yes, Egyptian Freemasonry is still alive and has a lot to give to anyone who is interested in a real inner experience.

And this is why Egyptian Freemasonry and esotericism are very often seen as a threat by the Masonic establishment.

From my previous experience in this field and the books I have written in other languages, I can go even further with you today. This book will be an opportunity for you to practice and experiment firsthand with this hidden part of the Masonic tradition. You will be able to realize in detail what is at stake here. You will unveil some of these secrets, not as a historian but as someone who is eager to experiment.

This is the reason why, even though I will give you clear historical references and access to rare details, my goal in this book is to go even further. I want to give you a real opportunity to individually experiment with this school of Freemasonry. You have in your hands a real guide for the solitary practitioner of Egyptian Freemasonry, Mason or not.

It is to this initiation that I invite you today.

Chapter 1

What Freemasonry Really Is

Before beginning this journey into esoteric Freemasonry, it is essential to understand what Freemasonry really is. I am aware that you can easily find definitions online. You can either access Masonic websites or check Google and Wikipedia. You can also read books on this subject. However, I am confident that you will always find the same things. Historians will provide a historical timeline. Masonic organizations will tell you all the good they are doing for every initiate and society as a whole. Detractors will explain how evil the rituals are and how dangerous the organization is. Digging a little more, you will soon discover that the so-called secrets were published a long time ago, in the eighteenth century. Of course, Masons will say that it is not possible to find the real secrets online, such as the signs, passwords, and sacred words. If you try, you will see that they are all there, clearly explained. You may think that you have all the elements you need to understand this tradition. You might say that there is no need now to waste your time on such a subject. In fact, if you have read the introduction to this book, you already know that things are not so simple.

First of all, these explanations are very often linked to a specific country. It is difficult to find online a clear and full vision of this organization worldwide. We know that any Masonic organization has a strong tendency to present a golden picture of what they are and do. Myths and reality are closely intertwined, with very few efforts to distinguish between these two aspects. The same peculiarity is found in the declarations of the detractors. Eventually, you will realize that few rituals and processes have never been published. It can be a surprise to know that, but it is true.

Before introducing you to esoteric Freemasonry, it is essential to give a simple presentation of this tradition. As I will explain in more detail later in the book, I have had the chance to be initiated into several Masonic organizations in France and in other countries including the United States. I have also had the opportunity to present lectures and participate in Masonic ceremonies in various countries and very different cultures. One of my main focuses has always been the study of the rituals in their symbolic and esoteric perspectives. The historic work is included in this research, but always in reference to these occult processes and not as an end per se. I have also been introduced to other initiatic Western organizations over the years. All of these gave me the opportunity to see this initiatic tradition from another perspective. This insight is what I will now share with you, but before we go any further, I need to remind you of a few basic facts about the history of Freemasonry.

Undoubtedly some groups of stonemasons at the end of the Middle Age in Scotland and England were organized into corporations according to some very simple rules.

The oldest Masonic lodge known was called Mary's Chapel. It was founded in 1599 in Edinburgh, Scotland, by someone named Schaw.

Each new apprentice was introduced to the group through the use of a short ritual called the *Ritual of the Ancient Duties (Obligations)*. In this short ceremony, the candidate put his hand on the book of the duties during a discourse reminding him of the duties inscribed in the book, the common rules to follow, and a warning of the consequences if this oath was not obeyed. This ritual continued to be used until the beginning of the eighteenth century (1729). A second ritual appeared also in Scotland around the beginning of the seventeenth century (1637) in the city of Kilwinning. A group of Masons and Calvinists developed a new approach less connected to the real work of Masons. They created a ritual called *Mason's Word*. The book used to listen to the obligation and pronounce the oath was the Bible. Secret signs and words were also present during the ceremony. This ritual was used officially maybe for the first time in the Lodge Kilwinning n°0. Then progressively over the years, rituals evolved to use symbolism, allegories, and more references to the Bible.

Progressively the number of real stonemasons or architects decreased and the number of nobles, gentlemen, artisans, businessmen, and bourgeois increased. The main purposes of the lodges became philanthropy and social assistance. The lodges helped their members in case of sickness or unemployment. In case of death, they helped widows pay for the funerals and other things needed for their orphans. At a time when social security didn't exist, it must have been a relief for the initiate to have the potential support from his brothers. It is sad to see that most of the time today, lodges and Grand Lodges don't do anything to help the brothers and their families in need, as was the case at the beginning. Individual assistance may exist here and there today, but it never quite comes from the Masonic organization itself.

Scholars and nobles began to join the lodges, and discussions on various social subjects began to take place in addition to ritual. You have to remember that rituals at this time were simple. Most of the time they were composed of discourse, oaths, obligations, teachings, and other secret signs.

Then on June 24, 1717, four lodges from London organized a celebration for the Holy Saint John. They created the first Grand Lodge. I don't want to go into the various episodes that took place during the development of this first structure, but it is from this organization that Freemasonry spread to Europe, America, Australia, Africa, and Asia.

After several years of opposition between two parties (called the "old" and the "modern"), an agreement was reached in 1813 creating the organization known today as the *United Grand Lodge of England*. Several landmarks were published as a basis of what should be Freemasonry and, consequently, a Mason. The respect of these landmarks by a Grand Lodge (group of lodges in a country) gives the status of Regular Grand Lodge,[1] officially recognized and validated by the so-called United Grand Lodge of England. The latter grants this recognition to only one Grand Lodge by state or country. It is good to remember that countries with several states or provinces do not have a Grand Lodge for the country, such as the "Grand Lodge of the United States." Each state has a Grand Lodge that is independent and has received validation from London, following a persistent form of colonialism.

---

1. These Grand Lodges are also called *Obediences* in European and African countries.

Chapter 2

The Birth of Freemasonry

Even if this is not obvious at first glance, history told in a linear way can give a false vision of the actual Masonic world. Historical facts are presented linearly because this is the usual way of presenting them but a linear timeline shouldn't be considered to be progress. Going from the first lodge in Scotland to the United Grand Lodge in England and maintaining a king cannot be seen as progress. This is the story of the largest organization of lodges in the world, but surely not the only one.

From the beginning of Freemasonry, every country has developed various rituals, interpretations, teachings, and secret signs. For historical reasons that I will detail later in the book, France has been a place where most of the esoteric Masonic rituals have been created, developed, and organized. Before the spreading of this English recognition, Masonic lodges were created one from another and self-regulated. They followed a set of common rules and were free to adapt their rituals or create new ones. It was a time of creativity. What made a Mason then was simple and relied on discourses, an oath, and a few words and signs. Consequently, it was easy to recognize as a brother someone who shared the same experience, even if the ritual or the words were not exactly the same. The organizations of Grand Lodges appeared progressively as an administrative necessity to maintain communication between the lodges and establish a common ground. This administration progressively created rules that have become more and more restrictive over the years. The creativity, dangerous for any form of central government, was almost eradicated. As you may have noticed, I used the word "almost." In fact, several of these rituals were preserved, sometimes inside

Masonic organizations, sometimes outside. Among these groups, some of them maintain their ritual work from previous centuries to disappear or hide. You have to keep in mind that mainstream Freemasonry doesn't mean there are no other kinds of Freemasonry. Even more importantly, there are several very interesting and respectable groups and materials. Eventually, worldwide Freemasonry appears to be a more complex organization than the previous linear story.

Chapter 3

The Two Masonic Families

Now we have to step back a little and see this Masonic world as it really is. First of all, you must be aware of something important: there are two large families of Freemasons.

The First Family

The first "family" of Freemasons is the largest in the world. This is the group of Grand Lodges that are validated by the United Grand Lodge of England. They have specific requirements and landmarks that are shared by all of these lodges and Grand Lodges. Among these rules, a few have been sources of numerous conflicts over the years. They are still applied even with some minor adaptations in some countries. They were published in full for the first time in 1856 by Dr. Albert Mackey. Among the most significant are the following:

Landmark 18: The candidate shall be man unmutilated, free born, and of mature age. That is to say, a woman, a cripple, or a slave, or one born in slavery is disqualified for initiation into the rites of Freemasonry.

Landmark 19: A belief in the existence of God as the Grand Architect of the Universe is one of the most important landmarks of the order. It has always been deemed essential that a denial of the existence of a Supreme and Superintending Power is an absolute disqualification for initiation.

Landmark 20: Subsidiary to this belief in God, [...] is the belief in a resurrection to a future life. [...] To believe in Freemasonry, and not to believe in a resurrection, would be an absurd anomaly, which could only be excused by the reflection that he who thus confounded his belief and his skepticism was so ignorant of the meaning of both theories as to have no rational foundation for his knowledge of either.

It is interesting to recall that the first Masonic constitutions written and published by Anderson in 1723 didn't mention anything of this kind. It seems that in its evolution, this Masonic family became less and less tolerant of other faiths. Even if the Grand Lodges are not currently keeping all the ancient landmarks, most of them still constitute the foundation of the order. It is clear to anyone who reads these documents that they were written in a specific social and religious context. This is why some of them have been abandoned and others reinterpreted. However most of the three landmarks I highlighted here continue to be considered as absolute references, even with surprising choices. For example, it is common today to initiate someone who is disabled and continue to decline any women candidates. It is also common to stick with the idea that Freemasonry is fundamentally rooted in Judeo-Christian values. In several large countries, this Masonic family continues to segregate according to these beliefs. I must highlight a very important element to keep in mind. All these current rules and taboos are the consequence of a politic of power coming from the government of these organizations. They are very rarely the opinions of the initiates. However, I should acknowledge that these kinds of principles are rarely challenged.

This first family of Freemasons calls themselves "regular Masons" and considers the second family to be "illegal" or "clandestine." These words mean that it is officially unlawful to meet with or talk to a Mason of the second family. If a regular Mason decides to attend a meeting of the second family or even to meet a member of the second family privately, he will be theoretically (and sometimes really) declared a perjurer and expelled.

The Second Family

The second "family" of Freemasons is also present all over the world, even if the number of initiates is significantly less than that of the first family. They are also organized in Grand Lodges. The requirements are sometimes different from and sometimes the same as those of the first group. Women can be initiated in most of these organizations. This is the family that is declared "clandestine" by the first one. It is important to explain the reasons for such a separation. As Freemasonry evolved over the years, independent lodges were federated by various organizations. Several of them followed the same rules as the United Grand Lodge of England. Then when the latter decided to pick only one Grand Lodge per country,[2] political competition emerged. Most of the time the number of lodges and initiates in an organization has been the key element for being selected as "regular." Consequently, all the others that constitute this second family became "illegal."

Progressively three main branches appeared in this second Masonic family, and they can be defined as conservative Freemasonry, liberal Freemasonry, and esoteric Freemasonry. Understanding these differences will give you good insights into this very important part of the Masonic world.

Conservative Freemasonry

You may recall that only one Grand Lodge has been selected in each country by the United Grand Lodge of England. In various countries, several other Grand Lodges were following the same rules or landmarks and lost the recognition most of the time by being outnumbered. However, losing this battle didn't mean they vanished. Many continue to exist and remain close to these initial standards. Their hope has often been to take the place of the "regular" Grand Lodge or to wait until the United Grand Lodge of England changes its rules and validates more than one Grand Lodge per country. As of the publication of this book, such a revolution has never really happened, except "Prince Hall" in the United States. I want to emphasize the fact that in regard to the Masonic initiation, there is almost no difference between conservative Freemasonry and the first family we talked about. Without the political power of their regular Grand Lodges, Freemasons of both groups should recognize themselves as initiates. Sadly, this is not yet the case.

Liberal Freemasonry

Rules and ideas can sometimes be very heavily influenced by the historical context. Masonic landmarks are a very clear expression of the religious and social views of English nobility in the eighteenth century. We can even consider Anderson's Constitution as an advanced

---

2. I have to acknowledge that one exception to this "absolute" rule exists in the United States. Besides the State Grand Lodges, the English institution recognize Prince Hall Grand Lodges (African American Freemasonry). Consequently, approximately forty-two State Grand Lodges did the same, with the exception of Grand Lodges largely in southern states. That doesn't mean the details of this recognition are the same in every state. For example, even with official recognition, some Grand Lodges ask for a brother to be reinitiated if he wants to switch from a Prince Hall Lodge to a mainstream Grand Lodge. From an initiatic point of view, such a process does not make any sense.

text for his time. Providing a place in England to meet and discuss without consideration of religious affiliation was a real achievement. However, keeping without modification what could be considered as liberal three centuries ago doesn't make it liberal today. This is why I used the term "conservative Freemasonry" in the previous paragraph. As a consequence, several Grand Lodges have evolved over time in various ways. Two main changes of the latter have been the religious beliefs and the initiation of women. The requirement to believe in one God and an afterlife was considered at the time of the French Revolution to be a way to enslave people. Freethinking was considered the best way to educate and promote science and philosophy. It was not a war against beliefs per se, but a war against the churches using beliefs to their own advantage. This is why the idea of separation of church and state was central to the eighteenth-century events.

Several French Freemasons were philosophers and freethinkers. As a consequence, their fraternal debates influenced the European Masonic institutions. The obligation to believe in (one) God was moved to a category of intimate and personal beliefs. From this philosophical point of view, no institution or group eager to defend freedom of thought should impose its views on others. Progressively liberal lodges became the place where it was possible to think about what being human should be. Learning to know yourself and becoming a better man or woman became not a matter of religious principle but a humanist attitude. This new point of view changed everything about the way to practice Freemasonry. We cannot be surprised then that initiating women or anyone without consideration of religious beliefs became logical. Of course, this Masonic movement abandoned a part of its spiritual roots, but not every aspect of it. As the present book is focused on esoteric Freemasonry, I don't want to go any further into this subject now.[3]

Today, the largest number of Freemasons in Europe are part of this liberal Freemasonry.

Esoteric Freemasonry

Another part of this book will explain more extensively what the expression *esoteric Freemasonry* means. In a few words, I can say here that from the beginning of its history, some Freemasons have been interested in something other than philanthropy and social development. Subjects linked to psychic abilities, ancient mysteries, religions, esotericism, occultism, and theurgy, to name just a few, were their main focus. Rituals were written or adapted to highlight this approach. Lodges assembling initiates sharing these interests

---

3. It will be the subject of my next book about Freemasonry, tentatively titled *Masonry in Your Daily Life*.

were created. Eventually Masonic organizations were also created to federate local groups. From the eighteenth century, Egyptian Freemasonry has become the major character of this part of Freemasonry.

Meeting the Masonic Families

To conclude, it is easy to understand that if you are a woman reading these pages, the second Masonic family is the only option for you. If you live in Europe and are eager to become a Mason, you are most likely to find a Masonic organization belonging to the second family (except in the UK). If you are a man living in other parts of the world (the United States, for example), you are most likely to find a Masonic organization belonging to the first family. However, knowing more about the characteristics of each Masonic group will allow you to choose according to your interests and beliefs. I think that the next few years could see the rise of other Masonic options in English-speaking countries. If this occurs, it will be a great benefit for the history of Freemasonry. Frozen systems are never a good thing. Life needs evolution and movement.

Chapter 4

What Makes Someone a Mason

Undoubtedly contemporary Masons are not real stonemasons anymore. In Europe, you can still find strong and beautiful organizations of "craftsmen." They are composed of workers who followed a professional training taught in a traditional way. Learning the skills of their field (mason, carpenter, baker, cook, etc.) is associated with the teaching of moral values, private ceremonies, and mentorship. The goal is to reach the mastering of the profession and moral standards. In this case, becoming a Master (Mason, for example) is to achieve this personal training and being recognized as such by the other Masters.

As I explained previously, Freemasonry was separated in the seventeenth century from the craft itself. That means the ways to become a Freemason today are subject to various interpretations. It is common to see stickers with the sentence "2B1 ask 1" (To be one, ask one). Asking to be a Mason is a good way to begin. Direct petitioning is very common all over the world. After being accepted, a ceremony called an initiation will be organized for you. Then you will become a Freemason and your journey will begin.

It is clear that today what makes a Mason is the initiation performed by a group of initiates assembled in a lodge. There are three main parts in such a ceremony: (1) the ritual itself, (2) the repetition of a solemn obligation in presence of the sacred book,[4] and (3) the communication of the secret words and signs.

---

4. Most of the time, the Bible.

At first glance, these criteria seem simple, but what happens if these three elements are published? This is not a trivial question. If anyone knows about this initiation, a large part of the effects may vanish. There are three ways to consider the situation:

1. The real initiation as the adoption of a new member by the group: In this case, neither the ritual itself nor the "secrets" are important per se. They are only here to give an identity to the group.

2. The ritual as a myth of remembrance, a teaching, and a meditation: In this case, if you have access to the text, you do not need a group to become a Mason. A self-dedication using a Masonic text performed in the privacy of your home will have the same result.

3. The ritual as an esoteric process: In this case, the ritual should be performed by officers who have been properly trained to understand and control the effects on a spiritual plane. An individual practice may produce effects, but to reach optimum results, other initiates are very useful. However, esoteric rituals rooted in the essence of the tradition can be a very fascinating and efficient approach to this part of Freemasonry. This is the process I will develop in this book and that has never been published until now. You will discover that you can perform self-initiations in your inner temple with amazing effects.

You can see now that you can become a Freemason at different levels. Using rituals and esoteric practices will allow you to follow the path of Masonic Mysteries. At the opposite end of the spectrum, relying only on your adoption by a group of good men is not enough to open these spiritual gates to you.

In short, we can say the Masonic initiation uses initiatic rituals and teaches a specific kind of morality designed to improve the human being.

The oldest texts linked to the Masonic tradition belong to the Roman, Greek, and Egyptian traditions. They are paradoxically excluded from the "official history" taught by the popular Masonic Grand Lodges.

Chapter 5

From Esoteric Freemasonry to Egyptian Freemasonry

It is worth remembering that *esoteric* comes from the Greek *esoterikos*, meaning "belonging to an inner circle." It usually refers to Pythagoras, who was the first to clearly divide his followers into two categories: exoteric and esoteric. The first step of his teachings was more open, but the second one, esoteric, was restricted to more advanced students, who were allowed to follow private and even secret teachings associated with various ritual practices.

Obviously, even if Pythagoras used this name for his students, he was not the one who created such a distinction. Almost all religions distinguish various levels in apprenticeship. This is easy to understand when we consider professional skills such as sculpting, cooking, drawing, etc. In this case, we cannot call the most advanced group "esoterists," although etymologically we would be correct. It is logical here to progress by levels, as if climbing a ladder. Basic skills must be mastered before the student can progress further. Operative masonry can be used to understand the consequences that later occurred in Freemasonry. Professional groups (craftsmen) in Europe organized themselves into brotherhoods [5] intended to maintain the integrity of the workers and the quality of the work done. The profession's reputation was guaranteed by this hierarchy of master craftsmen, wardens of the tradition. Several museums exist in France dedicated to these professional organizations.[6] In a way, they can be seen as the ancestors of unions. But they were more than

---

5. *Compagnonnage* in French.

6. You can check the English part of this website to find out more: www.museecompagnonnage.fr.

that. If you chose to become a professional mason, baker, or cook, you were not obligated to join one of these organizations. However, they reputedly were managed by the most skilled workers, the master craftsmen. To ascend the levels of mastership, it was necessary for the student to learn from the masters, to build his own experience, and to travel from one place to another. By meeting different masters, the apprentice learned more. Actually, it is not necessary to use the past tense, because these organizations are still active today. Linked to his professional work, the student is required to follow a high standard of morality. Nobody can become a Master if he is dishonest, even if he possesses a recognized professional ability. Achieving excellence requires following secret recipes that are not revealed to apprentices. They must first demonstrate their desire and seriousness. The way to build a framework, to make stained glass, or to make a sauce is not taught to novices.

Freemasonry was built on the same principles. As already mentioned, we are talking about speculative Masonry. The tools displayed are not intended for physical work but, paradoxically, to be symbols of another kind of work. If you ask the Freemasons around you what the secrets are, they will tell you they are mostly composed of secret passwords and signs. If they were only that, going further would be a waste of time. However, there is also the learning of outdated instructions concealed in a mysterious phraseology. When I describe the traditional method of professional apprenticeship in groups of craftsmen, the nature of the secrets is easy to understand. In the case of Freemasonry, it is less obvious. To know the reality of what is hidden, we should know the objective. What is the goal? The classic answer you can hear almost everywhere is to make good men better! I have always thought this goal was noble and essential and that the world would be better if everyone were able to achieve it as soon as possible. Having taught philosophy for years, I do not see the need to complicate such an important purpose with degrees and symbols. Philosophy and common sense work better and faster than meditation on the level or the square! If you want to become a good man (or woman), read philosophers, do not harm, and do not lie, and humanity will soon be better, I am not saying that such efforts are useless; on the contrary, they are essential, and this is why we must teach these ideas as early and as fast as possible. It can also be beneficial to help women become better women! Don't be fooled by nice speeches or declarations veiled by symbols. Always go straight to the point and ask for precise answers. Freemasonry should not be a Sunday school or a mere philanthropic movement. If we consider its roots, the Masonic tradition has more to offer.

I am sure you understand now that if there is a specific goal in Freemasonry, it must be something else, something hidden, something esoteric. In this book, you will discover a lot of keys that will help you to understand more about this branch of Freemasonry. You don't have to wait a long time to get a glimpse. The purpose of esoteric Freemasonry is to unveil to the initiate the mysteries of life and death through initiations and efficient individual practices. To achieve this goal, the system uses several techniques that can be found in the Western tradition. Obviously, it is not easy to find Masonic groups whose initiates know the keys and how to use them and who have the audacity to actually perform them. I have been lucky in my Masonic life to have met several Master Masons who knew these techniques and taught them to the initiates. Some of these principles are in this book, and some of the practices presented to you here have been organized according to these principles. You will benefit from their practice.

Writing about esoteric Freemasonry in general would have resulted in a larger book. In fact, there are several kinds of esotericism, and each one is related to an aspect of the Western tradition, whether Hermetic, Jewish, or Christian. Each one has its own history, myths, principles, rituals, and practices, and each one has generated a branch of Freemasonry. Some have disappeared, but others are still alive today. Some are organized in independent Masonic groups, while others are comprised of specific rituals inside mainstream Freemasonry. As I explained in the introduction, some countries such as the United States are doing their best to stop any initiative of this kind. My first initiation in Freemasonry took place in a remote place in the middle of France. The ritual practiced was Egyptian, from the tradition of Misraim. Everyone working in this lodge knew well the esoteric goal of the tradition and the practices required to achieve a real inner transformation. This branch of esoteric Freemasonry, called Egyptian Freemasonry, has a very long history. It is rooted in the earliest time of Western civilization. As you will discover in the next part of the book, the tradition coming from ancient Egypt was followed by Hermeticism and the "schools of Mysteries" that include Mithraism, Pythagorism, and Orphism. This branch succeeded in maintaining a strong identity that can be found today in Egyptian Freemasonry. Admittedly, even in this part of Freemasonry, all the aspects of this tradition, for example theurgy and philosophy, are not always known and practiced. But this Masonic branch is one of the very few places in Freemasonry where we can explicitly talk about these essential parts of this inheritance.

All throughout its history, ambition to keep this pre-Christian esotericism alive has drawn opposition, bans, and even persecutions. From the beginning of Freemasonry, small groups or larger organizations have continued the work and maintained the light of this sacred fire. This is what is unveiled in this book, keeping other Masonic branches, such as Qabalistic esoteric Freemasonry, for another volume.

Chapter 6
Eastern Tradition and Egyptian Religion

Many centuries ago, when Greek philosophers such as Pythagoras and Plato were looking for knowledge, they traveled to Egypt. They took extended periods of time to be received among the priests and be taught about their Mysteries. Even in the sixth century BCE, Egyptian civilization had already existed for more than 3,000 years. Large and fascinating temples showed the power of religion, and impressive and mysterious rituals attracted truth seekers. Then Alexandria was built. Its library, the largest in the world, began to attract scholars, philosophers, mathematicians, and all sorts of brilliant minds of the time. Until the destruction of this famous library, Egypt remained a beacon of spiritual and intellectual light. Thus, it's easy to understand why this land became a place of pilgrimage and, of course, commerce. Several of these philosophers were initiated into the principal cults of Mysteries, such as Isis and Serapis, and lived in Egypt for an extended period of time.

All of them knew that other important civilizations flourished in the East, so they also traveled to Mesopotamia to continue their studies. Certainly, ancient philosophers were not ignorant of the presence of the peoples of the Far East, whom they called "Gymnosophists," but it was a different world. Religious and philosophical ideas spread, one way or another, but the heart and source of the Western tradition remained the sacred land of Egypt and, by extension, the Mediterranean world. Freemasonry is a distant heir of these religious mysteries that became what today we call "initiations." But before talking about the modern development of esoteric Freemasonry, we should have a closer look at Egypt.

If you want to understand the background of Egyptian Freemasonry, it is necessary to know a few things about ancient Egypt. This civilization was complex, and knowing how its people lived in relation to the sacred will help you to understand what the Egyptian Masonic tradition tried to create. Indeed, the Masonic use of Egypt, its traditions and religion, were often out of step with historical reality. Myths and reality are not always in conflict, but it is worth knowing where their limits are.

First, realize that it is not possible to speak of an Egyptian philosophy. In fact, this was a method of thinking created by a Greek called Socrates in the fourth century BCE. The Egyptian world is deeply rooted in its religion, and the gods are the fundamental elements of this civilization. The relationship that men and priests maintain with them guarantees a cosmic equilibrium.

In contrast to the Greek divine world, the Egyptian pantheon seems not to offer any coherent framework. Myths were different according to the temples and the priesthood involved. Moreover, the absence of what could today be called a canonical book didn't facilitate the student's work. It is likely that gods and goddesses were the result of a sha-manic original religion, in which every location has its own deities. This is also a possible explanation for the therianthropic (part-human, part-animal) figures of Egyptian divini-ties. Through the centuries, a progressive development stabilized this prehistoric sacred manifestation in a set of stories linked to the temples and the geography of the land.

We should keep in mind that Egyptian priests were not a kind of mystic, worshipping a single and transcendent God. Priests were responsible for maintaining a social and cos-mic order, which was achieved by knowing the formulas, symbols, and rituals and then performing them with exactitude. Divinities were dependent on these ritual practices, and any wrongdoing would have placed the whole country in jeopardy. The gods and god-desses lived in Egyptian temples where divine statues, usually hidden in the Naos, were the subject of very precise rituals. These ensured that divinities would remain in this physi-cal world. Among these rituals were the opening of the mouth ritual and the daily ritual. By performing them, the priests, delegated by the king, maintained the link between the world of the gods and the world of reality in which we live. With this very specialized work, chaos was overcome. Today we would speak of the struggle against the forces of entropy, chaos being the return to primordial assimilation.

The whole principle of the Egyptian religion relies on a magical background. To suc-ceed in maintaining the safety and glory of Egypt, gods and goddesses must actually be alive in the temple. This was not a vain speculation. Texts written by hermetic philoso-phers who were initiated into these mysteries clearly indicate this magical approach; they explained that gods were embodied in their material representations. According to this perspective, it is the Ba of the god that descends into the statue through the opening of the mouth ritual. Contrary to what is generally written, the Ba cannot be compared to the soul. Among other things, it has the power to transform the god from one form to another. The god is not able to take a body on his own; he uses the statue as the receptacle built and prepared specially for him. The text of the *Corpus Hermeticum* precisely describes this religious magic: "God is the creator of the divinities of heaven and man is the creator of the divinities who reside in the temples and are satisfied with the company of humans. The images of the gods which men shape have been formed of the two natures: the divine and the matter which has been used to make it. These statues have a soul and a consciousness. They are full of vital breath and capable of doing wonders. Some of these statues know the future and predict it by spells, prophetic inspiration, dreams and many other methods. Others are able to cure men from diseases and give to us pain and joy according to our merit."[7]

Most of these sacred statues were desecrated and vandalized when Christianity spread in the land of Egypt. But these statues were not idols. They were real icons, animated manifestations of the real presence of the god, and thus the true heart of religion.

Since our understanding of the secrets taught in the priesthood is limited, we must rely on old books that have been found. Some authors speculate that initiations were performed inside the temples and that Egyptian Freemasonry adapted these rituals to a modern form. Of course, this is pure speculation and no Egyptologist could support this theory. However, practitioners of esoteric Freemasonry undoubtedly used everything they could to rebuild a kind of archetypal Egyptian temple, the source of the primitive Western wisdom. The *Sacred Order of the Sophisians* is a very good example of that, and you will learn more about it later in this book. Most of the time, Egyptian magic was not directly involved in Freemasonry, with a few important exceptions. Cagliostro, for example, appropriated several magical aspects in his Masonic rituals. Egyptian Freemasonry also implemented a set of degrees called *Arcana Arcanorum*, supposedly containing the theurgic aspect of ancient Egypt.

7. Asclepius, *Corpus Hermeticum*, chapter 8.

Chapter 7

Western Tradition and Egyptian Freemasonry

Several times now, I have used the term *Western tradition* as if it were self-explanatory. Now it is necessary to explain precisely and simply what this tradition is and how some parts of it have survived until today. As a matter of fact, I should have evoked the *spiritual (or philosophical) Western tradition* instead. This abstract concept of Western tradition didn't appear from nowhere but was the result of a mysterious event called the "birth of civilization," which took place in what we call the Fertile Crescent. The lands stretching from the Persian Gulf and following the Tigris and Euphrates Rivers to the eastern coast of the Mediterranean Sea and descending south along the Nile Valley have seen the birth of language, cities, social organization, and religion, to say the least. These great cultures then spread to Greece, Rome, and beyond. As I am not talking here about science or linguistics, let's focus on the spiritual part of this story.

It is plausible that religion, theology, and philosophy appeared from the minds of our ancestors as they tried to find explanations for the universe. These three concepts were linked for centuries, before splitting in the eighteenth century. Religion was born from an admiration of the cosmos and the desire to find a meaning for our existence. The point was not to answer the question "Why are things as they are?" which is the goal of science, but rather "Why are we here?" Myths gave answers, and religious rituals embodied them, making gods and goddesses easier to reach through prayer. Theologians of every religion rationalized these myths and developed complex systems and dogmas to justify this system. Among them, some courageous minds were eager to know more and actually meet the divinities. They were called theurgists or magicians. Simply believing in or studying philosophy was not enough for them. They wanted to meet the gods and discover their nature. These people, known as free thinkers, magicians, or Hermeticists, were true adventurers of the invisible, regardless of the main religion of their time or opposition from political or religious powers. What really constitutes Hermeticism and ensures its permanence is a desire to go beyond appearances, using free thinking that is liberated from any cult or dogma. The central axis of this philosophical and spiritualist tradition is rooted in the teachings of Hermes Trismegistus and two major books, the *Chaldean Oracles* and the *Corpus Hermeticum*.

Neoplatonists and Hermetic philosophers incorporated the initiations of the ancient mysteries into their studies. The initiatic rituals mentioned previously (Eleusis, Mithra, etc.) are very close to what Freemasonry tried to implement. They must be distinguished from religious practices. Masonic initiations, such as the ones given in the ancient mysteries, contain a hidden, esoteric knowledge that was taught to a small number of individuals, who were usually selected for their moral qualities. Initiates were (and still are today) bound by oaths that require them to keep their knowledge and experience secret, just as in certain schools of Greek philosophy, such as the Pythagoreans.

Proclus asserts that "Plato used mathematical names as veils covering the truth of things; Just as theologians use myths, just as the Pythagoreans used symbols."[8] Let us remember that these various ancient initiations were compatible, so people could be initiated into more than one group. As Apuleius wrote: "I was initiated in Greece to most religions. Symbols and memorabilia have been given to me by priests and I keep them piously. There is nothing extraordinary. There are many religions, a lot of ritual practices, a wide variety of ceremonies that I studied for love of truth and duty to the Gods."[9] As you can see, the Hermetic approach is very close to the spirit of the Mysteries. The requirement of learning the books revealed by Hermes was a plus. Students had to spend a long time in deep, solitary reflection of the texts entrusted to them in order to learn—but the tradition cannot be reduced to that. Indeed, we cannot separate the Hermetic tradition from the philosophical currents and schools directly or indirectly connected with Neoplatonism. The philosophical study as conceived by Plato in the wake of Pythagoras is closely related to the mystical currents such as Pythagoreanism or Orphism. However, at its outset, Hermeticism put more emphasis on philosophical study than on mystical revelation. It was

---

8. Proclus, *Commentary on Plato's "Timaeus,"* 36b.

9. Apuleius, *Apologia.*

between the second and sixth centuries that the fusion of the various philosophical, mystical, and even theurgic aspects took place. Among those who organized this tradition were Plotinus, Iamblichus, Plutarch, Syrianus, Proclus, and Damascus. Eventually, the visible light of the Hermetic initiations vanished, while new monotheistic religions, more dogmatic in their politics, increased. The books of the ancient masters such as Plutarch and Iamblichus disappeared during the Middle Ages, only to be rediscovered during the Italian Renaissance.

Initiates that still preserved the inner knowledge, such as Pletho, used this movement to help the rebirth. The Napoleonic campaign in Egypt two centuries later, in 1798, sparked a worldwide enthusiasm for this country and its mysteries. This movement, called *Egyptomania*, had a significant impact on all parts of society: art, movies, architecture, and, surprisingly, Freemasonry. Several lodges or groups of lodges began to use these ancient references; for example, in 1767 there was a group called African Architects, in 1780 the Primitive Rite of the Philadelphians, in 1801 the Sacred Order of the Sophisians, and in 1806 the Friends of the Desert. These little-known Masonic organizations were all inspired by the rediscovery of Egypt. Several studies were used as justification for such Egyptian evolution in the Masonic movement. The most famous were the *Sethos* by the Abbot Jean Terrasson (1761), the *Oedipus Aegyptiacus* by Athanasius Kircher (1652), and *The Primitive World* by Court de Gébelin (1773). The Judeo-Christian Qabalah, Hermetic Neoplatonism, and other esoteric small movements found a natural source of expression there. All these influences should be considered if one wants to understand the esoteric and Egyptian aspects of Freemasonry.

Chapter 8
The Sacred Order
of the Sophisians

As mentioned in the previous chapter, the Sacred Order of the Sophisians was one of the most ancient and secret Egyptian Masonic orders.[10] According to the story, this was the first one created by the officers of General Bonaparte, who participated in the campaign of Egypt. Before the Egyptian Masonic Orders of Memphis and Misraim even existed, the Sophisians were initiating men and women as early as 1800! This is a detail that very few people, including Masonic historians, mention or even know. As someone initiated into the high degrees of this tradition, I had the unique privilege of meeting the woman who is currently in charge of maintaining and reactivating this respectable tradition. I thought it best to ask her for a conversation about this organization, its history, and broadly about esoteric Freemasonry. I knew that Paris would be the place to meet the head of this organization, but the chosen location surprised me. Strangely, it was a famous cemetery called the Père Lachaise. Here is an account of this interview:

I arrived early and waited for some time at the north entrance of the cemetery. It was a beautiful day in November. As is usual in Paris at this time of year, the weather was chilly but the sky was blue: a perfect day to visit such a mysterious place. Then she arrived, appearing to be in her fifties and walking quickly. I wondered if she were doing some kind of workout to show such energy. She invited me to follow her: "Don't be surprised about

---

10. Website of the Sophisians: www.sophisians.org.

my choice. I know that you want to learn more about the Sacred Order of the Sophisians to share with your readers, so follow me."

We walked together, following the avenues until we reached the top of the hill. We didn't speak much, as the interview hadn't officially started. Then the paths narrowed. Old trees provided a shade that mothers love when they walk with their babies in this charming place. The most famous French artists and writers have been buried here for a long time. From a previous trip, I knew that I was not walking in the oldest part of the cemetery, which is linked to stories of vampirism and magic. This will be the subject of another book. On that day, I was walking amongst tombs dating mostly from the eighteenth and nineteenth centuries. You should realize that this cemetery is not a flat meadow scattered with tombstones. The building above each tomb is intended to show the passion of the deceased. Columns, pediments, towers, and a lot of statues surround you on the labyrinthine paths. A dolmen marks the grave of Allan Kardec, the founder of Spiritism. This is a silent city full of immobile inhabitants. Their stone guardians, standing on their graves, watch you with confidence and prudence. As we reached a narrow intersection, my guide slowed down, and I was surprised to see a stone pyramid, as tall as myself, slightly covered with moss, with some engraved inscriptions still visible. The woman smiled and said, "Where do you find a Master Mason, founder of the most authentic Egyptian Masonic organization, if not under a pyramid?"

First, I should tell you that the master buried there was not the founder of the order per se. The real founder was the General Jean-Louis-Ebénézer Reynier, who served under General Bonaparte in Egypt from 1798 until 1801. Remember that, although Bonaparte brought an army to war, several historians, botanists, and painters came along and documented in detail the discovery of this country. They composed a true scientific expedition.

The woman pointed southwest and said, "The General is buried on another hill, in an ancient church that is now a secular mausoleum, the Pantheon. This mausoleum contains the remains of heroes of the French nation."

"So who is buried under this pyramid?" I asked.

"His name was Jean-Guillaume Cuvelier de Trye," she said. "He was also an officer in the army, and after several years of fighting in central Europe, he retired to work in the administration. He became a very active Mason. As an author, he wrote several plays, and as a musician, he composed several pieces."

"If I am correct, Freemasonry was not an Egyptian Freemasonry back then. I don't see the connection."

"You are correct, but before we continue, let us sit on this bench."

We sat and remained silent for a few seconds, looking at the panorama and the peaceful and mysterious pyramid in the middle of the French cemetery. Then she continued:

"The Sacred Order of the Sophisians was founded by scientists and generals—Freemasons who were part of this expedition of Egypt. Of course, most of them were already Freemasons when they traveled to this country. They were very excited to perform rituals in the land of the oldest civilization. They visited the ancient temples, the pyramids, and the most famous places of Egypt. It is very likely that they had profound initiatic experiences while working ritually. They decided to create this sacred order. Coming back to France in 1800 with their precious discoveries of documents and artifacts, these proud successors of Egyptian priests decided to establish the Sophisians in their own country. They announced to other Freemasons what they had discovered in the pyramids, and began the organization."

"I remember that at this time some writers had already begun to unveil the mysteries of ancient Egypt," I said. "This was the case, for example, with Athanasius Kircher when he wrote the *Oedipus Aegyptiacus* (1652), and with the Abbot Jean Terrasson and his book *Sethos* (1761). As a matter of fact, the latter even depicts imaginary initiations in ancient Egypt. A few years later, the French writer Antoine Court de Gébelin wrote *Le Monde Primitif* (1773). So it is not a surprise to see at least two very small Masonic organizations created close to the same time: the Architectes Africains [African Architects] in 1767 and the Rite Primitive des Philadelphes [Primitive Rite of the Philadelphians] in 1780. Even Mozart composed a famous opera, which I discuss in my book. So we can see that the foundation of your order was not really a revelation of Egypt to the Masonic world."

"In fact, yes, it was!" she replied. "These books and previous groups talked about Egypt without ever putting their feet on this sacred land. They never received initiations into these fantastic temples. So their interpretations were very speculative. Even more, they didn't understand the duty and mission of the Egyptian Masonic organizations."

"Do you mean that there is a hidden mission in your organization? Are you using the name of Freemasonry for your own purpose?" I asked.

"Let me continue about our birth and you will understand. Our founder, Jean-Louis-Ebénézer Reynier, was the head of this small group. To stabilize and develop the order, they decided to connect it with a brand-new lodge created in the largest French Masonic organization, the Grand Orient de France. You know this group. You have been one of their Grand Officers for a few years. The first Worshipful Master was Jean-Guillaume Cuvelier de Trye, who is buried under this pyramid."

She looked at the pyramid in silence for a moment. Then she continued:

"He was immediately admitted into the Sacred College of the Sophisians. Everything he learned was pure pleasure for him. It was as if he already knew the essence of this tradition. He managed and organized this esoteric heritage into a clear and beautiful system. He soon became the Grand Isiarque of this beautiful institution and succeeded to supervise its developments."

"Grand Isiarque?" I said. "I don't know this Masonic title. ... I know that more recent Egyptian Masonic organizations used the term Grand Hierophant. Is it the same thing?"

"Yes and no," she replied. "Back then, the Sacred Order of the Sophisians was not a Masonic organization per se. It was the equivalent of the high degrees in Freemasonry. It was required that a Master Mason be initiated as a Sophisian. The three usual degrees in Freemasonry were not part of our curriculum. Our order was in fact a Masonic esoteric society perpetuating the cult of Isis. It was for this reason that this rite worked under the auspices of Isis and Horus. This is also the reason for this use of 'Grand Isiarque' as the official title of the head of our organization."

"I suppose that today you are the Grand Isiarque?" I said.

"Not exactly," she said. "When a woman is in charge of the order, she is called 'Grande Isiade,' which is indeed my official title."

"I understand that the founders felt this pressing need to create the Sophisians as a group dedicated to the goddess Isis before any other modern groups, but what was the real motivation?"

She seemed to be looking toward another world, with her eyes fixed on a distant horizon. After a few seconds, she continued:

"I don't know if you have read an ancient book called *Asclepius*? It is often associated with the *Corpus Hermeticum*. Both date back to the first centuries but are probably most ancient. This is an amazing book, and its ninth part talks about Egypt. If my memory is correct, Asclepius predicted a near future from his time, saying: 'A time will come when it will seem that the Egyptians have honored their Gods in vain. They will leave the earth and return to heaven. They will abandon Egypt. This country which was once the home of the holy liturgies, now widowed by its gods, will no longer enjoy their presence. Foreigners will invade this land and no rituals will be celebrated anymore. Then this most holy land, the home of sanctuaries and temples, will be all covered with sepulchers and death. Then, without God or humans, Egypt will be nothing but a desert.'"

She looked me in the eye and said, "The gods and goddesses cannot die, you know? They exist or not. If they exist, they are immortal! You cannot decide that they must disappear! Therefore, after their secret experience in the Egyptian temples during the campaign of Egypt, the initiates came back with the sacred duty to reorganize the cult of Isis. The Masonic cover was the best way to go. By the way, did you know that the goddess Isis was worshipped all over the Roman Empire and even in Paris? For some, the name of this city, Paris, comes from 'Bar-Isis,' the 'bark of Isis.' Strange, isn't it?"

"I see," I said. "But why is your order called 'Sacred'?"

"The nature of the rituals we practice and the intimate connection with the Egyptian divinities elevate each Sophisian into a sacred dimension. The whole order creates by its rituals a sacred space in which the initiates can approach the goddess and the gods."

"Okay, but today the Masonic group called Memphis-Misraim seems the only one to claim the Egyptian heritage, so is your order still relevant?" I asked.

"Our founders did not hide the fact that the Masonic tradition had been distorted and twisted over time," she said. "The keys of the Mysteries had been forgotten and the goddesses and gods rejected. What was true at the beginning of the order remains true today. If we want the Masonic tradition to manifest its full power, both on the human and spiritual levels, it is fundamental to use these original keys. Now, it is clear to everyone that most contemporary Egyptian orders, Memphis-Misraim as you noticed, claim to have secrets. It does not take long to see that most of them are just classic Freemasonry, dressed in some Egyptianized symbols. It is difficult to find in these organizations something that can give a candidate a real Egyptian experience different from other Masonic organizations. These are just facts. Look at the history of these Masonic orders; you will see the behaviors of their officers and Grand Officers. This is often painful. So we decided to proceed as it was the case at the beginning. We connected the system of the Sophisians to a Grand Lodge using the best version of the rituals of Memphis and Misraim. However, the three degrees performed in the lodges of this Grand College have several characteristics coming from our structure.

"The Sacred Order of the Sophisians represents the Egyptian Masonic tradition of the origins. It harmoniously and effectively combines self-knowledge and progression toward the divine under the protection of the goddesses and gods of ancient Egypt. This is far different."

"I don't want to be rude by asking inappropriate questions," I said, "but I am sure my readers would love to know about the kinds of rituals you practice. You already said to me on the phone that they are among the few that have never been published. Can you tell me something more about them?"

"Of course, I cannot reveal the nature of the initiatic rituals we practice," she said. "However, I can say that the rituals of the Pyramids—they are the equivalent of the

Masonic Lodges (also called blue lodges)—include purifications, invocations, practices of protection and divination. In addition to these spiritual and theurgic practices, the meetings involve individual speeches. Lectures, discussions, and readings allow each person to deepen his esoteric knowledge and to discuss the essential questions of existence."

"I remember I read somewhere that the Sophisians used in their rituals a strange stele depicting the sacred mysteries of Isis. Although your rituals are secret, can you tell me if this is true?" I asked.

"As someone has already talked about it and even published a bad drawing of it, I can tell you that this is true," she said. "This stele was discovered in Italy and is very interesting. It was made by Romans according to ancient Egyptian artifacts. You can still see it today at the entrance to the Egyptian museum of Turin in Italy. I will send you a rare booklet describing this stele, which you can then share with your readers." [11]

"Thank you!" I said. "I really appreciate that! Let me come back to something unusual for most of the readers in English-speaking countries. Obviously, you are a Freemason woman. Today, this is common in Europe, but it was unusual at one time."

"Yes!" she said. "This is totally correct. In fact, many believe that Maria Deraismes was the first to be formally initiated in France on January 14, 1882. She was present at the creation of the mixed [men and women] international Masonic order called the *Droit Humain* [Human Right]. However, to say that she was the first woman initiated into Freemasonry is not correct. The Sacred Order of the Sophisians and the Masonic Lodge of the Frères artistes [Artist Brothers] officially initiated women from the very beginning. This lodge was a unique example of its kind. These feminine initiations began in 1797 and were reinforced in 1800. Several names of initiates can be found on the documents of the order. As you can see, this was eighty years before Maria Deraismes!"

I must say that the order is very proud of this heritage and of being the first Masonic order in history to initiate both men and women formally and regularly!

A young couple walked in front of us and we stopped talking to acknowledge them. Then, after a moment of silence, looking at the fascinating pyramid, the Grande Isiade said, "I think that I unveiled for you most of what can be said about the Sacred Order of the Sophisians. Do you have another question before we end this interview?"

---

11. There are several studies about the Mensa Isiaca (Isiac Tablet). Several were written before Champollion deciphered the Egyptian writings, and others after. This tablet was made in the first century in Rome, probably for an Iseum of this city. This is a very precious artifact for anyone eager to understand the cult of Isis outside of Egypt. I will post regularly the booklets I find about the Isiac Tablet on my blog (www.debiasi.org) and Facebook page (www.facebook.com/jeanlouis.debiasi).

I hesitated for a long moment, as I still had a lot of questions. I decided to ask a little more about this Egyptian tradition.

"I am grateful for this interview, but since you asked, I still have a few questions regarding Hermes. In a previous book, I spoke about the Hermetic tradition, stating that he is a common ancestor of the Egyptian or Esoteric tradition. What do you think of that and how do you see the place of Hermes in esoteric Freemasonry?"

"For a final question, this is very complex!" she said. "But you are right. This is important. Everyone should know that Djehuti, also called Thoth, was the Egyptian god of magic, like the goddess Isis, by the way. Hundreds of years later, Greek initiates associated Thoth with Hermes. As most of them were also philosophers and scientists, they emphasized the importance of reason and critical thinking. Their goal was to avoid religious dogmatism and fundamentalism. By promoting a balanced practice of reason and spiritual practices, it was possible to reach the highest level of the human mind and maybe meet the gods."

"But is it really a Masonic practice?" I asked.

"Yes," she replied. "It is the expression of man's virtue and intelligence: a manifestation of the part of us that transcends the animal part. We are truly at the heart of the Masonic tradition, in its richest and most noble expression. An ancient Masonic instruction says, 'We are here to dig tombs for vices and to raise temples to virtue.' The sacred text of the *Corpus Hermeticum* says, 'But the vice of the soul is ignorance. On the contrary, the virtue of the soul is knowledge and the one who knows is good and pious and already divine.'[12] Freemasonry at its best is the continuation of this effort to use critical thinking. Egyptian Freemasonry, such as the Sacred Order of the Sophisians, tries to combine the two sides of Hermeticism, even using theurgy to achieve its goal."

"I understand this inheritance," I said. "Is it the same thing that I called esoteric Freemasonry?"

"Etymologically, as you may know, esotericism is the knowledge beyond the veil of appearances," she replied. "Esoteric Freemasonry is not Egyptian per se. It can be Christian, for example. However, Masonic history shows us that esoteric Christian Freemasonry often goes back to religious dogma, and doesn't really succeed in maintaining the ideals of Hermetic philosophy that I just mentioned. Therefore, we are talking about Christian Freemasonry and Egyptian or Hermetic Freemasonry. The latter is closer to the idea of the esoteric quest."

---

12. Treatise 10, chapter 9.

"You know that if someone wants to find this kind of Freemasonry, most of the time they will first discover what today is called Memphis-Misraim," I said. "As there are many organizations using this very name. Do you have any advice about that?"

"It is true that the rituals of both Misraim and Memphis have been known for a long time," she said. "Those called Memphis-Misraim were published by a famous French Freemason called Robert Ambelain. I recommend first that you read these rituals, then see if you like them. You know, for most of these rituals Egypt is just a pretext … and everything remains very close to mainstream Freemasonry. Maybe some high degrees are more interesting than the first degrees as they are practiced in this lineage."

"What do you think about Masonic individual practices or even self-initiations?" I asked.

"Everything that helps someone to experiment by himself is good," she said. "Then maybe he or she will have the desire to look further and find an authentic group. This is what I wish for your readers."

A silence followed these last words and I knew the interview had ended.

She stood up and invited me to come closer to the pyramid. Taking a strange Masonic apron out of her bag, she placed it around her waist, then touched the stone and invited me to do the same. I must admit that I had a strange feeling, as if time were no longer a reality. The founders of this tradition were around us and at the same time in a different world. I was still in Paris, but also in Egypt, and in the United States. From the bottom of my heart, I thank the invisible powers who gave me the opportunity to meet this Grande Isiade and this hidden pyramid.

Chapter 9

The Masonic Lodge

Mainstream Freemasonry

There is a vast amount of literature about the origin of the Masonic lodge. According to mainstream Freemasonry, the "Masonic lodge" or "lodge room" is the representation of the temple of King Solomon as described in the Bible. It is true that a few elements, such as the two columns, can be linked to it. However, it takes only a few seconds to realize that the two temples have nothing to do with each other. The Temple of Jerusalem was a place of worship. Thousands of animal sacrifices were performed on the forecourt of the temple throughout the year. But although a lot of activity was taking place close to the temple, the inner space containing the Ark of the Covenant was not accessible to people other than priests. Even more, the Holy of Holies was accessible only to the Grand Priest. In this case we cannot imagine meetings, administrative discussions, or initiations occurring in such a sacred space. This is totally contradictory.

It was the same for Egyptian temples, the Naos being restricted to some classes of priests. Eleusis in Greece, a place where famous initiations took place, didn't have the same layout. If we want to find the origin of such a layout, we must rely on history and archaeology. Researching facts helps us to understand the real meaning and purpose of the Masonic lodge. Imagine you are using a transparency of a Masonic lodge and trying to place it on top of archaeological sites. Of course, this process could be seen as ludicrous because we are trying to find an old justification for a modern creation. The fact that the modern

Masonic lodge has been developed unintentionally allows us to do so. As I just stated, Solomon's Temple does not fit, nor does one that is Sumerian, Egyptian, Roman, Greek, etc.

The only kind that corresponds totally is called a Mithraeum. There is no need to expound about these initiatic mysteries to show how connected these buildings are to Freemasonry. We can find such structures all over the ancient Roman empire. They are rectangular and usually underground, or at least closed to any light coming from outside. Consequently, there are no windows. The entrance is on the west part of the temple, and there is an altar in the center. The initiates sit along the two sides of the room. The sacred representation of Mithra is located in the eastern part, while the ceiling represents the starry sky and the floor may have mosaics representing the symbols of the initiatic degrees. Among these, we found a representation of a sword close to the entrance.

Statues of the wardens and other sacred powers are placed around the temple in locations where today you can find the officers in Freemasonry. There are two guardians, or torch bearers (*dadophoroi*), called Cautes and Cautopates. Cautes holds a torch raised up, and Cautopates holds a torch downward. The first one is linked to the sun and the second to the moon. The Mithraeum summarizes the cosmos. Its directions are symbolic and are linked to the initiations performed. The axis of the temple is west-east and represents the equinox. At each equinox, the sun rises exactly from the east and sets in the west. The north represents the summer solstice, while the south represents the winter solstice. The top of the ceiling is the location of the north celestial pole, while the floor represents the south celestial pole. There are two niches, one facing the other, respectively, in the north (astrological sign of Cancer) and the south (astrological sign of Capricorn).

There are very few accounts of the initiatic mysteries of Mithra, as secrecy has been carefully observed. One symbolic story comes from Porphyry and is called "On the Cave of the Nymphs." Porphyry wrote this text to comment on an excerpt from Homer, stating that a cave in Ithaca had two double doors. The one in the north was a way for men to go down, while the other toward the south was the way of immortals. Porphyry explains that these two doors, present in the Mithraea, represent the movement of the soul crossing the gate of the north to descend in the body and going out from the gate of the south to ascend to the spiritual world as an immortal reborn. This circular movement of the soul found its late adaptation in the circumambulations of the initiate Freemason looking for the light in the darkness of the lodge.

Parts of the Lodge Room

The setting of the temples I will describe now corresponds to the usual requirements for Masonic temples in which Masonic groups meet. Keep in mind that besides these symbols, creativity is largely allowed and a lot of things without a direct link to the initiations can be found, such as portraits, paintings, and more. Usually, esoteric Freemasonry is stricter about what can be placed in a temple. The belief that symbols have an effect on the psychological and spiritual levels leads to a precise selection of what is on display in this sacred place. Let us now consider the various parts of the lodge room.

The Ceiling

It represents the sky at night. The ceiling can feature specific aspects of the cosmos, such as the zodiac or the planets.

The Walls

There is nothing specific on the walls, except sometimes a representation of the twelve zodiac signs that surround the temple. They can be represented with their symbols and associated with twelve columns. Even if a Masonic temple has no windows, we can find representations of three blind windows. In some Masonic organizations, a cord with eight knots surrounds the temple. On the east wall, an allegory of the divine power is used, such as a triangle, a pentalpha, or something similar. The eye is often associated with the triangle, while the letter G is with the pentalpha. In many countries, representations of the sun and the moon are also placed on the east wall.

The Floor

It is common to find a black-and-white mosaic pavement in the center of the room. Sometimes it is surrounded by a border of black and white triangular tiles. In some temples, this mosaic covers the full room. From time to time, tracing boards are placed on this pavement in the axis of the temple. In this case, they are often printed on carpets or banners rolled out for the ritual. Placed in the northeast corner, this first stone or cornerstone represents the real foundation of the temple and its balance. It symbolizes the point of the spring equinox.

The Seats

Besides the seats of the officers, several rows of seats are placed on the south and north sides of the room.

The Two Pillars

Two pillars are placed on the west side of the temple. They can surround the gate by which the initiates enter the temple. They are called Jachin and Boaz. Usually Boaz has a terrestrial globe at its top and Jachin has a celestial globe. There are a lot of comments regarding the names of these pillars. Obviously, their names and descriptions come from the Bible (II Chronicles 3:13–17). The pillar Jachin is derived from the word *Jehovah* and the verb *establish* and traditionally means "God will establish his house." The pillar Boaz is derived from the prefix *in* and the word *strength* and traditionally means "in strength." We find also these pillars on the Qabalistic Tree (which has a total of three columns). The first pillar is associated with the idea of "Mercy" and the second one with "Severity." As previously stated, this comparison doesn't mean that they were used in a similar way. As they were placed on both sides of the entrance door of the holy place, nobody except priests was supposed to walk between them.

Anyone who has seen Egyptian temples knows that there are two obelisks at the entrance, usually to represent the rays of light illuminating this sacred place. This symbolism is highlighted by the small pyramid at the top, covered in gold.

The Altar

The altar is located at the center of the room. It is common for ancient temples, from the Egyptian religion to Mithraism, to have a central altar and a symbolic display of the divine being close to the wall that faces the celebrants. The function can be slightly different, but the location remains the same. In Solomon's Temple, incense was burned on this altar. Egypt offers a variety of altars that were used for offerings, including liquid such as milk, flowers, fruits, food in general, perfumes, etc. The idea is that divinities who are present in the temple will enjoy these offerings and in return bless those who brought them. In some stories, we can also see that divinities consume these offerings. In a Masonic temple, the three lights of Freemasonry—the square, the compass, and the sacred book—are displayed on the central altar in a way that corresponds to the specific degree performed. On this altar, the initiate pronounces his oath of secrecy and allegiance to the institution of Freemasonry.

The Tracing Boards

These are explained and presented in the section in chapter 14 called "Animation of the Tracing Boards."

The Chamber of Reflection

This room is specific to European Freemasonry. It has a very rich symbolism rooted in ancient tradition. This room is always dark and ideally should be placed underground. A cell with humid and earthy walls would perfectly symbolize introspection. As this step is the beginning of the initiatic process, symbolism linked to alchemy began to be progressively implemented, associated with the human skull and bones. Everything is intended to develop the idea of the initiation as a process of transformation of the basic elements into a whole, well balanced and ready to help the soul to be received.

This chamber is full of alchemical and hermetic symbols, along with mottos and words on the wall, a mirror, a table and a seat, a paper and a pen for the candidate, a candle, sulfur, mercury, and salt, as well as a piece of bread and water, a human skull (most of the time fake), and the Bible (or any sacred book you choose).

This room is where the candidate must make a choice after a period of introspection: continue his path toward the Masonic light and reach a new life, or stay in the dark and death of the soul.

Preparing Your Own Egyptian Masonic Lodge

It is common to believe that Masonic work happens only in a group assembled in a lodge room, a place restricted to initiates. Never forget that almost all the rituals were already published a long time ago. Usually, the only recommendations concerning work outside the group meetings are those related to intellectual studies, moral ethics, and philanthropic activities. Without rejecting these important parts of the Masonic life, we must go further if we want to walk on the other side of the veil.

I spoke before about two different temples: a hidden temple inside your own self and a visible one into which you can walk. This inner temple cannot be built without some real esoteric work. To begin and achieve this process, you must use techniques of meditation and visualization. In order for the building to become an inner reality, you will have to bring life into it, to animate it. This is possible for everyone, no matter if you are an initiate or not, although initiation may help.

In most of its rituals (three first degrees), Egyptian Freemasonry follows the Greek habit, associating wisdom with ancient Egypt. The considerable number of Egyptian sites and artifacts available for centuries in all of Europe has drawn attention to this famous civilization. Hieroglyphs, untranslatable back then, added to this mystery. Scholars and religious men tried to understand these symbols with little success. The trend appeared to move those who were asking more of Freemasonry to a more ancient horizon on the other side of the Mediterranean Sea. It is obvious that the third degree of Master is a true copy of the Osiris myth. From here, the Egyptian lodges adopted various symbols taken from Egypt and applied them to modern Masonic uses. Sometimes the tools were just redecorated according to this prevailing atmosphere of Egyptomania. Talking about the Masonic temple, I have explained that obviously the layout and symbolism of modern Freemasonry have been linked by esotericists to the symbolism of the cult of Mithra and the architecture of the Mithraeum. Consequently, the esoteric setting of your individual temple will follow this blueprint. When needed, it will be associated with Egyptian symbolism. We can call this combination a syncretism, which often took place in Masonic history. The esoteric perspective allows us to use Egypt as the real foundation and add on top of it what will be helpful in the Masonic work.

Although ideal, it is not always easy to have a whole room dedicated to a ritual work. This is why I will first describe the ideal Masonic temple and mention, when necessary, how you can adapt it. Keep in mind that you can freely alter these instructions according to your own needs or what you like to see.

Ideally, the shape of the temple should be rectangular. Following the teachings coming from the Mithraic mysteries, the cosmic organization of the temple interior is a system unto itself, and there is no need to try to associate it with the four cardinal directions. Symbolically, the east wall of the temple faces the entrance, which should be at the center of the western wall. A few stairs should be present inside the temple in front of the entrance door, to symbolize the underground descent. When I lived in France, I had several occasions to visit very old medieval churches. They are part of an architectural group called "Roman churches," built between the tenth and twelfth centuries. I remember opening the entrance door and immediately descending a few stairs to walk into these very dark churches. The windows were very small, the walls very thick, and the ceiling was arched. To one who knows the layout of Mithraea, the connection was obvious. The thickness of the stone walls, the absence of sound, and the reduced light recreate the original cave where the divine mysteries of Mithra took place. It was also in a similar underground cave that the *Accademia dei Segreti* (Academy of Secrets) had its meetings in Naples, Italy.

As for the pedestal present on the east side, you can symbolize these stairs in two dimensions with rectangular strips, a drawing on the floor, a painting, or pieces of wood or vinyl. On the east side of the temple, you will do the same with three stairs between the floor and the pedestal.

If you are working alone in your temple, there is no need to add rows of chairs on each side. These are needed only if you are performing rituals or doing practices with friends.

As before, it is interesting to display the symbols related to this sacred place. The north and south walls will be divided into two sections. On the upper part will be the signs of the zodiac, and on the lower section, representations of the divinities associated with the planets. In the center of the wall and close to the floor, you will display the representation of an alcove or a small dark door, and the same on the opposite wall. These two alcoves should be exactly one in front of the other.

On the north wall (beginning from east) on the upper section: Aries, Taurus, Gemini, Cancer, Leo, and Virgo. On the lower section: Jupiter, Mercury, and Luna.

On the south wall (beginning from east): Pisces, Aquarius, Capricorn, Sagittarius, Scorpio, and Libra. On the lower section: Saturn, Venus, and Mars.

On the east wall: You have several options here, and they can change according to the degree in which you are working. Here are some examples you can use: triangle with a central Egyptian eye (Oudjat), triangle with the representation of the Pythagorean Tetractys inside, or the pentalpha with a central letter *G* with the Greek shape. You can also display a representation of the Tauroctony, as was the case for each Mithraeum. On the same wall and to the left (northeast) of the central symbol will be a symbolic representation of the sun, and on the right (southeast) a representation of the moon.

Although not absolutely required for the practices of this book, it is good to use a rope called a Masonic knotted rope. It should be long enough to surround your Masonic lodge. If you work only in part of the room, use the rope to delimit the sacred space, including the chair where you will relax and meditate. You can also add knots in a shape called the *love knot* (sometimes called the *infinity knot* or *figure-eight knot*). The number of knots can vary according to the rites. I recommend in this case using the number 12. You should prepare the knots symmetrically.

On the floor will be placed a black-and-white mosaic pavement. You can print it or order a vinyl banner for it. You can find files to use on my personal website (www.debiasi.org). You have the choice of covering the floor with it, using it only in the center of the room, or placing a smaller one between the central altar and the entrance. You can even use a smaller one placed on your altar. I suggest you do the latter; the reason will be obvious when you read about the mystical gate of the temple in chapter 14. The tracing boards will be displayed upon this mosaic pavement. You can print these tracing boards on paper or vinyl. When not in use, they should be rolled and stored in a part of the temple or outside and close by.

The ceiling should represent the starry sky. You can either paint it a deep blue or keep it white, projecting the sky onto it with devices that are easy to find.

The central altar should be placed on the axis of the temple, close to the east edge of the mosaic. This can be stone or wood, and although there is no rule regarding the material, metal or plastic are not the best when you consider the occult effect of the furniture's function. As we are considering here an occult aspect of Freemasonry, you can add a specific symbol on each side of the altar; this will bring more occult power to the place. Add the following representations: east, a serpent rolled up in a spiral at the top of an altar; south, a representation of the god Harpocrates carrying in his left hand a horn of plenty; west, the three divinities Isis, Serapis, and Harpocrates (the first two are half-human, half-serpent); and north, the god Anubis carrying a short caduceus in his right hand and a large feather in his left hand.

You can add a table cloth to it, although this is not a requirement. If you do, it should be white with gold fringes. Be careful not to cover up the symbols on the sides of the altar.

As this book is about individual Masonic work, you can consider using it to place the sacred book, the square, the compass, the black-and-white mosaic, the tracing board, and the three lights. Of course, in this case everything will have to be a smaller size to fit on top of your altar.

Stones are an important part of the foundation of your Masonic lodge. Following the esoteric teaching, you can place twelve stones on the floor, one in front of each zodiac sign. The size is not important. The best stones are meteorites, which you can easily find online. If you choose to use these celestial stones, glue them onto a small piece of wood about three inches square. As you may already know, meteorites carry a powerful symbolism because they represent the presence of the celestial world. In the northeast corner of the room, place the cornerstone. There are many ways to do this. As you are working here in the Egyptian Masonic tradition, I recommend considering your lodge as a temple. As such, you will use a brick made of clay. Its description and making can be found in the ceremony of consecration of your lodge.

Three columns should be placed around the center of the temple. They should be as high as your heart, with candles (and candlesticks, if needed) placed at the top of each one. The usual positions of these columns need not be considered here, as they are obscure. They must be placed according to an esoteric principle that will create a specific effect on the invisible level. This is why you will place a column at both the northwest and the southwest corner of the mosaic. The third one will be placed on the axis of the temple halfway between the altar and the east wall. If you want to add more to this nice preparation, you can use an Egyptian style for these columns. They don't need to be three different styles. This is a late addition to the use of the three visible lights, which is the most important point here. If you place the lights on your altar, these three columns are symbolically replaced by candlesticks.

Just in front of the entrance or slightly on the south side, place a bowl on a pedestal, as high as your lower belly. This bowl will be filled with water before you begin your practice and will be used to purify yourself (hands and face).

In front of the doors and below the stairs, place a cushion on the floor. It should be dark red. On top of it, place a sword or a dagger, with the tip pointing toward the door and the length of the sword exactly on the axis of the temple. If you need more space to move during your practices or rituals after you enter the temple, move it closer to the door.

A cabinet can be used to store your books, notebooks, incense, and other objects needed in your practices. Place it in the northwest or northeast part of the temple.

The first initiation uses the chamber of reflection. You should use a representation of this place and display it in the north when you need it. There is no need to keep it afterward. You can also install a small table in the northwest with all the required symbols on it before your self-initiation. This chamber may be used whenever you feel the need to practice deeper introspection.

Choose a comfortable chair for the periods of relaxation, meditation, and other inner work.

I do not suggest adding too many things to the temple, as they will only be a distraction and lead to lower efficiency on all levels.

As you can see, the lodge can become a real sacred place, allowing you to perform genuine inner work. In many situations, however, you cannot create such a place, so it is important to know how to make adaptations without losing the desired effects.

There are three main kinds of adaptations possible:

1. This may be obvious, but you can install your temple temporarily. Everything can be stored and installed in a room you will clear for this time. Of course, it will not be possible to fully consecrate this sacred place, but in chapter 17 I provide a simple consecration you can use for this temporary purpose.

2. You can use part of a room to install your altar, depending on the available space. I remember using a corner of the room I had separated from the bedroom by a curtain. In such a case, you can simply open the curtain, pull up your chair, and begin your spiritual work. Here, you would not need to install every element just described. On your table, place the center of the room materialized by the mosaic pavement, the three candles, the three Masonic lights (square, compass, and sacred book), the tracing board (when needed), and the symbols on the east wall.

3. There is an ancient Masonic tradition that has been the origin of a large number of amazing artistic creations. Scale models of Masonic lodges have been made to represent this sacred place. Several Masonic museums have such charming and interesting creations on display. Here I give you one photo of a model scale representing a lodge room, made in the nineteenth century. Some of these representations would close like a box. You can do the same by building a model scale of your Masonic lodge with all the information I just gave you. It's best to have the ceiling and the west wall removable, or to have the north, south, and west walls able to be opened and moved horizontally to each side.

Chapter 10

The Officers

Mainstream Freemasonry

As in any initiatic tradition, a Masonic lodge is composed of several officers, each of whom is in charge of part of the ritual. According to ancient Masonic teachings, we can consider that three officers govern the lodge: the Worshipful Master and the Senior and Junior Wardens. Five officers give light to the Lodge: the three just mentioned plus the Secretary and the Orator. Seven officers are needed to operate the lodge.

Each officer has a specific jewel and a precise position in the lodge. The following list gives you the essential elements needed to understand this organization.

Worshipful Master: Jewel: the square. Position in the temple: east. The Immediate Past Master often sits beside him.

Senior Warden: Jewel: the level. Position in the temple: west. He is the second in charge in the lodge.

Junior Warden: Jewel: the plumb. Position in the temple: south.

Secretary: Jewel: two quills crossed. Position in the temple: southeast.

Treasurer: Jewel: two keys crossed. Position in the temple: northeast.

Senior Deacon: Jewel: the sun in the middle of the square and compass. Position in the temple: northeast, in front of the pedestal of the Worshipful Master.

Junior Deacon: Jewel: the moon in the middle of the square and compass. Position in the temple: southwest.

Marshal—Director of Ceremonies: Jewel: two wands crossed. The first title (Marshal) is more common in the United States, while the second one (Director of Ceremonies) can be found in other parts of the world. Their duties are almost the same. The Marshal sits at the left of the Senior Warden.

Master of Ceremony: Jewel: two swords crossed. The Master of Ceremony is more common outside the United States. He oversees the preparation of the temple and the candidates.

Senior and Junior Stewards: Jewel: horn of plenty. Positions in the temple: The Senior Steward sits at the right of the Junior Warden and the Junior Steward sits at the left of the Junior Warden. These are assistants, and their position in the lodge may vary.

Tyler: Jewel: sword. Position in the temple: southwestern door. Also known as *Outer Guard*.

Inner Guard: In some Masonic jurisdictions, this officer replaces the Deacons.

Chaplain: Jewel: open book. Position in the temple: southeast, in front of the pedestal of the Worshipful Master.

Almoner: An officer present in some Masonic organizations outside the United States. He is in charge of assisting and supporting members who are in need.

Director of Music: Jewel: harp. Officer in charge of the musical program during ceremonies.

Orator: Jewel: page of parchment. Officer in charge of summarizing the speeches and discussions presented during the lodge meeting. He is often in charge of the welcoming speech during the visits of dignitaries and new initiates. This officer is almost never present in the United States.

Historian—Librarian: Jewel: page of parchment and a quill. Officer in charge of recording and researching the history of the lodge and related subjects.

Egyptian Freemasonry

There were countless rituals in the early days of Freemasonry. Every group of initiates, eager to highlight a glorious past and esoteric heritage, created original rituals. As I stated previously, Egyptian Freemasonry was very diverse. Several groups created a system in which various new names were chosen for the officers. In some cases they were taken from old texts coming from Latin or Greek. For example, in the Sacred Order of the Sophisians, the Worshipful Master became the 1st Philisiarque and the Deacons the Mystophores. In other rituals of Misraim, these names became something else. This is one of the beautiful things about Freemasonry: to have found a way to express this desire for research and creativity.

In the case of an individual practice, officers are of course not needed. You will perform the rituals and the self-initiations yourself. There is no need to worry about details that are more for historians. If you are interested in exploring further some historic point of view, a few links found in the bibliography will help you. I will regularly update this list on my own website (www.debiasi.org).

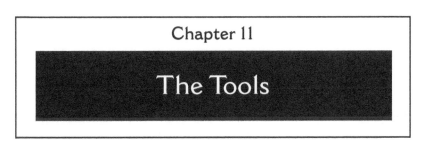

Chapter 11

The Tools

Mainstream Freemasonry

The Square and the Compass

The square is often associated with the idea of squaring our actions, while the compass should help us to circumscribe our desires.

The square symbolizes equity and achievement. It also combines the symbols of two operative tools: the horizontal line (the level) and the vertical line (plumb line).

The function of the compass, the other operative tool, is to trace plans, but also the initiate's personal limits.

The square and the compass are two of the three lights of Freemasonry. The third is the sacred book. These lights are used in a certain way when the candidate takes an oath.

The Letter G

A symbol of deity, God, this letter is often associated with the square and compass, and represents geometry (Gymateria) to measure spiritual values. The rules of geometry are applied to the Freemason's inner work.

The Pentalpha

See the comments in the section of chapter 14 called "Individual Practices of the Second Degree: The Pentagram and Pentalphas."

Sacred Book

This is the third light of Freemasonry (the Bible), along with the square and the compass. The candidate takes his oath on the sacred book, which is on the altar in the center of the lodge. This book is present at every meeting.

24-Inch Gauge

This is a symbol of the three divisions of time: eight hours of service to God, eight for work, and eight for refreshment and sleep.

The Square

This is a symbol of equity and achievement. It also combines the symbol of two operative tools: the horizontal line (the level) and the vertical line (plumb line). The square is the jewel worn by the Master of a lodge.

The Level

Symbol of equality between the brothers and in front of Death. This is the jewel worn by the Senior Warden of a lodge.

The Plumb

Symbol of integrity, honesty, and justice. This is the jewel worn by the Junior Warden of a lodge.

The Trowel

Used to spread the cement of love and affection within the initiates. It erases the differences between the brothers.

The Chisel

Used to carve a stone, it represents education and knowledge.

The Rough Ashlar and the Perfect Ashlar

Various states of the initiate, from the beginning of the work until mastership. The rough ashlar is the symbol of the new initiate. He will become a perfect ashlar with work and time.

Rods and Staffs

Commonly, rods or staffs are used by Deacons, Stewards, and Marshals of a lodge. They represent authority and can also symbolize Hermes, the messenger of the gods. They are usually as tall as a standing adult. They can be distinguished by the top, which is often metallic and differs according to the office.

The Sword

In European Freemasonry, the sword was a symbol of spiritual equality between the initiates, aristocrats, and others. In some Masonic organizations, there is a straight sword and another one called the *blazing sword* (appearing at the beginning of the nineteenth century). This blazing sword refers to the Bible and is described in the book of Revelation (1:9–20). However, the interpretation doesn't stop there. There is a rich symbolism especially linked to Qabalah and the Tree of Life. According to this system, the divine power called Mezla, descending from the highest sphere, Kether, follows a serpentine path to reach the lowest sphere, Malkuth. The representation of this descent of power on the Qabalistic Tree is compared to the flashing of a blazing sword. This is the symbol of enlightenment in action when the initiate receives the divine light, when the veils of darkness are opened and the light of the soul reveals its divine and immortal presence.

In European Freemasonry, the worshipful Master is the warden of this sword, which is placed in front of him. He uses it to pronounce the solemn invocation opening the lodge. Even more importantly, this specific sword is used to consecrate the candidate during the initiation. The power of the divine planes associated with the inner light of the Worshipful Master flows into the initiate to reveal for him the real inner light. Several years ago, when I was Grand Officer of the main French Masonic organization, I had the privilege to experience firsthand the power of this office and this specific tool. As I was conducting an important initiation into the high degrees in the headquarters of the organization in Paris, the custodian of the museum allowed me to use the Masonic sword of General Lafayette. For the duration of the ceremony, I kept this historic sword and consecrated the initiates with it. The intensity was amazing and the emotion indescribable. Then the sword was returned to its showcase in the museum. It is interesting to recall that tools can accumulate a power that can be felt and used. This is what happened at that moment. What is true for a sword is also true for the other tools. This is why it is important to choose them carefully and to cherish them.

In mainstream English Freemasonry, only the Tyler, or Outer Guard, used a straight sword, while in other Masonic organizations the sword is still used in the ritual.

The Gavel

This tool is used to divest the initiate from vices and reveal the real hidden stone, which is the soul. The gavel is a symbol of authority and is sometimes confused with the mallet. The shape indicates which one you have in front of you. The difference is not universal and should not be a cause for worry; moreover, in many Masonic organizations there is no difference at all. Like the sword, the gavel may have a power by itself, and the symbols painted or engraved on it increase its effectiveness. I had the opportunity to experience that many years ago when I directed an initiation using the ebony gavel of a famous French occultist named Papus. This gavel had specific symbols set on its side, and I found it more efficient for knocking precise sequences than the modern gavel I generally use. Unfortunately for me, I kept this gavel only for the duration of the ceremony. It would have been amazing to keep it forever!

The Mallet

This tool corrects irregularities of the stone. The mallet is a symbol of power and strength.

Tools of the Degrees

There are tools that are used in relation to the practice and the initiation into a specific degree. In mainstream Freemasonry, here are the usual tools you can find.

Tools of the First Degree (Entered Apprentice)
- The 24-inch gauge [13] and the common gavel

During this first initiation, you can also find the following:
- The blindfold: It symbolizes secrecy and the state of darkness and ignorance of the candidate.
- The cable tow: This is a rope that symbolizes the limitations of our physical body, like the umbilical cord.

Tools of the Second Degree (Fellowcraft)
- The square, level, plumb rule, compass, and gavel

---

13. Even if this gauge is commonly used in the first degree, a considerable number of organizations are using it in the second Masonic degree. This is what I did in this book.

During this second initiation, you can also find the following:

- The blindfold and the rope

Tools of the Third Degree (Master Mason)

- The pencil, skirret, and compasses

During this third initiation, you can also find the following:

- The blindfold and the casket

Egyptian Freemasonry

Egypt is well known for a specific kind of writing called hieroglyphics. This is not the place to speak extensively about this writing system, but a few things should be said to understand its use in Egyptian Freemasonry. Jean-François Champollion was the French scholar who deciphered this mysterious writing. He wrote, "It is a complex system, writing figurative, symbolic, and phonetic all at once, in the same text, the same phrase, I would almost say in the same word." [14] Before the nineteenth century and this discovery, hieroglyphs were mostly understood as symbols, ideas, and not sounds. This theory was developed mostly by Athanasius Kircher, a German Jesuit scholar who published more than forty books on subjects ranging from ancient Egypt to China, biology, medicine, and more. The engravings on his books are fascinating. However, regarding the interpretation of this specific writing he was partly wrong, because he failed to see that the signs were mainly phonetic. Surprisingly, his discovery didn't much change the approach of esotericism. As some signs were still considered to be figurative and symbolic, the sacred nature of these writings was saved.

We know that hieroglyphic writing evolved into simplified systems, Hieratic and Demotic, which facilitated its use in daily life. However, the traditional hieroglyphic system continued to be used until the closing of the last Egyptian temples in 391 by the decree of the Christian Roman emperor Theodosius I. No doubt this writing was a way to maintain the authentic Egyptian tradition. Every sociologist knows that when a writing system and a language disappear, a culture dies. There is a tight bond between concepts and words: losing the words makes the concepts disappear. Civilizations stand and survive through their architecture, but more importantly through their visible written language.

---

14. Jean-François Champollion, letter to M. Dacier, September 27, 1822.

After being used essentially for sacred purposes for thousands of years, Egyptian hiero-glyphs gained a different nature. They were considered capable of creating a spiritual effect simply by being seen, written, and maybe pronounced. As we have lost the pronunciation, only the writing remains. Hieroglyphic writing has a kind of performative effect. Consider, for example, the following prayer: "O Djehuti, I am the servant of your house. Great are you, Djehuti, and great are your actions!" This declaration is a humble prayer to Thot-Djehuti. As such, it has an effect on the worshipper while building a link between him and the god. But writing this text in ancient Egyptian will materialize the invocation, giving it an action on the spiritual and invisible levels. This effect is even stronger if the name of the user or the worshipper is associated with it. The action will continue as long as the writings are not erased. Following this idea, the Western esoteric tradition used talismans and tools from ancient Egypt, which were often decorated with symbols or sacred texts. This is true in some theurgic initiatic orders and also in a few Egyptian Masonic organizations. The Sacred Order of the Sophisians is a good example of such reconstitution of Egyptian material and tools. This is also true for the Masonic Egyptian regalia.

As you build your own individual temple to experience this esoteric tradition, I suggest adapting the usual Masonic design in an Egyptian style. The internet can be a great help here. Of course, in this book I give you several indications and representations of tools that have been designed for this branch of Freemasonry. As many tools have been found in Egypt, feel free to conduct your own research. When specific tools have been used in Egyptian Freemasonry, it's best to use them. Otherwise, use what you like from this amazing civilization.

Here are some tools that are not commonly found but are sometimes used in esoteric Freemasonry.

The Square and the Compass

The square is used on the central altar, but the Worshipful Master also wears it as a symbol of his function. In ancient Egypt, squares were numerous, often used as amulets and placed on mummies, on the deceased's left side, close to the heart. These amulets were simple, without any hieroglyphs. Obviously, their position on the body had to do with the meaning of the amulet. Several models were developed in Egyptian Freemasonry, such as what is shown in figures 13, 14, and 15.

As the compass was not used in ancient Egypt, the Masonic models are modern and you can be creative here. Figure 17 is an example that associates Egyptian designs with the meaning of this important Masonic symbol. Remember that the compass was created in the first century by Romans, so you can find examples in this civilization.

The Letter G

As previously explained, the letter G is often shown in the pentalpha or the radiant triangle in the east. Based on what I have seen around the world, I suggest three possibilities: (1) the Greek letter G, which is a square open on the right; (2) The Oudjat, which is an Egyptian eye, also called the Eye of Horus; and (3) the Pythagorean Tetractys, represented by ten dots in a pyramid. You can also replace the dots with the representation of the sun in the hieroglyphs, which is a dot surrounded by a circle. I give you an example in figure 8.

The Pentalpha

This geometric figure is often used on the east wall. You can use the Egyptian representation of a star that has five points (see figure 16).

Sacred Book

I spoke extensively about the nature of the sacred book in my 2014 book *Rediscover the Magick of the Gods and Goddesses*. I mentioned that the Bible is the sacred book most often used in Freemasonry around the world. The principle is to place in the center of the lodge the sacred book corresponding to the initiate's religion. Since he must pronounce his oath upon it, it is necessary to provide the book he considers sacred. Implicitly, this is not some ordinary book. The word *sacred* indicates a book in which a divine being expresses his will or message. Simply put, it should be a book that is the foundation of a religion. At the outset of Freemasonry, the Bible was not used, but progressively it became an absolute requirement. Maybe you've heard of the "Masonic Bible." This is not a specific version of the Bible like we find in some Christian cults, but one wearing the emblems of Freemasonry. This copy is signed by Master Masons present at the initiation and offered to the new initiate after his third degree. I must also emphasize that not all religions are welcome in mainstream Freemasonry. Consequently, not all the sacred books are authorized. According to the principles, they should be, but the reality varies widely according to the Grand Lodges.

In Egyptian Freemasonry, the sacred book commonly used is the *Egyptian Book of the Dead*. When this book is opened, the part chosen is often the "weighing of the soul." It depicts the moment when the soul of the deceased is placed on the scale of Maat to measure his moral attitude during his past life. Other sacred Egyptian texts can also be used.

As this tradition continues through Hermeticism, the *Corpus Hermeticum* has also been used. To my knowledge, this is the only sacred book in the world that does not contain any harmful commandments or stories full of hatred for people. As a Hermetist, this is the one I personally chose for my Masonic initiation.

24-Inch Gauge

In the practice related to this tool (in chapter 14), I extensively describe the Egyptian equivalent of this 24-inch gauge. I highly recommend using it instead of the classic tool.

The Level, Plumb, Chisel, and Trowel

All these tools except the trowel were used in ancient Egypt, and you can use their ancient design to remain in harmony with the other instruments. The trowel can be adapted for use as well.

The Rough Ashlar and the Perfect Ashlar

Previously, I presented the stones you should use in your individual lodge. If you want to place these two ashlars somewhere, choose the types of rocks you like the most. Since the ashlar represents your inner being, your soul, it is a good idea to choose rocks that were used in ancient Egypt to make statues. These include soft rocks such as limestone from desert cliffs, sandstone, calcite, and schist; harder rocks include quartzite, diorite, granite, and basalt. The perfect ashlar can be a perfect cube or a cube crowned by a semi-pyramid (see figure 7).

Rods, Staffs, Scepters

It is difficult to call staffs "tools," but as they are used during ritual ceremonies, I place them in this category. These staffs are extremely interesting and were important in ancient Egypt. The discovery of Tutankhamun's tomb revealed to the world amazing furniture, sculptures, and jewels. Among these were a considerable number of staffs and scepters. Other discoveries and the temple walls themselves provide us with numerous examples. Some staffs are short, while others are long. With some, artists kept the natural shape of the branch, just covering the wood with gold leaves. Others are associated with hieroglyphs, representations of divinities, decorated with gold and semiprecious stones. Their names are numerous. They were part of the pharaonic regalia, as Tutankhamun's tomb demonstrates. They were also used by officials, priests, and even master craftsmen. It is likely that Egyptian ceremonial rods owned by architects were used as symbols of their authority and function.

Among them I can specifically highlight the following:

- The Sekhem, still used as a scepter of power by the Worshipful Master in the Order of the Sophisians
- The mekes that was used in the Great Offering ritual
- The lotus-bud scepter, an authority on the living and the deceased
- The Payprus scepter, mostly associated with female deities
- The staff crowned by Anubis, the pillar Djed, the ankh, or even the combination of these three symbols

Each one can be used for a specific function in your lodge. Besides the Sekhem, the staff crowned by Anubis is an amazing symbol you should make and use. The name of the lodge can be painted on it. Usually this staff is black, with gold writings. It represents the presence of Anubis, the one who guides the dead in the afterlife. It should be carried by the officer in charge of escorting the candidate during the initiation. When you are performing your individual rituals, use it during the circumambulations and when you are working at the third degree. It can remain in the southwest corner of your lodge.

To follow the Hermetic tradition, you can also use the caduceus, a symbol of Hermes, which was also associated with Anubis in Egypt during the Ptolemaic period. There are several examples showing Anubis holding a small or large caduceus. In this case Anubis is called Hermanubis, whose role is to guide the souls from earth to the world of the dead. The Greek etymological term for the "guide of the souls" is *psychopomp*. The shape of a caduceus differs according to the period. In figure 21 I give you an Egyptian example of a wand I made years ago and offered to a Masonic lodge.

The Sword

Swords in ancient Egypt were curved, while Masonic swords are straight. Egyptian daggers have inspired various designs. They are often long enough to be symbolically considered short swords. You can use them as a model if you want to make your own. Archaeologists found that the blades of some of these ceremonial daggers were made of meteoric iron. One of these is the famous ceremonial dagger found in Tutankhamun's tomb. These blades were called "stars," and because the metal was considered sacred, there was strong symbolism attached to them by Egyptian priests. To follow this tradition and use this very powerful symbol, here is what you can do: buy a fragment of meteorite and affix it onto the blade of your straight or blazing sword. If you believe this metal contains a kind of energy or memory, be careful not to isolate the meteorite from your blade with a layer of glue. Try to maintain direct contact between the meteorite and the metal of your blade, even if not on the whole surface. To complete the sword with its symbols, and invisible energy, I suggest using real gold and silver. As you may know, these metals are associated with the sun and the moon, respectively. Gold and silver leaves can be easily found and applied on your sword, to the cross-guard or the pommel. (You can do the same with your staffs.)

Gavel and Mallet

These tools were used in ancient Egypt and usually have nothing specific. However, it could be beneficial to place specific Egyptian symbols on them, because there is a belief that the sound will project the power of the symbol placed on it. If you choose, for example, the ankh, the power of life will be activated. It is not always necessary to paint these symbols yourself; you can use metallic gold or silver tattoos and affix them on your gavel. You can find such tattoos at www.theurgia.us.

The Djed Pillar

This pillar can be found on walls all over Egypt. It was used as an amulet, at the top of the staffs, and in jewelry, to name just a few of its uses. A full book would be necessary to describe its endless symbolism. It represents stability: it is associated with the god Ptah, creator of the world, and with the god Osiris as his spine. In my presentation of the Masonic myths later in this book, I explain the story of Osiris. His coffin followed the Nile and ended in the roots of a tree, which eventually was cut and transformed into the pillar of a temple. Isis found it and extracted the coffin from this pillar. As such, the pillar is sometimes represented with two eyes and even with arms supporting the sun above it. Several Djed pillars were placed on mummies, almost always in a symmetrical position, in the center of the body. The symbolism of this pillar is deeply linked to the tree, the bridge between earth and heaven, and, more importantly, eternal life. A festival for "raising the Djed" was dedicated to it. In this festival, Pharaoh, surrounded by priests, raised the Djed to represent the cosmic order and the resurrection of all life. This is one reason why it can be used in the third Masonic degree in Egyptian Freemasonry.

I suggest you make a Djed pillar that is ten inches tall. For the rituals described in this book, it's best to make it of wood. Choose an evergreen tree, then paint it gold or cover it with gold leaves.

To Conclude

Understand that the tools described here are Egyptian transpositions of the tools used in the Masonic tradition. I explained that esoteric Freemasonry has a different goal, which is spiritual. This is why amulets and tools were used in Egyptian Freemasonry with a sacred perspective in mind. It's good to remember this when you prepare your own tools and lodge.

Chapter 12

The Masonic Regalia

Mainstream Freemasonry

Freemasons are supposed to wear formal apparel for the ritual meetings. Bow ties are often used by officers in charge and, following an ancient tradition, the Worshipful Master wears a hat. You should know that although this is common, it is not true everywhere. As previously mentioned, there are no absolute rules in Freemasonry.

However, one item that can be found everywhere today is the apron. For the first two degrees, it is made of lambskin or white leather. It is considered an emblem of innocence and the badge of the Mason. Interestingly, in past centuries it was not always white, and had symbolic representations linked to the degree. The Master has a different apron, and the design changes with various countries, Masonic organizations, and rituals.

Freemasons also wear collars, sashes, and sometimes gloves. The Masonic regalia often includes jewels that correspond to the office, and other medals.

I have to emphasize something essential here, which is the love of honors and medals. Humility is always preached while an unbelievable number of honors are placed on the chests of Freemasons. It's even worse when we go further than the three degrees: the office regalia is endless. It can be regarded as exuberant, eccentric, and almost ridiculous. Possibly the worst side effect of the Masonic initiation is self-importance! Don't be fooled by the declarations highlighting the necessity of humility. Every meeting and every medal or pin added to the regalia demonstrates the opposite.

Esoteric Freemasonry, on the other hand, sees these things differently. Humility should be at the core of an initiation. Everything that flatters the ego and encourages self-importance should be banished. Medals, collars, and other parts of the Masonic regalia should be preserved only as long as the symbol is used to teach something or to have a specific effect.

Egyptian Freemasonry

If you are already a Mason, use the regalia of your degree. If you use white gloves during group rituals, don't use them here. If you have not been initiated into Freemasonry, nothing prevents you from buying and wearing Masonic regalia in your individual practice. Esoteric Freemasonry usually maintains the use of aprons with specific symbols. In Masonic museums, it is common to find aprons depicting the initiatic degrees from an Egyptian perspective. In the case of the third degree, Master Mason, representations of pyramids, Egyptian temples, sphinxes, and obelisks are numerous. You can look for this kind of apron if you so desire. There is also a very interesting esoteric process you can use in this case: use a white apron, even the one you used in the first two degrees, and paint it with your own understanding of the third degree. You can take your time doing that and visit museums for inspiration.

In Egyptian Freemasonry and other esoteric groups, a ritual robe, a tabard, a tunic, or a shawl is frequently used. The colors used in the past have been diverse: light blue, deep blue, black, or white. I recommend light blue. Although this is not an absolute requirement, there are several advantages to such clothing. It is always important to find a process to disconnect from daily life. Having specific regalia with which to perform the ritual work gives us a huge help and benefit. We can consider that the preparation of your practice is a part of it. According to archaeological findings, it seems that in ancient Mithraic ceremonies, the initiate was fully naked during some parts of his initiation. Today in Freemasonry (male, of course), the candidate is still partly stripped. Depending on the degree, parts of the leg, arm, shoulder, and chest are visible. The link with this ancient initiatic tradition is clear, even if prudishness has obviously modified the original process. As you are working alone here, you can choose to perform self-initiations as Mithraic initiates did: naked under your ritual robe, or wearing the blue robe over your usual clothing. Your apron will be placed over the ritual robe. It is good to add a medal in the center of your chest. Even if you do not use a medal with the square and the compass intertwined according to the degree, you could wear a square jewel when you have reached the third degree. It is interesting also to consider some Egyptian amulets related to the symbolism of the degree and the work.

All this individual preparation will help you to feel a sense of solemnity. During your practice, you will be in a different time than the rest of the world. You will enter into a sacred world. Your thoughts and behavior will become more and more different.

Chapter 13

Spiritual Training

Individual Process

I am always taken aback when I hear Freemasons talking about the benefits of an initiate practicing Zen, yoga, or any form of Eastern meditation in general. From the beginning of my Masonic journey, when hearing such remarks, I always ask the same question: *Why?* As you can expect, the answer is about the benefits of meditation on the human mind. I completely agree, because I have personally practiced meditation and I'm learning yoga today. I have no doubt that we can obtain benefits from these practices, but that is not the point. Who would be willing to be initiated into an organization that would encourage its members to practice the techniques from another school? Wouldn't it be better and faster to go directly to the other school?

One explanation could be that most Masons don't know anything about their own techniques. In fact, I have been the first to write about them. Now, some Masons seem to discover or pretend that a kind of Masonic meditation exists. But to present a coherent, traditional, and efficient system is different. It's not just a matter of sitting, relaxing, and breathing; a real individual practice can help you on a spiritual level. If some branches of Freemasonry are the heirs of the Western tradition, they should have keys you can still use for your own benefit, if you dare try. The fact of whether you are already a Freemason or not does not have much impact on this individual journey.

If you are already a Mason with an open mind, you may go faster in this inner work and maybe improve your understanding of the group rituals you perform regularly.

When it's about inner practice, the best understanding comes with feeling and experiencing it. Nevertheless, I am among those who want to understand some general principles before beginning. So let's get started now.

Mental Preparation

We are a beautiful mix of flesh and spirit. The activity of the brain is the basis of our thoughts, whether we believe in the existence of a soul or not. Everyone should recognize that we have a real mental power: the power of our thoughts on our body. I am not talking about a magical action outside our own body, but only on the effect we can have on ourselves, for good or bad. I will give you two examples that show the power of the mind. Stress may produce excess acid in the stomach, leading to painful ulcers. Knowing this, we can modify the effect of stress on our stomach by changing our mental attitude. The second example is the well-known *placebo effect*, where someone receives a supposed treatment that is really pills made only of sugar. The person's belief in the effectiveness of the treatment creates a genuine improvement in their case. Some symptoms may even disappear.

These two examples illustrate how our mental attitude can make our life miserable or enjoyable, even if we are unaware of the cause and the process involved. Imagine the huge importance of being aware of these inner processes and mastering them. This is what Eastern techniques are doing and also what Western practices can do. It is possible to go even further, introducing the idea of a spiritual world, the goal of our mental preparation. This is why the path of esoteric Freemasonry can change your life.

Breathing and Relaxation

Life came to you with your first breath, and death will come when you will release your last breath. Breathing is life. This is true for the sake of your body, for the health of your brain, and for the clarity of your thoughts. Diet is also important, but without breathing, it is not enough to maintain a healthy life. Therefore, you should learn how to use breathing. This is the first step. In yoga, these breathing techniques are called *pranayama*. They can be very complex and challenging to master, requiring months or even years to achieve good control. It is not necessary to aim for such a lofty goal now. As in many things, you should begin with small steps that will eventually lead to big realizations. The first thing you must do is to become aware of your breathing. This is simple to say and easy to do for a few seconds but is more complicated to maintain for a few minutes. You must become an observer of your own breathing. Sit on a chair, with your back straight, and breathe normally. Observe the air entering and leaving your body. Observe this movement, focus on it, and maintain this observation for a few minutes. Keep doing it from time to time until you can do it for five minutes without thinking of something else. This is simple but is a very effective first step.

After that, begin to improve the way you breathe. When you inhale, focus first on filling your lower belly, then your lungs. Do the same when you exhale, by pushing out the air. Do these movements slowly, just as regular waves break on a beach. You do not need to perform this exercise for an extended period of time. If you do it for a few minutes a day, every day, you will progressively attain a feeling of well-being. Five minutes per day is enough. Try to simply observe what is happening. It is recommended that you do this before your individual practices described in the next parts of this book.

When your mind can easily follow this natural movement, you can add a short pause at each step of the cycle. When your lungs are full of air, stop breathing for a few seconds, keeping the air inside. Then exhale. When the lungs are empty, stop breathing for a few seconds. Then inhale. I want to highlight the important fact that these two periods should not be extended too long. Fifteen seconds of lungs full and ten seconds of lungs empty are good at the beginning. After a few weeks, you will find the correct timing for yourself, but do not go too far. Remember to keep your back straight.

Another interesting step that is very good for your health is to practice the same technique, but outdoors. The more your environment is free of pollution, the better your practice will be. If you have the chance to practice on a beach or in the mountains, don't hesitate. Experiment also in a forest or close to a waterfall or a rocky beach. These places produce a large quantity of negative ions [15] that positively affect your personal energy and, eventually, your mood. Practicing breathing techniques in this type of environment is even more beneficial.

As we are living creatures, we are in motion. We are walking, running, hiking, swimming, and doing all kind of physical activities. During this whole time, we breathe. Try

---

15. Negative ions are oxygen atoms charged negatively by their extra electron. They are created by the moving of water, thunderstorms, etc. Their nature allows them to attract airborne particles such as pollutants, allergens, dust, and more. Then they ground these particles, clearing the air and letting you breathe only good air that will rejuvenate your body.

practicing your breathing exercises while walking, for example. Proceed in the same way, but without the retention. During these periods, just focus on your breathing, letting your thoughts go away. You can do the same in a smaller place. Think about monks doing their circumambulations in the small garden of their monastery. They are doing a kind of similar exercise.

After a few weeks of practice, you will realize that you can use this technique to reduce stress and even make it disappear. When you are in a stressful situation—driving on a busy highway, for example—just begin to breathe and to focus your mind on the air. Then your stress will progressively vanish and you will be in a better condition to interact with your environment.

I haven't spoken about relaxation yet because it is better to see it as a consequence of your breathing. If you are practicing at home on a chair, just let your mind scan your body. Continue to keep your breathing in your thoughts and at the same time focus on your head, then your shoulders, your arms, etc. As you focus for a few seconds on them, imagine that they are slightly heavier and relaxed. The feeling of relaxation will progressively extend to your whole body. There are several ways to achieve good relaxation, but this one is easy to do. You can do the same when you are outdoors and even when you are walking. Keep an open mind and explore what you can do with that. Even when you are not working with the individual Masonic techniques provided in this book, it is helpful to use breathing and relaxation just before going to sleep. Your night will be better, and you will wake up well rested.

Clear the Mind

You already know that clearing your mind can be a real challenge. It is easy to focus for a few seconds or even minutes, but then a flow of distracting thoughts rapidly slips into your mind, breaking your peaceful meditation. Trying to repel them often strengthens their power. Imagine a dam stopping a flow of water: it must be a strong structure that cannot fail. This is not the best way to clear your mind. Peace is always better than restraint. It's a fact that thoughts are produced constantly, and our Western culture does nothing to slow this down. On the contrary, there is almost no peaceful place: noise and music are everywhere all the time. I love hiking, and in past years I was shocked to run into some people on the trail who were carrying speakers with music playing. They were often teenagers or young adults. You cannot find peace if your brain is constantly attacked by this kind of noisy aggression. Even more, the neurological system of such people is destabilized and can even be damaged. This is not the fault of listening to music, but it is a situation in which there is no time for silence or for natural sounds.[16] If you want to clear your mind, you must first be quiet and create a silent environment around yourself. Use the opportunity to go outdoors to find this peace, and you might be surprised by the effect. It is the same when you are doing your spiritual practices: you can use music during your rituals, but doing this all the time would be a mistake. Do not exceed fifty percent of the time. During your preparation for a ceremony, keep the place quiet. Then you will be able to do some real inner work.

I now give you two techniques to help you in this process. The first one is comprised of an addition of perceptions. As your brain generates thoughts without your consent, you will choose which ones to focus on. The average person has a limited number of simultaneous thoughts the brain can handle. If you focus on one thing, there is room for other thoughts generated by your brain. If you focus on two, there is less room, and so on. When you are focusing on your breathing and simultaneously observing your physical activity, being aware of walking, for example, you are beginning to clear your mind. You can incorporate the awareness of the sounds of your environment, the feeling of the air on your skin, or the awareness of the smells. Adding these elements will shut off the production of new thoughts, for lack of room. When you have succeeded in producing this effect, you will go back, reversing the process by diminishing the number of thoughts you chose. You will think about your breathing and walking, then keep in mind only the movement of the air, and eventually nothing. Then you will be surprised to discover that the simple fact of focusing on your breath for a few seconds will naturally trigger the process of emptying your mind.[17]

The second method, which is not incompatible with the first one, consists of observing the flow of your thoughts. Here is the process you can use: When you are breathing peacefully with nothing specific to focus on, you will see thoughts appearing. Suddenly, you will realize that you are following a chain of thoughts that drive you far from your starting point. Don't try to stop them. Follow the flow of these thoughts but as a disinterested observer: be aware of the movement without being part of it. Don't worry about losing control by being taken away by the flow. Come back to your breathing. Then when

---

16. I use this opportunity to invite you to discover a set of ethics promoting conservation in the outdoors. It is called "leave no trace" and can be found on the following website: https://lnt.org. The section about natural sounds will help you to continue this reflection.

17. This is a method I personally teach in workshops and that you can master rapidly. Don't hesitate to visit my website (www.debiasi.org) to find out about the next workshop on this topic.

you are the observer, focus on the breathing more intensely for a few seconds. The next step is to allow the flow to come back. You will see that this back-and-forth will help you to decrease the flow.

To begin this step, choose the method you feel is most appropriate for you. Experiment and be patient. This step is not always the easiest one, but once you feel it, you will have made considerable progress.

Visualization

I like to say that visualization is the main key to a successful spiritual practice. If this skill is not mastered, it can affect your whole life for better or worse.

First, you should know that the word *visualization*, although correct, can be misleading. Visualization is not necessarily a mental picture! You can build a very efficient visualization without mentally seeing anything.

Building a clear, strong, and precise mental image is difficult and challenging to maintain for a few minutes. Of course, we can be trained to do this, but it is not necessarily the best way to learn. When someone says to me that they have difficulty with this, my answer is often this: Do you think that someone who is blind from birth can visualize? Do you think he will use visual representations? Do you think he will draw a kind of mental picture? Certainly not! He will create a mental representation composed of sounds, feelings, and smells.

It is the same for us. We don't all memorize in the same way. Some people will clearly remember a picture; for others, it is a scent or sound. Even if we are not blind, one of our senses often dominates the others. An interesting first step is to discover which one. If it is hearing, for example, you will build your inner representation with sounds. Then progressively you will incorporate other senses, such as smell, touch, and sight. Keeping this in mind will help you to choose which sense you should begin with.

The goal is to build a mental representation of what you are trying to achieve and to focus on it.

The example of a flashlight will illustrate what I mean. In this case, sight is the main sense involved. Imagine you are camping in a remote place. Night comes and everything is dark around you. Then you grab your flashlight, turn it on, and point it in front of you. Suddenly that area becomes visible. When you begin to mentally visualize, you are in the same situation. The main object you are focusing on is in the center, but is surrounded by many other ideas, which may disturb your focus. The trick in your visualization is to isolate the single image you chose. As you do with a lamp, you will reduce the focus to include the diameter of the space that is lit up. If you have done this once, you know that by so doing, you isolate the object, but you also increase the light's intensity. This is exactly what will happen with your visualization. When this is done, keep it in mind for a few minutes. As I explained before, it is the same process for a sound; you always hear a multitude of them, but you can focus on one and isolate it. Then the other sounds seem to diminish and almost disappear. You can understand now why *visualizing* can also be called *focusing*.

The process is simple but requires several training sessions in order to master it. Here is how you can proceed in two simple steps. First, focus on a memory of something from your daily environment. Choose a simple object you see or use every day, such as your bed, your car, or your computer. While sitting down, breathing and relaxed, focus on this object and keep it in your mind for a few seconds or minutes. To increase the focus, move the object in your mind. Imagine the bed moving up, spinning, slowing down, and coming back to its place. Try not to be disturbed by other ideas during this exercise. When you are done with this, proceed in the same way with someone you know—a child or spouse, for example. Once you have this person precisely in your mind, do the same thing and move him. Connect this practice with the breathing explained above. Try to maintain this visualization for five minutes.

I also suggest immediately applying the following practice for yourself. Visualize one of your organs. The purpose of this is to increase its proper functioning or to cure it. The only thing you must do after focusing on it is to incorporate the idea of a perfect organ. You will be able to see firsthand the effect of your visualization.

As this book is about Freemasonry, the second step is about selecting a simple symbol that you will visualize during your period of esoteric work. Again, it is important to focus on it while keeping in mind the observation of your breathing. Do not try to interpret the symbol. An important key here is focusing on a single image without interpretation. Change the symbol the next time you perform another individual practice; it's important not to use the same one every time.

When you feel that these exercises are easy for you to achieve, you can go a step further and enlarge your focus to include other elements that will interact with each other. You can find more details in the part about tracing boards in the next chapter. They are a good example of groups of symbols that are related to each other. You can proceed the same way you did before until you reach a satisfactory level of control. The last piece of advice I want to give you here is this: Always stay in control of what you are doing. Just as you turn a flashlight on and then off again so as not to wear out the battery, it is the same for you. You must be the one who decides when to start and stop the exercise. Control is paramount. Then you will be able to go further with your training.

Invocations

Rituals are composed of many elements that must be mastered to achieve reliable and beneficial results. After learning how to breathe and visualize, you must understand how to invoke. The rituals provided in this book are not magic. They provide a way to enlighten your spirit and reach a higher level of consciousness. They also open for you a mysterious gate to an inner understanding of a timeless tradition. All these goals are worthy and will help you in your daily life, as long as you keep dogmas away.

Every technique that has been previously learned must be kept and used. It is easy to understand that spoken words must be harmonized with breathing. Just breathe normally, fully aware of the movements of your body while you speak. Don't push too much or exaggerate your breathing. Stay as close as possible to a natural rhythm.

It is common to say that spoken words should be filled with emotion and understanding to be efficient. This is true but with the following exception: emotion must not overwhelm your inner work and control of your visualization. This is why you should begin with an absence of feeling. You don't need to understand all the philosophical meanings of the texts spoken; a basic understanding is enough at this point. In fact, some ancient Egyptian words have no meaning today. So to begin, find the right way to place your voice: it must be clear and intelligible. There is no link between a loud declamation and a powerful one. Your environment will determine what is the most appropriate level, but usually it is enough if you can hear your own voice. You can pronounce the texts outside of the ritual to detect the difficulties.

Then go ahead. Remember never to let your intellectual mind disrupt the focus and control you have of your mental process. The success of the practice relies on this.

Movements

You can perform most parts of the practices while seated. However, you will have to move in your lodge, including your arms. These movements support your inner work by moving the energy inside you and around you. None of them should be accidental. They are usually precisely described, and you must follow the indications provided. They must be associated with your breathing. If you must raise your arms, for example, you should inhale at the same time. If you knock with the gavel, the movement of knocking will be done while exhaling. Walking will be accompanied by regular and harmonious breathing. To add all these indications in the text would be confusing, and you would lose the main purpose. This is why these precise teachings are often given orally. Nevertheless, the information about breathing and visualization explained previously will help you to feel what is right regarding movement.

As a daily training, while walking, for example, try to associate everything you've learned. Breathe, open your eyes without interpreting what is around you, ground your body, and walk in harmony, feeling every step under your feet, until unsolicited thoughts disappear naturally. It will be easy afterward to do the same in your spiritual practices.

Meditation

Almost everyone today seems to know about meditation, but although the word is well known, explaining it is not always easy. I can write about Masonic or Christian meditation, but in this case, there are specific characteristics on which we need to comment. There is no need to talk about the benefits of meditation, as they are well known: lowering blood pressure, reducing stress, improving focus, and much more. Meditation as such was defined in the Middle Ages by a monk named Guigo II. He was the first one to name meditation as the second of four steps that composed the "ladder of paradise." As this Carthusian monk explained, there are four steps to ascend from the world to God: *lectio, meditatio, oratio,* and *contemplatio* (reading, meditation, prayer, and contemplation). As Guido II explained: "Meditation is a laborious activity, with which our mind uses the lights of our reason to find a deep understanding of a hidden truth." The more the soul progresses in the meditation, the more God seems large to his eyes. Then the soul uses prayer to continue the ascent until he reaches silence and solitude to progressively be in contact with the divine. Meditation is not limited by our understanding, but rather is an activity of the soul, a spiritual process.

As you can see, meditation today usually combines the three upper steps of this mystical ladder. If you follow the process I explained previously, you already have reached this second step and created this step of consciousness in which thoughts have vanished. The mind appeased can focus on a target point. It could be the resolution of an intellectual or spiritual problem, the cure of an organ, the visualization of a divinity, or simply an inner silence. All these aspects are consequences of your preparation and are part of meditation.

Nonetheless, a spiritual path does not end with meditation. This medieval image of the ladder was correct. When this state of meditation has been reached, another tool is used: prayer. I want to associate the latter with meditation because several techniques are closely connected. Prayer will be based on breathing, visualization, specific positions, and invocations. Mantras are often used as a way to intensify this complex inner process. Prayer beads are tools to help your progress. [18] In this book, I give you an example you can use to experiment and feel the benefits of this practice. The "ascent to the Good" described by Plato is followed by the step called *contemplation*. This step can be seen as an extension of your consciousness, an opening of your mind to a planetary, or even cosmic, awareness. This very intense emotion, being part of a cosmic harmony or beauty, can be obtained through this ascent of the soul, but also during an aesthetic experience.

Now, it is useful to know what the specifics of an esoteric Masonic meditation are. It can be understood by considering another parallel system. Christian priests and monks learned from pagan philosophies and adapted the techniques to their own purposes. The symbol of the cross and the episodes of the life of Christ were visualized in their daily prayers. Sometimes cycles of many days were used to follow the episodes of his life and identify with it. Visualization, prayers, and mantras help the believer in this inner process. As you may realize, this combination of techniques is the core of the spiritual work. Then specific symbols are coherently organized, based on the myths of the group. Stories, such as the death and resurrection of Osiris or Hiram, become the focus of the initiate. Consequently, Masonic meditation is not just a meditation, but a very precise process following the main symbols and sequences of the myths of each degree. Furthermore, to be efficient, this spiritual practice must follow natural cycles such as those of the moon and the sun. Sacred stories of the tradition should also be used at precise dates, such as the birth of Christ and Mithra on December 25.

Obviously, all of the above has been neglected or ignored, and it is time for those interested to put their tools to use.

Building of the Inner World

Everything just explained has a very interesting side effect: it will help to make the system real inside you. When a Mason is initiated, he goes through the process of the initiation; then he must learn and remember traditional teachings. Most of the time, the teachings

---

18. I wrote a book about this fantastic tool called *The Magical Use of Prayer Beads*, published by Llewellyn.

are outdated, so apparently the goal is not to use them in real life; rather, the point is to create an identification between the beliefs involved in the system and the mind of the new initiate. Progressively, the words repeated, the lessons remembered and recited, turn out to be real for the follower. The system stops being a tool and becomes a truth that cannot be discussed. On the contrary, esotericism is supposed to aid in the development of critical minds that understand and respect its tradition. As such, initiates use these tools to make the inner experience happen. All the symbols and stories related to the degrees help to build an inner scenery. Each degree becomes an act of the play, which is the whole system. As you can see, the point is not to know whether the story is true or not, but to realize that it will affect us. The techniques must help us build this inner theater and make it as real as possible. It must become an inner reality used as a tool, but you must be careful, because the border between spiritual practice and delusion is very thin. You should find the right balance between skepticism and confidence in the effectiveness of this inner work. I am using the word *effective* and not *faith*, which is related to religion. In the Western tradition, such an initiatic journey is an inner experience aiming to escort you in this ascent to another level of consciousness. Freemasonry often uses the Platonist injunction "Know yourself," without saying how. Esoteric Freemasonry provides more practical keys, as you can see. This discovery of who you are is not a question of faith, but a matter of clearheadedness. As the philosopher Nietzsche once wrote: "If you wish to strive for peace of soul and pleasure, then believe; if you wish to be a devotee of truth, then inquire." [19]

Group Process

This book is about individual practices. The techniques explained in the previous paragraphs are intended to help you in your journey into Egyptian Freemasonry. Of course, Freemasonry has existed mainly as a brotherhood, a structured organization managed by a hierarchy of officers. Today, each lodge follows the official ritual. A few details or local traditions are sometimes added to it, but nothing that can endanger the permanence of the system. You know now that it has not been this way at all times and in every place, especially if we consider Freemasonry worldwide in all of these organizations, large and small.

Some Masonic lodges can be considered esoteric, since they are aware of these techniques, are open to them, and talk about them. Others try to implement elements of more traditional symbols, such as the elements during the initiation of the chamber of reflection.

19. Nietzsche, *Twilight of the Idols.*

Then a third category explicitly teaches some of these techniques to the initiates and asks them to continue the practice at home. In this case, the whole group benefits greatly from the efforts of each one. In fact, the common ritual performed by initiates who are working individually is even greater than the sum of its participants. The whole is superior by the addition of its elements. This is the beauty of a common ritual, but it begins with the real action of each one.

Individual Rituals and Self-Initiations

This step combines all the previous techniques into a whole that is structured and organized. Steps and degrees for the training are essential. The rituals and the practices have been prepared to escort you on this spiritual journey.

The rituals of the degrees provided here are not simple copies of what you can find in a lodge. They have been adapted for individual use. Throughout its history, Egyptian Freemasonry created a large number of rituals. Some are very close, while others (such as the Sophisians) are very different. The first three degrees are usually more similar than the high degrees. However, even in this case they are choices to make. The goal has been to keep the Egyptian Masonic traditional basis, but to go further. Several rituals contain important keys on a practical level that make the ritual more efficient. Sometimes the rituals even needed to be corrected, which has been done.

The rituals in this book provide the most efficient Egyptian Masonic individual work you can find. It is not philosophic, philanthropic, or social. These rituals and practices can really raise your state of consciousness and open for you a different view of the world. They can even improve your inner abilities and have a very positive effect on your daily life.

I must emphasize two important statements about self-initiations:

1. Nothing can totally replace a real initiation performed by the officers of a lodge upon a candidate. The ritual work creates an interaction between people present in the room that may deeply impact the psyche of the initiate.

2. Almost all the Masonic rituals presented here have already been published and are available in books or on the internet. Sometimes the passwords are provided, and sometimes not, but it takes only a few seconds on Google to find them. In any case, they are not worth searching for, because they are not the interesting part of the esoteric process.

Additionally, the ritual texts are not typically useful for the non-initiate. This is why these adaptations will be useful for someone who is eager to experiment or to reactivate what has already been experienced in a lodge.

Keep in mind that self-initiations really work on a spiritual level and can sometimes be more powerful than initiations performed in a lodge. We must admit that not all Masons are able to perform a good initiation, even one that has real action on the spiritual plane.

Consequently, don't hesitate to experiment and explore. Just reading and thinking about it are not enough. You should try. Without action, nothing really exists. Real individual work is the key to success.

Chapter 14

Rituals and Practices of the Three Degrees

First Degree

Opening Ceremony of Your Lodge in the First Degree

When your lodge has been installed, you should begin with a short and silent relaxation. Just sit and breathe for a few moments. Music is allowed but not mandatory. The light should be soft and indirect. Artificial light is not a problem as long as it is not too bright and allows you to read your ritual text easily.

The sacred book is still closed, the square and the compass placed on it but not intertwined. The compass is not open. The representation of the lodge carpet is rolled up, or its front side is hidden.

When your breathing is deep and slow, stand up and put on your Masonic regalia.

Light the small candle, the symbol of the sacred fire.

Sit again on your chair, back straight, facing east. Place your hands flat on your thighs. Close your eyes, relax, and breathe quietly. Take a moment to mentally prepare yourself for the ritual that is about to follow. Let your thoughts come and go freely. Then after a few minutes, focus on your breathing. Observe the air moving in and out of your lungs. As you are in a period of preparation, limit this time to approximately three minutes. Follow the spiritual training I explained in the previous chapter.

Stand up and move the chair to have more room around you.

Take the gavel and knock once on the table. Raise the sacred fire. Breathe deeply and regularly as you keep the fire raised.

Then say:

I invoke your presence, divine powers, and I humbly bow down in front of you.

Extend your arms, holding the fire as you bow down. Stay in this position a few seconds, then rise up straight, the fire at the height of your heart. Then continue:

I salute you and welcome you to this sacred place.

Set the fire in its place on your altar. Raise your hands toward the east, palms up, and say:

May this light be the manifestation of your spiritual light!
 May this lodge be duly tiled and protected against all creatures, visible and invisible, that would desire to threaten me!
 May silence prevail!

Meditate for a few moments in peace, establishing in yourself that inner silence. Then continue by saying:

I stand in this lodge to work sincerely under the auspices of the pure Masonic Egyptian tradition of the origins.
 As the temples of the sacred land of Egypt were protected visibly and invisibly, so now is this place.

Place your right hand on your chest. Breathe and stay silent for a few moments, aware of the solemnity of the moment. Then sit down and meditate. After a few minutes, stand up and continue, saying:

As a Mason of ancient Egypt, I work tirelessly to help humanity to become better and live in peace.
 Every day, I build altars to virtue and dig tombs for vices.
 As an initiate, I must illuminate this lodge, calling the spiritual light to be visible again, bringing its blessings upon those who are in its presence.

Take the small candle you will use to light the three larger candles. Light it to the sacred fire, raise the flame, and say:

The shining Eye of Horus is coming! The luminous Eye of Horus is coming! Peaceful and radiant as Re on the horizon, he is coming!

With his fire and heat, he repels the power of Seth. Following Re, his flame left the sky and is coming. The Eye of Horus is living in the Ouryt. The Eye of Horus is alive. He is Ioun-moutef.

You can have soft music playing in the background during the lighting of the candles. (You can find examples on my website at www.debiasi.org.)

Light the first candle, which represents Wisdom. (This candle has been placed at the east side of the black-and-white mosaic.) As you light it, say:

May the divine Wisdom be present in this Lodge!

Light the second candle, which represents Strength. (This candle has been placed at the southwest side of the black-and-white mosaic.) As you light it, say:

May the divine Omnipotent Strength be present in this Lodge!

Light the third candle, which represents Beauty. (This candle has been placed at the northwest side of the black-and-white mosaic.) As you light it, say:

May the divine Beauty be present in this Lodge!

Breathe deeply one time and light the three candles that are in front of the representation of the triangle in the east. Start with the left candle (north), then the right candle (south) and the central one. While lighting the candles, say:

O Isis, I light the fire for you and I repel Seth, as he threatened you.

Extinguish the small candle you used to light the others. Breathe deeply one time, then light the incense you prepared at the beginning of the ceremony. While the smoke of the incense is rising, turn your hands toward the sky and say:

The Eye of Horus was hiding you in his tears and his perfume is rising to you, O Isis. It rises to you who are among the goddesses and gods.

Divine perfume, twice good, rise as a god. Ra-Horkhouiti loves you and his nostrils welcome you. Be pure resin. The eye of Re makes you rise to the sky. Gods welcome you as their hearts love you. Be in peace!

The big crown of perfume rises to the head of Isis and shines on her head.

May this sweet perfume bring peace to my soul, decrease my troubling passions, and help me to become fraternal to every human being, raising my mind and heart.

Breathe deeply one time and say:

The architect who built the first pyramid worked with tools that still exist today. They are, for Freemasons, precious symbols of the construction of the temples of gods and the temple of each of us. Sometimes they are called "Jewels of the Lodge."

With the word of Thot, they manifest the invisible in the visible. These are the compass, the square, and the rule. Without them, nothing can be achieved. May these three symbols manifest their presence and power.

Open the sacred book, place the square, the compass, and the rule according to the position of the first degree, and then say:

Now, the Jewels shine from the center of the Naos.
So may the divine be invoked.

Kneel, bow your head, and say:

O Isis, you are the nature, mother of all things, mistress of the elements, original principle of time, supreme divinity, queen of dead souls, the first among those who live in the sky, universal image of gods and goddesses. Heaven and its luminous ceiling, the sea and its cool wind, hell and its silence chaos, obey your laws. You are the unique power worshipped through as many shapes, devotions, and names as there are people on earth.

O Supreme Architect of the Universe, bless this lodge and my work. Give me light. Disperse the darkness that veils truth. Let me see the order of the cosmos and then my soul will rise and contemplate the beauty of all things that have been, are, and will be!

Stay silent a few seconds, then stand up and sit on your chair. After a few moments of contemplation, continue the ritual, saying:

Symbolically, an apprentice Freemason is three years old.

I am a Mason from Egypt. As such and according to the tradition, our work begins when the sun rises on the sands of Memphis, at noon when the shadow is the shortest.

After a few moments of contemplation, keep saying:

As this lodge is now purified, protected, and lightened, as it is time and I have the symbolic age required, may the sacred words be again spoken.

Stand up and face east.

Place your left hand upon your chest, then knock three times with your gavel (or your fist) according to the following sequence: 2–1 (2 knocks, pause, 1 knock).

Then place your right hand on your left hand. Hold this position and say:

To the glory of the Supreme Architect of the Worlds, to the glory of the gods and goddesses of the sacred land of Egypt, by the divine powers that are part of every human being, I declare open this ceremony working at the first degree of the Masonic order!

Release your arms and say:

I'm not in the profane world anymore. May my works and those of all Freemasons all over the earth who are working as I am remain consistent with the Universal Harmony. May my work proclaim only the glory of the Grand Architect, the gods and goddesses of the sacred land of Egypt, the permanence of True Freemasonry and the Happiness of all Beings.
    So mote it be!

The following are the specific texts to use when you are working toward the second or third degree. Then you can sit and start your esoteric work, which I will explain in the next section.

Closing Ceremony of Your Lodge in the First Degree

When your esoteric work is achieved and after a moment of rest and relaxation, stand up, open your arms toward the east, palms up, and say:

May the Supreme Architect of all Worlds, the goddesses and gods of the sacred land of Egypt, be praised for their assistance and protection!

Now place your right hand upon your heart and your left hand upon the right. Then say:

I swear to live every day according to the high standards of morals that have been taught to me by this Masonic tradition.

The vice of the soul is ignorance. When I am not learning who I am, what nature is, neither the Good, then my soul cannot resist corporeal desires. She becomes enslaved by my body. She carries it as a burden. This is the vice of the soul.

On the contrary, the virtue of the soul is knowledge, as the one who knows is good, pious, and already divine.

I have been following this rule today, working in my heart in this lodge, uniting myself fraternally with all initiates present under the square, for the happiness of all beings.

May the Supreme Architect of all Worlds, the goddesses and gods, continue to support my inner work!

After a moment of silence, open your arms, raise your eyes to the sky toward the east, and say:

Eternal power, I salute you. My soul and my heart praise you!

As I am about to close this spiritual work, allow my eyes to be liberated from the veil of illusions.

Enlighten my soul as you have illuminated me.

May these lights, soon to be veiled, place in my soul their power and their strength.

Close your eyes, creating a perfect inner and outer silence. Imagine around you all Freemasons of the earth receiving this divine light. Visualize that you are part of this universal chain. Feel the love and brotherhood coming from this shared desire to perfect themselves and rise to the best of humanity.

You can use music during this meditation.

Keeping this scene and feeling in your mind, say:

May this fraternal chain be so strong that nothing can ever alter it.

Open your eyes, then release your hands and your visualization.

After a few moments, say:

May wisdom enlighten me!

Extinguish the candle located on the east side of the mosaic. Then say:

May strength give me good health!

Extinguish the candle on the southwest side of the mosaic. Then say:

May beauty guide me on the path!

Extinguish the candle on the northwest side of the mosaic. Then extinguish the three candles in the east in reverse order from the opening (central candle, then the right and the left).

Separate the rule, the square, and the compass, saying for each tool:

May this rule keep me in the path of the Truth.
   May this square always govern my actions.
   May this compass allow me to moderate my passions.

Close the sacred book.

Knock three times as you did for the opening (2–1), and place your right hand on your chest. Then say:

To the Glory of the Supreme Architect of the Worlds, to the glory of the gods and goddesses of the sacred land of Egypt, by the divine powers that are part of every human being, I declare closed this ceremony working at the first degree of the Masonic order!

After a brief moment of silence, say:

I have only one vow to ask. I want to keep in me Wisdom and Knowledge, revealing the divine presence within me as I go further on the sacred path of return.
   May the regular practice of the sacred Mysteries protect me forever from falling off this kind of life!
   So mote it be!

Your lodge is now closed and you can store all your tools.

Ceremony of Self-Initiation to the First Degree Apprentice
Preparation of the Ritual

I can understand the temptation to read the text of the initiation before proceeding. If you can resist, don't read it beforehand. If you can't resist, don't read it carefully. Stay superficial. In any case, I will give you all the indications and items you need for this initiation so you can be completely ready before you begin.

Time

I recommend performing this initiation during a quiet period. It is important not to be disturbed during the process. Turn off your phone and choose a time when nobody is at home. Night is often a good idea. If you live in the country and can be sure of being undisturbed, you can even perform this ritual outside.

Your Preparation

As this is your first initiation, it is obvious that you will not wear an apron. Wear a kind of clothing that expresses the respect you want to show to this tradition and to the divine powers invoked during this ceremony.

Without any specific indication in the ritual, do not wear anything on your head or your hands.

Prepare the apron needed for the Apprentice. Even if it has not been an absolute rule in the history of Freemasonry, almost everywhere these days this first apron is usually plain white.

Preparation of the Room

As you begin your Masonic path today, you are not supposed to know the installation present in the lodge room. So here is how to proceed before you begin. First, set up the scenery. Install the black-and-white mosaic and the three columns around it. In the center, place your sacred book, the square, and the compass. To the east, install the representations of the columns and the pentalpha.

On the left (north), install a second small table covered with a black cloth. It will play the role of the chamber of reflection. I have already described this hidden part of the lodge. After placing all the items needed on it, cover them with a light black veil.

For the initiation itself, you should prepare the following items: a black veil that is large enough to cover your head and face, a cup of water, a censer, and incense.

The Oath

Here is the text of the oath you will have to copy by hand during the ritual. As you will recall, this text is specific, so follow the guidelines given in chapter 13 in the section called "Invocations."

I, (your name), I stand in the presence of this invisible respectable assembly of Masons, the wardens of this sacred temple, and in union with the egregore of the Egyptian Freemasonry.

In front of me are the sacred symbols, and I swear upon them to keep secret what the invisible masters will reveal to me in the process of this ceremony and during my individual practices.

I swear to work with zeal, constancy, and regularity to understand the Masonic tradition and apply its highest principles in my life.

I swear to practice assistance to the weak, justice to all, devotion to my family and my country and to humanity, and dignity to myself.

I swear to become an example of what mankind has best, by studying and practicing the precepts contained in the universal code of morals.

I swear to consider every individual as a human being, regardless of social class, tribe, color, sex, religion, or nationality.

I swear to reject all vain desire for honor and ambition, as long as the unique goal is my own glory.

I swear to reject vanity.

I swear to defend the principles of reason, tolerance, and fraternity.

So mote it be!

Ritual

When you are ready and all is in place, stand in front of your altar (which is the representation of the lodge) and breathe in silence. Dim the lights in order to create a more meditative atmosphere, but keep enough light to be able to read.

Turn to your left and face north. The chamber of reflection is covered by the thin black veil. Breathe, and in silence, remove it, carefully placing it beside you.

Take a few seconds to look at the symbols placed (or represented) in front of you. Then read the following text:

After going down in the deep ground, I stand now in the cold, mysterious cave, symbol of my corporeal envelope. In front of me are the representation of the human death and the elements of its alchemical transformation. One of the main objectives of the initiation is to allow my soul to regain its original faculties while establishing a harmonious balance with the physical body.

   Everything here reminds me of the inevitability of this passage. As Lucius Apuleius said: "To have a good life, first we must meditate on death."

Sit and take a few moments to meditate on the meaning of your death and its importance in your life. If you want to write a few words about that, feel free to do so on the blank page you prepared previously. Take whatever time you need for this meditation.

Then take the white page and write in black the text of the following oath you will have to pronounce later during the ritual.

When you are done, roll the page like an ancient parchment and place it at the west side of the black-and-white mosaic, which is the closest side to you.

When you are done, say:

O you who escort the perfect souls to Osiris, hear my voice and guide me to him. May my soul listen as you listen, see as you see, stand up as you stand up, and sit as you sit.

   O you who open the gates and guide the soul to Osiris's house, assist my soul in such a journey. May my soul leave this place in peace and love, because I am just.

Stand up. Place on your head the black veil. Place it so that your face remains uncovered. Then face the east and kneel. Stay silent for a few seconds and join your hands, with the fingers of both hands crossed.

Keeping this position, say:

O you, the One who rises with the moon!

   O you, the One who shines as the moon, help me to ascend to the outer world. Untie me to allow me to reach the light and the company of the inhabitants of this world. Open for me the door of the Duat.

Open your hands and raise them toward the sky, palms up. Then say:

I search the sky, I search the horizon, and I walk all around the world. I entered as a falcon and I leave as a phoenix. Morning star, open for me the gates, and may I enter in this new world in peace. Show me the path to worship Osiris, the master of life!

First Journey: Water

Replace the document you just read and raise your hands toward the sky. Then say:

The sky opens. The earth opens. The chapel of the west opens. The chapel of the east opens. The chapel of the south opens. The chapel of the north opens. The doors open to welcome Re standing on the bark of the day as he breathes Maat!

Release your arms and face west. Then say:

I am standing in front of the west as a free and honest man (woman).

Knock your gavel four times on the altar.
Take the cup of water in your left hand and raise it to the sky for a few seconds, saying:

From the west, I place myself under the protection of Osiris.

Lower the cup and plunge the thumb of your right hand in the water. Then trace an equal-armed cross (four branches of the same length) on your forehead, saying:

From the west, may this water purify all parts of my being.

Face north and proceed in the same way, using the same invocations while replacing the name of the direction with the correct one. The sequence is north, east, and south.
Face west again and replace the cup.

Second Journey: Air

Facing east, light the incense and place it in the censer. Then say:

I am standing in front of the east as a free and honest man (woman).

Knock your gavel four times on the altar.
Take the censer in your left hand and raise it to the sky for a few seconds, saying:

From the east, I place myself under the protection of Osiris.

Lower the censer and plunge the thumb of your right hand in the smoke of the incense. Then trace an equal-armed cross (four branches of the same length) on your forehead, saying:

From the east, may this perfume purify all parts of my being.

Face south and proceed in the same way, using the same invocations while replacing the name of the direction with the correct one. The sequence is south, west, and north.

Face east again and replace the censer.

Third Journey: Fire

Facing south, light the candle previously prepared. Then say:

I am standing in front of the south as a free and honest man (woman).

Knock your gavel four times on the altar.

Take the candle in your left hand and raise it to the sky for a few seconds, saying:

From the south, I place myself under the protection of Osiris.

Lower the candle and place your thumb over the flame for a few seconds to warm up your finger. Then trace an equal-armed cross (four branches of the same length) on your forehead, saying:

From the south, may this heat purify all parts of my being.

Face west and proceed in the same way, using the same invocations while replacing the name of the direction with the correct one. The sequence is west, north, and east.

Face south again and raise the candle for a few seconds. Then lower the candle to heart level and face east.

The Sacrifice

Place the candle, still burning, on the altar in front of you, and say:

Now purified, it is time for me to take the decisive step that will manifest my renunciation of the profane world and my commitment to this spiritual path of virtue and light.

Many Masonic groups have forgotten the profound significance of this renunciation. Their ignorance led to the dangerous use of the physical suffering of the candidate to conclude a pact with the invisible. The effect of this is to reduce the freedom of the initiate and to bind him magically to an egregore that can control him.

The real Egyptian Freemasonry of the origins does not practice this form of magic harmful to the initiate.

The goal of my renunciation of the profane world is intended to manifest my will to dedicate myself to the service of the Light.

This is why I will now proceed to the sacrifice of a physical part of myself. This will constitute the physical mark of my renunciation.

Take a pair of scissors and cut a small lock of your hair. Place it inside a small piece of folded white paper. Place it close to the roll of the oath that has been placed on the eastern part of the black-and-white mosaic.

Kneel and say:

I have been purified and I have now to leave this mundane world to unite my soul to the esoteric Masonic tradition.

I know that an oath pronounced in the presence of spiritual powers is binding and will have consequences for me if I don't fulfill its terms.

This is why, I, (your name), agreed to proceed further in this ceremony.

The Light

Say:

The shining Eye of Horus is coming. He is coming in peace, shining as Re in the horizon. His flame is coming and rejects the power of Seth. The light is coming from the sky following Re. The Eye of Horus is alive and he is bringing me light!

Knock your gavel three times on the altar, first a sequence of two knocks and then a final one.

Remove the veil from your head and look up, feeling the presence of this spiritual light. Breathe in peace for a few seconds.

Stand up. Raise the candle burning in front of you while saying:

Ineffable Wisdom, Unknown God of the Temples of Memphis,
*   Let there be Light!*

At the time of the pronunciation of the second sentence, light the first candle that represents Wisdom. This candle has been placed at the southeast side of the black-and-white mosaic (the top right from you).

Breathe deeply one time, then raise the small candle again while saying:

O Omnipotent Strength of the first Manifestation,
   Let there be Light!

As you did with the previous candle, light the second candle, which represents Strength. It is located on the southwest side of the mosaic, at the bottom right in front of you.

Breathe deeply one time, then raise the small candle again while saying:

O Eternal Beauty, who arranges and harmonizes everything in all Worlds,
   Let there be Light!

As you did with the previous candle, light the third candle, which represents Beauty. It is located on the northwest side of the mosaic, to the bottom left in front of you.

Breathe deeply one time and light the three candles that are in front of the representation of the triangle in the east. Start with the left candle (north), then the right candle (south) and the central one.

Replace the candle you used to light the others close to your oath.

Breathe deeply one time and say:

The work of architecture that was given to the Freemasons at the dawn of all time is carried out using three tools that bear the beautiful name of "Jewels of the Lodge." These are the compass, the square, and the rule. Without them, nothing can be achieved. May these three symbols be manifested accordingly.

Open the sacred book, place the square, the compass, and the rule according to the position of the first degree (see figure 13), and then say:

Now, the Jewels shine from the center of the Naos in the presence of the spiritual light.

Kneel again, then roll out your oath and say:

Here is the time in the presence of this spiritual assembly and in union with the egregore of the Egyptian Freemasonry to pronounce my oath.
   May all the invisible presences witness my commitment.

Now read the text of your oath.

When you are done, continue, saying:

This commitment has become part of myself. It must now be sealed and activated on subtle planes. For this, it must be united with the sacrifice I made earlier in the ceremony and burned ritually in the presence of the invisible wardens of this sacred temple.

Stand up and place the white paper containing your hairs inside your oath. Take the container you choose in which to burn these papers. With care, light your oath and hairs before placing them burning in the container. While they are burning, say:

May the invisible wardens and masters of the Masonic tradition witness this act and seal it on the invisible plane.

Human words fly away and disappear, but what is handed over the fire lives forever.

So mote it be!

Let the ashes cool down. At the end of the ceremony, store them in a small box.

Investiture

Cross your arms on your chest, right over left, with the crossing point of your arms upon your heart. Bow your head and say:

To the Glory of the Sublime Architect of the Worlds, in the name of the Masters of the Egyptian Freemasonry, in the presence of this invisible respectable assembly of Masons, and by the power of the ritual I just performed, I solemnly enter into the room prepared for the Apprentice Freemasons.

Release your arms, take your apron, and wear it. From now on, every time you perform a ritual practice, wear this apron, as it is the reminder of your initiation.

Take time to read the following paragraph. You can sit if you want.

You have entered into the world of the Apprentice Freemasons. As you recall what has been explained previously in this book, since the revival of modern Freemasonry in 1717, the symbolism of construction has assumed great importance. Many tools of architects and builders have been associated with Masonic rituals. A number of them have become symbols with an esoteric meaning. As an initiate Mason, you have to practice and learn to better understand the meanings of these tools.

However, you decided to learn more about esoteric Freemasonry. As such, you will have access to the roots of the true Freemasonry of the origins. This is not in the eighteenth century, nor in the Middle Ages, nor even in Israel. It appeared in Chaldea, Egypt, Greece, and Rome. It is these constructors who have associated a moral value with the symbols of architects and builders.

We can go even further and affirm that the source of Freemasonry is found in the temples and religious teachings of ancient Egypt. Remember that the true stone is yourself, and it is upon yourself that this work must take place, under the protection of the Great Architect of the Universe.

During your journey, you will find and learn many signs and passwords. Be aware of this privilege.

For now, it's important that you focus on what you've just experienced and learned. It is a complex internal process that must be respected. It should not be disturbed by unnecessary explanations at this stage.

Take time at the end of this ceremony to take a few notes about what you felt, your thoughts, and whatever seems good and useful to you.

You can now proceed to the simplified closing ceremony.

Closing Ceremony

After a moment of relaxation, say:

The only way I can assist the Supreme Architect of All Worlds as a Mason from the land of Memphis is to behave everywhere like a man of duty, fully loyal to the Supreme Architect and following as absolute laws the voice of my conscience. It is by the latter that a human being is linked to the divine.

I have been following this rule today, working in my heart in the shade of the north and south columns, uniting myself fraternally to all initiates present under the square, for the happiness of all beings.

Stand up, then put your right hand on your heart and say:

Under the Egyptian palm tree, I prepared the temple of wisdom and worked as my Master from noon until midnight.

Now is the time when the night is all over Egypt, and the Star of the nights shines its light on the sleeping Sanctuaries.

After a moment of silence, maintaining the same position, raise your eyes to the east and say:

Eternal and Sovereign power that is invoked under a hundred different names, Supreme Architect, organizer of All Worlds, from this Temple and to You only, my prayers are addressed from my heart. In that way my loyalty is manifested!

As it is time for me to interrupt my mystical works, allow my eyes to be liberated from the veil of lies, errors, and prejudices.

Enlighten my soul as you have illuminated my work, as that worthy of You. Made better by the rejuvenating Fire of the True Masonry, I can one day realize the Perfect organization of Your Wisdom.

May these lights, before being veiled, place in my soul the Fire of their power and their Strength.

Close your eyes, creating a perfect inner and outer silence. Imagine around you all Freemasons of the earth receiving this divine light. Visualize that you are part of this universal chain. Feel the love and brotherhood coming from this common desire to become better humans.

You can use music during this meditation.

Keeping this scene and feeling in your mind, say:

Let me rejoice for this work loyally performed. May I continue to work every day to improve my abilities. May I strengthen in my heart the love of my neighbor and the understanding of my duties, to dedicate myself to the services of immutable Truth, Liberty, Equality, and Fraternity. May this fraternal chain be so strong that nothing can ever alter it.

Open your eyes, and release your hands and your visualization.

After a few moments, say:

May your Wisdom, Grand Architect, be always in my mind!

Extinguish the candle that symbolizes Wisdom, located on the southeast side of the mosaic.

Then say:

May your Strength support me!

Extinguish the candle that symbolizes Strength, located on the southwest side of the mosaic.

Then say:

May your Beauty guide me!

Extinguish the candle that symbolizes Beauty, located on the northwest side of the mosaic.

Then extinguish the three candles in the east in reverse order from the opening (the central candle, then the right and the left).

Separate the rule, the square, and the compass, saying for each tool:

May this rule, symbol of the Eternal Architect, keep me in the path of the Truth.
   May this square, symbol of moral rectitude, always govern my actions.
   May this compass, symbol of measure, allow me to moderate my passions.

Close the sacred book.

Knock three times as you did for the opening (2–1), and place your right hand on your chest. Then say:

To the Glory of the Supreme Architect of the Worlds, by the divine powers that are part of every human being, I declare closed this ceremony working at the first degree of the Masonic order!

After a brief moment of silence, say:

It is in my soul and the soul of my peers that I must sow the Word of Horus, so that it produces fruits of all kinds. For the soul of man is the natural ground over which is the flight of the divine hawk.

   And as the Nile waters fertilize the land of Memphis during the season Akhet and the month of Thoth, may the celestial waters fertilize my inner Temple in the same mysterious season.

   So mote it be!

Individual Practices of the First Degree

Each of the following three ceremonies helps you to select the kind and level of energy that will allow you to raise the vibrations of your sacred space in the degree concerned. Several consequences can be highlighted:

- Your ritual and invocations will modify the kind of astral vibrations of your individual temple. This specific energy surrounds you until the closing of the ceremony.
- Your level of consciousness will also be modified, along with the vibrations of the place.
- You will be connected to the egregore of Freemasonry.
- You will be able to perform specific practices in the best possible psychic conditions.

It is time now to explain some esoteric practices that will allow you to start this exciting work.

Animation of the Tracing Boards

We already talked about the origin and definition of tracing boards. Now it is time to explain how esoteric Freemasonry uses them. This is a process that is usually taught in some lodges to help the initiate really progress in his inner work.

Obviously, this practice can be done with all kinds of tracing boards. Remember that although most of the symbols used on the various boards are the same, their organization may vary according to the years, rites, or intent of the masters of the lodge. Keep in mind something important: if you consider Freemasonry worldwide from its creation until today, you cannot find a real consistency in the use and organization of the symbols.

The process described here can be used for your own purpose for any Masonic degree. You can easily adapt it.

Historically, tracing boards were used to draw plans of the Freemasons' buildings and calculations related to the work of craftsmen. Most of the time they were cleaned after being used. This contributed to the secrecy of the work in progress. Architects usually kept the details of their projects secret. For example, Filippo Brunelleschi, the famous architect who created the dome of Florence's cathedral in Italy, refused to reveal the details of his plan before construction began. Leonardo da Vinci was another renowned artist who used mirror writing, contractions, and shorthand symbols to record his projects. Even if several theories have been developed to explain his motives, it is worth mentioning that this kind of writing has been considered a mystical process from very ancient times.

Anyone who has seen voodoo symbols or Hopi healing symbols temporarily painted on the floor for a ceremony could make a connection with the original Masonic tracing boards. We can also mention the pentacles used in Ptolemaic and medieval magic to invoke spirits or attract invisible powers. Whether chalk or paint is used, the use and purpose of these religious processes give us clues about the esoteric use of this Masonic tool.

According to mainstream Freemasonry, tracing boards are used to teach the lessons of the degree. They are seen as a symbolic summary of the teachings of the degree. As Freemasonry is speculative and no longer operative, these symbols are associated with a moral teaching and should help the initiate to build his inner temple. It is clear that overblown language has often been used to emphasize this brilliant approach. I have never really been convinced by such high expectations. Simply stated, each symbol shown on the board has its own meaning. Like any idea, each one can be developed and associated with our own experience. However, to say that the sun, for example, is the symbol of the light, the square, and of righteousness is charming but limited. Building upon this statement, esoteric Freemasonry went further. Some initiates understood the connection with the ancient magic traditions, using such drawings for a spiritual goal. In this case, the representation itself was supposed to become a magic writing, able to give life to a specific energy. Thus, the design is considered to have a power by itself. This is called a performative design, which is used in radionics. Beginning in ancient Egypt, initiates added a second layer of mystery by creating a specific way to realize the magical figure. Pigments were not chosen randomly but according to mythological and astrological rules. Colors were linked to specific myths and divinities. Then the method of tracing the representation carefully followed a precise sequence.

We should understand that a magical or spiritual symbol is realized like an actual building. There is a logical way to make it, starting from the foundation to the top. To use an analogy, imagine that the invisible power around us is like a cloud in the sky or humidity in the air. The water dispersed in the air needs a mechanism in order to be extracted, bottled, and used. Technicians build several systems, such as specific kinds of wire mesh or fencing. Placed at precise locations, these obstacles are able to catch the surrounding water, gathering all the drops present in the atmosphere. I am sure you have already applied this analogy to the making of a performative representation. The invisible energy that surrounds us should be caught with the help of a specific mechanism. Ancient initiates in all cultures used various ingredients such as a sacred alphabet and symbols. Likewise, esoteric

Freemasons applied these symbolic rules to Freemasonry, specifically to the making of the tracing boards. Most of the time this process was shared orally. Understand that the esoteric process will work even without making or painting the tracing board by yourself. Of course, using the full traditional process will amplify the effect.

As I want to give you the most of this esoteric tradition, I recommend that you print a black-and-white representation of the tracing board at the desired degree. Then you can color the tools and symbols according to your understanding of the symbols. When your tracing board has been completed, you can begin the process.

Remember that one of the most important works is the inner animation of the symbols, as we have just seen with the practice of the compass. Tracing boards are symbolic summaries of the entire structure of the lodge prepared at a specific degree of initiation. You will mentally build not only an isolated symbol but a composite picture as well. This mental process will take several sessions to be completed. This is an essential step in the inner work of an esoteric Freemason.

On the internet you can find a lot of different tracing boards to use. If you are a Mason, you can use the one displayed in your lodge. You can download various interesting examples from my website (www.debiasi.org). Consequently, the process of memorization will be different. The practice described here involves several steps you should follow gradually:

1. Observation of the symbols displayed on the board

2. Memorization of the symbols

3. 3-D creation of the symbols

4. Projection within the board

It is important now to give you some explanations of these steps.

The first one is obvious, and the main challenge is not to associate thinking with observing. Seeing something is different from identifying it. Seeing the symbols means simply to allow their shapes to enter into our minds without any filter. This could be more complicated to master than you previously thought, so do not underestimate this phase.

The second step is very important. This is the memorization of the full picture. Again, do not intellectualize. Start by memorizing the board from the bottom to the top. Alternatively, you can follow whatever sequence seems logical to you. Memorization is different for everyone. For some, it could be to see mentally, while for others it means thinking of something. These differences have no impact on the process. Just memorize in your own way. Using a blank page, you should be able to redraw or place the symbols using their names in their proper locations.

The third step is essential. It consists of a creative mental exercise: transforming the 2-D representation of your board into a 3-D mental model. Many years ago, I attended a Masonic meeting that performed this exercise in a unique manner. During the opening ritual, when the time came to reveal the tracing board placed in the middle of the lodge room, the officer in charge proceeded differently. Instead of bringing a tracing board ready to use, he brought real tools and organized them according to the location they were supposed to have. Rough stone, cord, square, compass, etc., were placed in the center of the room, creating a real 3-D representation. The innovation stopped there and nothing was taught regarding the use of such a remarkable adaptation of the ritual. However, the intuition was correct.

You should proceed in the same way, but mentally. This inner representation should be accomplished with your eyes closed. The representation of the three stairs should appear as three real steps, the two columns as real columns, and so on. Usually this process will take a few sessions to master. I recommend proceeding to the next step only when you begin succeeding in making a 3-D mental representation of these tools. Obviously, to keep all the symbols together can be quite challenging, but you do not have to wait for complete success in order to progress to the next step. Each of your ritual sessions will train you to reinforce this inner faculty. Everything will gradually improve.

The fourth step manifests an occult process used by the initiates of the Renaissance. This is the projection of your mind into a world you have built according to traditional principles. The method is simple but needs time to become natural. Your goal is to imagine that you are in the center of the board, surrounded by the symbols you created. This is where you will meditate and later learn the real and spiritual meaning of the symbols.

Ritual Process

Once the opening ritual in the first degree has been completed, unveil the tracing board you prepared and place it upon the representation of the black-and-white mosaic.

Begin by the same inner process described in the previous exercise. This is an effective way to prepare yourself for a spiritual practice.

Then, still relaxed on your chair, look at the tracing board. Do not intellectualize or identify what you see. Let your eyes move from one symbol to another without focusing on a specific one. Come back regularly to your breathing, so that you remain relaxed and receptive. You can slightly open your eyes for few seconds, then close them again. If you already have mastered this step, it will be a reactivation of the symbols.

Close your eyes while breathing deeply and regularly. Remember the various tools that are on your board and begin to give them a 3-D shape. Begin with the representations that are linked with the building itself: the steps, the door, the pediment, the columns, the walls and their windows, the celestial vault above you, and the two stars toward the east. Imagine that you are standing in the center of this place. Your breathing is deep and you enjoy seeing the lodge room from the inside. As our purpose is esoteric Freemasonry, I recommend using the traditional representation. Once you feel that the board has been properly set, mentally place the other objects required for this degree in a Masonic lodge. If you have not been initiated into Freemasonry, use the representation of your individual lodge as it is explained in this book. Once this process is completed, begin your meditation as if it takes place within this spiritual location.

After a few moments, come back to your physical body, open your eyes, and take some notes on what you felt or understood.

Replace the 2-D representation of the tracing board, and if necessary return the candles to their previous positions around the black-and-white mosaic.

You can now proceed with the closing ritual in the first degree.

The Mystical Gate

The position and nature of the door of the temple is a mysterious and recurring question in Masonic symbolism. As a matter of fact, many tracing boards and Masonic aprons seem to indicate that we stand in the forecourt of the temple. The door is seen from outside, often at the top of three degrees and surrounded by two columns. This could represent the entrance of the temple of Solomon, or an Egyptian temple. In this case, the lodge meeting would have taken place in this forecourt, or perhaps in what is called the "peristyle" of Egyptian temples. Today the two columns, which have only a symbolic function, are often placed inside the temple, to the southwest and northwest. Consequently, the temple is symbolically placed in a different spacetime. Egyptian Freemasonry, specifically Memphis-Misraim, as defined by Robert Ambelain, describes the east as a door of ivory and gold, closed, without apparent lock, framed by two columns of Egyptian style, ending as the Djed, or *occult pillar of Osiris*. Between the columns, a semitransparent veil of turquoise color is suspended, masking a part of the gate. It is clear in this case that the gateway to the temple is located to the east.

These examples demonstrate an inconsistency in the representation of a Masonic lodge and, more importantly, the location where the secret meeting takes place. The locations should differ according to the initiatic degree (Apprentice, ..., or Master). Esoteric Freemasonry considers this question from another perspective. It is said that there are at least two entrances in a Masonic temple, one on the material plane and another on the spiritual. This idea of two levels of reality is common in spiritual traditions around the world. In India, for example, the city of Allahabad is at the confluence of two great rivers, the Ganges and Yamuna. However, according to Hindu belief, a third, invisible river, the Saraswati, conjoins them. Sometimes it is said that this river flows from the sky, or underground, joining the other two rivers from below. This place is considered sacred, and the famous pilgrimage called Kumbh Mela takes place here every twelve years. Any pilgrim bathing at a specific moment at the confluence of these rivers has his sins washed away.

Both Kabbalah and paganism have such places in which communication between the spiritual and material worlds is possible.

Initiates believed that it is possible to build a spiritual gate to cross this threshold and visit the invisible plane. The same idea exists in esoteric Freemasonry. Consequently, it is important to know where this mysterious door is, and how to use it. Several years ago, I attended a meeting performed according to the Egyptian ritual. I had the opportunity to talk with an ancient master of the lodge who unveiled for me an ancient practice related to this mysterious gate. As he explained, one of the essential keys has been placed for a long time in the most obvious spot, in the center of the lodge room. He was referring to the black-and-white mosaic that should be used for this purpose. This is what I invite you to do with this practice.

As in the previous exercises and once the rite is open to the first degree, take the time to meditate and relax. Your black-and-white mosaic should be placed in front of you, surrounded by the three candles. While maintaining regular breathing, focus your gaze on the center of the mosaic. Your gaze should go throughout the mosaic, as if you were looking beyond the physical surface itself. This technique is used to perceive three-dimensional effects in photos or drawings prepared for this purpose (see figure 28). You should use the same technique, directing your gaze into the depth of the mosaic tile while keeping the tile as clear as possible. Gradually, you will discover how to "place" your gaze. You will realize that each of your practices will help to develop this interesting faculty. It is essential to remain relaxed, to breathe regularly, and to wait until this phenomenon begins to manifest. The surface of the black-and-white pavement, hitherto flat, will seem to acquire a real depth. You will get the impression that the pavement is moving and taking on a different thickness. When you reach this stage, you will feel internally that you can project yourself into it. Do not be afraid; continue to breathe calmly. Some people will tell you that this process is only the result of an optical effect. Although this is true, it also constitutes a mental technique that can allow you to reach another step of consciousness.

At this point in your esoteric practice, you can keep your eyes half closed or shut them completely. Simply do what you feel is most appropriate, while allowing images and feelings to emerge spontaneously in your mind.

After a few moments, come back to the perception of your physical body, open your eyes, and write some notes about what you felt or understood.

You should know that you have just crossed one of the temple gates, and this experience will leave you with a strong inner understanding for a very long time. If you have already practiced the animation of the tracing-board lodge previously explained, I suggest you do this exercise immediately after the crossing of the mystical gate.

You are truly in what is called the *inner temple*. It is both an archetypal reality of Freemasonry and a very specific inner space. It is within this sacred temple that you should study and practice your art. The visible temple is only the exterior of this inner reality. I strongly recommend practicing this process regularly to get into this dimension easily and quickly. It will then be easier for you to work simultaneously on the two levels: visible and invisible.

The Compass

I explained before what we can call a symbolic work. You will recall that an efficient symbolic work does not start theoretically. That would make Freemasonry a purely intellectual exercise and not a real inner practical work. This is what a real philosophical work is about. This is the way to know yourself. When you learn a practice involving your body, such as a sport, art, etc., you can easily understand that your mind should not be placed at the first location.

A Freemason is supposed to be an architect, but he remains in the Masonic mythology as a hand-worker who became an architect, which is very different. It is therefore appropriate to begin by doing things and progressively find the keys inside oneself, by working. If we were working on a rough stone, we would have to look, to take a chisel, a mallet, and start. The learning will come from confronting reality, understanding failures and successes. You should understand that this feeling can only come from experience. Strangely, it is the same process for symbols, and Masons who are not interested in the esoteric aspects of the work cannot really achieve an inner work. The individual process we are talking about is intended to help Masons and put anyone on the same path with the same efficiency.

Once the opening ceremony is completed in the first degree, sit down and start a relaxation. After around five minutes, open your eyes halfway, breathing regularly and peacefully. Look at the compass placed on your sacred book. Welcome the vision of this tool, its shape, its position, its opening, etc. Do not intellectualize, but simply observe that compass. It is useful to highlight here the importance of choosing symbols that meet your aesthetic requirements. They must please you during this moment of silent contemplation. Close your eyes and mentally recreate the compass without everything around it. If necessary, open your eyes again and contemplate the compass a little more. You can follow this process two or three times until you reach a clear inner vision of this tool. I am not talking about a perfect inner photo, but a very good memory of the shape of this tool.

Now stand up and push back your chair to make more room around you. Stand up straight, arms along the body, head vertically above your body. Your chin should be slightly tucked so that your neck is stretched. Do this without excessive tension, without exaggerating the movement. Your legs are placed in contact with each other. Your feet are very close together. Your position embodies the compass in its closed position. Your head is the axis on which the whole revolves. Tighten your legs and arms for a few moments, sometimes exaggerating the tension and allowing spontaneous ideas to emerge—emotions could also emerge while in this position. Take your time and breathe slowly and deeply during this exercise. Do not worry if a particular idea appears. This work consists of embodying a symbol. This inner process will yield progressively more and more results as you practice this exercise several times.

After a few moments, open your legs slightly apart. The first opening of your feet should be the width of your shoulders. Your hands are still in contact with the exterior of your thighs. Hold this position and in the same way as before, breathe slowly and deeply. Let everything that can come from that feeling emerge in you.

After a few moments, spread your legs a little more and do the same as you just did. After holding this position, you can return to your original position, then sit down. End with a short relaxation. Open your eyes and take a few notes about what you felt or understood.

You may have noticed that the Masonic tradition opens the compass differently depending on the ritual or the degree. The symbolic tradition gives little explanation of the reasons for these openings. The symbolic limit of the compass is 180 degrees until it becomes a line. At the third degree of Master Mason, the compass should be open at 45 degrees.

The usual opening in Freemasonry is 90 degrees. The latter indicates that the compass becomes a "straight square." I will now explain to you an extension of the previous practice that you will use in the third degree. It will allow you to understand some meanings linked to specific degrees.

After performing the opening ceremony to the third degree, practice the exercise just described, but when you move your legs apart, open them at approximately a 45 degree angle. Before doing that, you can put two markers on the floor to get a better idea of what this angle is. However, do not focus on precision that is impossible anyway. The key lies elsewhere. As I explained, a part of esoteric Freemasonry comes from what I called Hermetic Kabbalah. It is often the case for numbers used in this tradition. This is the case here. Anyone interested in Qabalah would have noticed that 45 degrees, transcribed in Hebrew characters, corresponds to the word *Mah*, composed of two letters: Mem = 40 and He = 5.

From the Kabbalistic point of view, the cup (Mem) symbolizes the first visible manifestation, the female principle that defines and constrains. It is connected to the sephirah Binah and the planet Saturn.

Water is the primordial undifferentiated liquid. This is the chaos, the Nun. This chaos, however, is ready to become the original energy from which the material world will be shaped.

The representation of the first letter, *Mem*, is open on one side, like a matrix awaiting fertilization. This letter Mem is also the first letter of the word *maïm*, which means "water" in Hebrew. This word is composed of three letters: Mem, Yod, and the final Mem. This word corresponds in Qabalah to the primordial water.

The Yod symbolizes the fertilizing power of the sephirah Hochmah. It is the *Logos Spermatikoï* that carries the divine breath. It is the one who separates the waters in Genesis, starting the creative process by an act of differentiation. The form of the final letter Mem is closed, as is the womb of the Mother after the act of conception.

Acting as a Freemason and manipulating the compass allows you to "play" this myth of creation. You will become gradually aware of this demiurgic process. The creation not only is a moment of the past but can be reproduced analogically to enlighten your inner soul.

The second letter, *He*, represents the vital breath, called in Qabalah the *Rouar*. It was the breath that hovered over the waters during the Genesis myth of the Bible. It was this Rouar who animated the first man and made him a living being. Freemasonry often linked this opening of the compass to the book of Proverbs 8:27–28, and we understand why: "When He established the heavens, I [Wisdom] was there. When He inscribed a circle on the face of the Abyss [Mem]; When He made firm the skies [He] above, [...]." So unite the circle, water, and breath in that pure symbol of opening the compass. It is essential for us to embody it to continue the first part of the exercise.

Once your legs are open according to the markers you put on the floor, close your eyes. Visualize in front of you at the height of your shoulders a cup about six inches tall. The cup should be visualized approximately thirty inches from your chest.

While maintaining this visualization, become aware of your breathing, of the air moving in and out of your lungs. Continue until you feel well breathing like that.

Focus on your visualization, and let the color and the shape of the cup be spontaneously manifested. Hold this visualization for a few minutes.

Extend your arms forward, palms facing the cup. Move your hands as if you were taking a material cup into your hands.

Visualize water in the cup and the shape of the letter Mem in the center of it. Feel the energy shining from the cup.

Pronounce the sound *Ahh* by directing your breath to the liquid in the cup.

Release your hands and place your arms back on your legs. Breathe quietly while maintaining the presence of the cup in front of you, at the height of your chest. Then extend your arms toward the cup and imagine that you place it in the center of your chest. Once you have done that, keep your right hand upon your chest a few moments, the left being placed on the right hand. Breathe deeply and release your hands, placing them back on each of your legs.

Breathe and let the feelings emerge with every breath. After a few moments, return to your starting position, legs closed, then sit down and take a few breaths without focusing on anything in particular.

Open your eyes and take a few notes about what you felt or understood.

You can then perform the closing ceremonies of the second and third degrees, followed by the closing ceremony of the first degree.

Second Degree

Opening Ceremony of the Second Degree

It is sometimes interesting to change the energy of the place in which you work to practice esoteric techniques of the second degree. It is necessary for that to use the following sequence, associated with the opening ceremony of the first degree of Apprentice.

Before starting the sequence, you should add extra candles. Place five candles around the sacred book as if located at the five corners of a pentagram.

After placing these extra candles, breathe in silence for a moment and then say:

A Fellowcraft is symbolically five years old.

With full knowledge of the letter G, the Egyptian Freemasons of which I am a member traditionally begin their work at noon, when the light shines at the zenith of the Temple. As the Master Hermes says, "It is from the Light and Life that Humans were born."

Breathe deeply one time and say:

This is from the east that light is coming and this is where the origin of our tradition can be found.

May the light of this degree shine once again!

Light the incense, arrange the tools on the sacred book according to the intertwining of the second degree, and meditate for a few moments. Then say:

May the power of the four elements—earth, water, air, and fire—that compose my body be now invoked.

Light the first candle placed at the top of your sacred book. You will progressively follow the sequence as mentioned in the following invocations.

While lighting this first candle, say:

From the realm of Ether, I invoke the power of Jupiter!

Light the second candle, placed at the southwest point of the pentalpha.

From the realm of fire, I invoke the power of Mars!

Light the third candle, placed at the northeast point of the pentalpha.

From the realm of air, I invoke the power of Mercury!

Light the fourth candle, placed at the southeast point of the pentalpha.

From the realm of water, I invoke the power of Venus!

Light the fifth candle, placed at the northwest point of the pentalpha.

From the realm of earth, I invoke the power of Saturn!

Raise your hands to the sky, palms up, and say:

I invoke the powers within me!

Take your sword and draw in the direction of the east a pentagram on a vertical plane. You should start from the upper angle and continue to draw it clockwise.

Then replace the sword and knock five times in the following sequence: 2–1–1–1 (2 knocks, pause, 1 knock, pause, etc.).

Stand up, put your right hand on your heart, and say:

To the Glory of the Supreme Architect of the Worlds, to the glory of the gods and goddesses of the sacred land of Egypt, by the divine powers that are part of every human being, I declare open this ceremony working at the second degree of the Masonic order!

Now you can proceed to your work in the second degree.

Closing Ceremony of the Second Degree

When your work to the second degree has ended and prior to performing the full closing ceremony of the first degree, you should proceed as follows.

Stand in front of your altar, and after a moment of silence, say:

It's midnight. The night has come over Egypt and the sacred bark of the Sun is traveling through the dark world.

Extinguish the five candles of this degree that are placed around the sacred book. Proceed in the reverse sequence from the opening ceremony.

Then you will knock five times as follows: 2–1–1–1.

Still standing, put your right hand upon your heart and say:

To the Glory of the Supreme Architect of the Worlds, to the glory of the gods and goddesses of the sacred land of Egypt, by the divine powers that are part of every human being, I declare closed this ceremony working at the second degree of the Masonic order!

Continue with the closing ceremony of the first degree.

Ceremony of Self-Initiation into the Second Degree
Time Preparation of the Ritual

As for the self-initiation into the first degree, I recommend performing this initiation during a quiet period.

Your Preparation

Remember that you are already an Apprentice Freemason, so you will wear your white apron during the ceremony.

Preparation of the Room

Install the lodge room according to the instructions provided with the opening ceremony of the first degree.

For the initiation itself, you should prepare the following items:

- A 24-inch gauge (Egyptian rod), level, plumb rule, square, compass, and gavel
- A black tablecloth with a golden pentalpha painted or embroidered on it
- Five candlesticks, with the candles placed on each of the five points of the golden pentalpha and a cup of water placed in its center

Entrance in the Temple for the Ritual

When you are ready and all is in place, stand in front of your altar (the representation of the lodge) and breathe in silence.

Using your gavel, knock 3 times (2–1) as an Apprentice on your altar and return the gavel. Say:

> I, (your name), stand in front of the mysterious door of the second degree of Freemasonry.
> I have meditated upon the teachings of an Apprentice and I began the work on the rough
> stone that is my own self.

The 24-Inch Gauge

Take the gauge in both hands. Place it on the palms of your hands and raise your arms to the sky, saying:

> Life, Prosperity, and Health!
> As Khnum lives, the sun goes down and that which is in heaven arises.

As initiate, I invoke the presence of Re to protect me during the crossing of the night.
I invoke the presence of the serpents that guard the double doors!
Open for me these gates to your very realms to achieve my journey in peace!
May all the powers of the divinities present in the twelve realms of the night give me their blessings and protection to come to rise at sunset as the sun does in its radiant glory!

Silently pause, then place the Egyptian rod upon your heart (chest) for a few seconds, and place it on the altar between you and the square and compass.

Take the cup of water in both hands. Raise the cup, saying:

I swear to always practice virtue, reject vices, and work to my own improvement!
May this water purify my body and my soul!

Return the cup to the altar. Plunge the index fingers, middle fingers, and ring fingers of both hands in the cup and moisten the top of your head.

Dry your hands before continuing. Then say:

The star is the light that every initiate following his path should follow. For that I must be resilient and learn what the real tools are that will help me to advance to the mastership of my life. Only by a correct use will my life be transformed.
Such as the star that has five points, I must accomplish the five journeys that will balance the inner symbols always present in my soul.

First Journey

Take the gavel and chisel you previously prepared (or their representations). The gavel should be in your left hand and the chisel in your right. Cross your arms upon your chest, the right over the left.

Bow your head in front of the east of the temple, saying:

I have begun the sacred work of sculpting my own stone, revealing progressively the beauty of my inner soul. May the divine powers of the east continue to assist me to achieve this Great Work.

Stand straight, turn to your right, facing south, then bow your head again and speak the same invocation, changing only the name of the direction. Proceed in the same way for the west and the north, coming back to face east. Return these two tools to the altar.

Kneel and say:

My first work has been achieved.

Stand up.

Second Journey

Take the square and the compass you previously prepared on the altar. The compass should be in your left hand and the square in your right. Cross your arms upon your chest, the right over the left.

Bow your head in front of the east of the temple, saying:

I have begun the sacred work of righteousness, correcting progressively my daily behaviors. I have begun the hard work of tracing the plan of my life and the consequences of my choices. May the divine powers of the east continue to assist me to achieve this Great Work.

Stand straight, turn to your right, facing south, then bow your head again and speak the same invocation, changing only the name of the direction. Proceed in the same way for the west and the north, coming back to face east. Return these two tools to the altar.

Kneel and say:

My second work has been achieved.

Stand up.

Third Journey

Take the Egyptian rod and the lever you previously prepared on the altar. The lever should be held vertically in your left hand and the Egyptian rod vertically in your right hand. This time do not cross your arms upon your chest, but hold them on both sides of your body, with your forearms extended and horizontal in front of you.

Bow your head in front of the east of the temple, saying:

I have begun the sacred path crossing the worlds to learn more about the wonders of the cosmos and the divine powers. I have begun the work of understanding the spiritual world. May the divine powers of the east continue to assist me to achieve this Great Work.

Stand straight, turn to your right, facing south, then bow your head again and speak the same invocation, changing only the name of the direction. Proceed in the same way for the west and the north, coming back to face east. Return these two tools to the altar.

Kneel and say:

My third work has been achieved.

Stand up.

Fourth Journey

Take the level and the plumb you previously prepared on the altar. The level should be in your left hand and the plumb in your right. This time do not cross your arms over your chest, but hold them on both sides of your body, with your forearms extended and horizontal in front of you.

Bow your head in front of the east of the temple, saying:

I have begun the sacred work of standing straight. My feet are stable on the floor and my head rises to the sky. I have begun the work of straightening up my Self. May the divine powers of the east continue to assist me to achieve this Great Work.

Stand straight, turn to your right, facing south, then bow your head again and speak the same invocation, changing only the name of the direction. Proceed in the same way for the west and the north, coming back to face east. Return these two tools to the altar.

Kneel and say:

My fourth work has been achieved.

Stand up.

Fifth Journey

Extend your arms toward the east, palms up and open, and say:

As Isis said to her son Horus: All things in this world are shaped by words and actions; the source of everything is in the ideal world, which emanates to us through the principles of order and measure, and all is manifested. Everything in existence came from above, and everything in existence will rise to go down once again.

May the power of the four elements—earth, water, air, and fire—that compose my body be now invoked.

Light the first candle, placed at the top of the pentalpha on the east side of your altar. Follow the sequence as mentioned in the following invocations.

While lighting this candle, say:

From the realm of Ether, I invoke the power of Jupiter, royal and magnanimous giver of abundance from a cup unfailing, Shepherd of the golden Stars, Lord of the tides of fortune! Glorious dispenser of mercy, divine patron of paternal and filial love!

Light the second candle, placed at the southwest point of the pentalpha.

From the realm of fire, I invoke the power of Mars, all-powerful defender of justice and truth, noble inspirer of courage and endurance and of bold resolve, inculcator of loyalty, giver of the joy that springs from shared endeavors, divine patron of fruitful debate and of good order.

Light the third candle, placed at the northeast point of the pentalpha.

From the realm of air, I invoke the power of Mercury, swift and unconstrained traveler in the ways between the Worlds, divine imparter of secret tidings to gods and to humankind.

Light the fourth candle, placed at the southeast point of the pentalpha.

From the realm of water, I invoke the power of Venus, radiant giver of love, Egyptian rod of the forces of life, divinely robed in light and girded with invincible beauty.

Light the fifth candle, placed at the northwest point of the pentalpha.

From the realm of earth, I invoke the power of Saturn, sublime and shadowed one, austere awakener of high aspiration and mystic hope, art giver of the silent will to endure, art patron of the spirit's creativity and of the forces of preservation and renewal.

Raise your hands to the sky, palms up, and say:

Powers that are within me, sing in concert with my Will!

Blessed Gnosis, by Thee illumined, with your assistance I can celebrate the Light of the Divine and rejoice in Joy of Mind.

Turn off all artificial lights and sit in silence for a short meditation.

After a few minutes, knock one time on the altar with your gavel. Take a few seconds to contemplate the symbol of the pentalpha and the five candles burning around it.

Increase the light in your temple so you can continue the reading more easily. You can stay in your chair to read this short text written by Vitruvius:

No building can be said to be well designed without symmetry and proportion. As a matter of fact, they are as necessary to the beauty of a building as they are to the well-formed human figure, which nature has so fashioned, that in the face, from the chin to the top of the forehead, or to the roots of the hair, is a tenth part of the height of the whole body. From the chin to the crown of the head is an eighth part of the whole height, and from the back of the neck to the crown of the head the same. From the upper part of the breast to the roots of the hair, a sixth; to the crown of the head, a fourth. A third part of the height of the face is equal to that from the chin to the underside of the nostrils, and thence to the middle of the eyebrows the same; from the last to the roots of the hair, where the forehead ends, the remaining third part. The length of the foot is a sixth part of the height of the body. The fore-arm is a fourth part, the width of the breast a fourth part. Similarly have the other members their due proportions, by attention to which the ancient Painters and Sculptors obtained so much reputation. Just so, the parts of Temples should correspond with each other, and with the whole. The navel is naturally placed in the center of the human body, and, if in a man lying with his face upward, and his hands and feet extended, from his navel as the center, a circle be described, it will touch his fingers and toes. It is not alone by a circle, that the human body is thus circumscribed, as may be seen by placing it within a square. For measuring from the feet to the crown of the head, and then across the arms fully extended, we find the latter measure equal to the former; so that lines at right angles to each other, enclosing the figure, will form a square. If nature, therefore, has made the human body so that the different members of it are measures of the whole, so the ancients have, with great propriety, determined that in all perfect works, each part should be some aliquot part of the whole and since they direct that this be observed in all works, it must be most strictly attended to in temples of the gods, wherein the faults as well as the beauties remain to the end of time.20

Stand up and say:

---

20. Vitruvius, *De Architectura* (published as *Ten Books on Architecture*), 3.1.

I have organized and harmonized the elements that structure my body.

    My soul is coming to light in the sacred eternal temple!

Open the sacred book as you usually do, and arrange the tools on the top of it according to the intertwining of the second degree.

Using your gavel, knock five times on your altar in the following sequence: 2–1–1–1. Stand up, put your right hand on your heart, and say:

To the Glory of the Supreme Architect of the Worlds, by the divine powers that are part of every human being, I declare this temple fully open in the second degree of the Masonic order!

The Oath

Speak now the renewing of your oath:

I, (your name), stand in the presence of this invisible respectable assembly of Masons, the wardens of this sacred temple, and in union with the egregore of the Egyptian Freemasonry.

    In front of me are the sacred symbols of the second degree, and I swear upon them to keep secret what the invisible masters will reveal to me in the process of this ceremony and during my individual practices.

    I swear to work with zeal, constancy, and regularity to understand the Masonic tradition and apply its principles in my life.

    I swear to continue the practice of the highest moral principles.

    So mote it be!

Investiture

Cross your arms on your chest, left over right, with the crossing point of your arms upon your heart. Bow your head and say:

To the Glory of the Sublime Architect of the Worlds, in the name of the Masters of the Egyptian Freemasonry, in the presence of this invisible respectable assembly of Masons and by the power of the ritual I just performed, I solemnly enter into the room prepared for this Fellowcraft degree.

Release your arms and turn back the upper triangular part of your apron in order to have it upon the rectangular part. From now on, every time you perform a ritual practice, wear the apron this way.

Take the time to read the following paragraph. You can sit if you want.

You have entered into the world of the second degree of Freemasonry.

As expressed during this ceremony, may my desire to evolve be accomplished! As I commune with myself, my bodily sensations fall asleep and my mind awakens. May I cleanse myself from the torments of the world and matter, for many fearful persecutors are in me.

The first is ignorance, the second is sadness, the third is intemperance, the fourth is concupiscence, the fifth injustice, the sixth avarice, the seventh error, the eighth envy, the ninth cunning, the tenth anger, the eleventh imprudence, and the twelfth wickedness.

They are twelve and have under their orders a greater number. They subject my mind to being imprisoned in the jail of my body to suffer through the medium of the senses. It is in this that resides the process and the teaching of the rebirth.

I invoke the first power, knowledge, so that by its manifestation in me, ignorance will disappear.

I invoke the second power, joy, that I may cast out sadness from myself and from all who acknowledge its presence.

I invoke the third power, the virtue of temperance, that it may sustain me in the face of intemperance.

I invoke the fourth power, perseverance, a force opposed to concupiscence.

I invoke the fifth power, righteousness, which alone drives out injustice without fighting. Becoming myself just, the unjust has no place.

I invoke the sixth power, generosity, which comes into me to fight against avarice.

I invoke the seventh power, truth, to scare away error and reveal reality.

I invoke the eighth power, sharing, to flee jealousy and reveal fraternity.

I invoke the ninth power, frankness, to flee envy and reveal honesty.

I invoke the tenth power, appeasement, to escape disputes and reveal dialogue.

My spiritual birth is now beginning to manifest.

I invoke the eleventh power, wisdom, to avoid imprudence and reveal discernment.

I invoke the twelfth power, goodness, to flee from wickedness and reveal generosity. So, freeing myself from the yoke of bodily sensations, the power of my mind is revealed.

There are no longer in me persecutors of darkness, and I can finally know myself in peace.

I am in heaven, on earth, in water, and in the air. I am in animals, in plants, in the womb, before the uterus and after the uterus. I am present in all things.

Here is the regeneration: no longer seeing oneself according to the limitations of our bodily senses but as being part of the cosmos and the Whole.

Take time at the end of this ceremony to take a few notes about what you felt, your thoughts, and whatever seems good and useful to you.

You can now proceed to the simplified closing ceremony.

Closing Ceremony

After a moment of relaxation, you should close this ceremony with the closing ritual in the second degree, followed by the simplified closing of the first degree, as you did in the self-initiation of Entered Apprentice.

Individual Practices of the Second Degree
The Pentagram and Pentalphas

The pentagram has been discussed several times in my previous books, where I developed some of its aspects: *theurgic* in *Rediscover the Magick of the Gods and Goddesses*, and *practical* in *The Magical Use of Prayer Beads*.

Writing about esoteric Freemasonry, I will now highlight some reasons why this important symbol has been used in this tradition. From the beginning, the Masonic tradition did its best to link its rituals and symbols to a more ancient past. This is how most initiatic traditions work. Real historic lineage can sometimes be demonstrated, but even when this is not the case, a spiritual tradition is chosen and used to found a new school of thought.

It is interesting now to ask ourselves a simple question: Why did Freemasonry choose the pentagram to be set at a place of honor in Masonic lodges?

Remember that the pentagram is very often associated with the letter G, the square, and the compass to represent Freemasonry. There are several obvious reasons for this:

1. Having an initiatic structure, it is logical to link this tradition to the first initiatic order documented, which is the *Pythagorean Order*.

2. As a building tradition, this figure is important in geometrical architecture. Freemasons consider it their duty to summarize the world and the human being; thus, the pentagram is used to symbolize important concepts.

3. Deeply intertwined with the Judeo-Christian tradition, it was important to highlight the connection with this theology of salvation.

4. Rooting several of its degrees and concept on Qabalah, the latter was unavoidable.

5. As Egypt was considered by ancient Greeks to be the origin of all ancient knowledge, creating an Egyptian ritual was logical.

To begin, I should note that the name *pentalpha* is more appropriate for a five-pointed star drawn from the points of intersection of a pentagon. The word *pentalpha* comes from the association of the two Greek words: *Pentes*, meaning five (5), and *Alpha*, the first letter of the Greek alphabet (*A*). This is the word I will use here. Let us now examine the five points.

Point 1: The pentalpha appears in Mesopotamia circa 3000 BCE and corresponds to the sign UB. It represents a "Heavenly Quarter" and the "four directions plus the zenith."

It seems that Pythagoras discovered the representation of the pentalpha during his travels in Egypt and Babylon. When Pythagoras organized his initiatic order during the sixth century BCE, he chose this symbol and used it as a sign of recognition. He associated the pentalpha with the six Greek letters U-G-I-EI-A, which means "health," "divine blessing," or "blessed." The fourth and fifth letters were associated by visual reduction to just one sign, usually the Greek letter *Theta*. From this, Pythagoreans began to use the expression "Be blessed!" as a password associated with the sacred sign of the pentalpha. A late interpretation of the Pythagorean sign associates it with the Latin word *Salus*, which translates to the Greek word *Ugieia*.

Point 2: The pentalpha is a summary of endless captivating properties that can help us develop our meditation skills and imagination. Undoubtedly, it was used for such purposes at the time of Pythagoras and Plato and in Freemasonry. I give you here some insights, and you can continue to play with these intertwined symbolic meanings. One of the essential teachings of Pythagoras's school was that "All is number" and "God is number." Pythagoreans effectively practiced a kind of numerology or number worship, considering each number to have its own character and meaning.

Following a similar approach, let us consider the number 5 at the geometric level. This number can be represented by a regular polygon: equilateral, equiangular, and transcribed in a circle. Each of the outer five angles are 108° (1 + 8 = 9), and each of the inner five angles are 72° (7 + 2 = 9). The sum of all angles is 900° (9 + 0 + 0 = 9).

For Pythagoras, the number 10 was the representation of the full cosmos. It is called the Tetractys and is represented by a pyramid of dots organized in four lines that correspond to the numbers 1, 2, 3, and 4, for a total of 10. As you can see, the number 9 is not visible. Paradoxically, this number has unique, interesting properties. Some authors talk about the "9 code." If the circle represents the universe, you should realize that 9 is everywhere. Every time you cut a circle in two parts, the sum of the number of the angles is 9. For example, a circle has 360°. If you divide it in two, you obtain 180° (1 + 8 + 0 = 9). If you divide again by two, the new angle becomes 90° (9 + 0 = 9); again divided by two, you obtain 45° (4 + 5 = 9); and so on. The pattern is the same if you consider the regular polygons drawn in a circle. The sum of interior angles of any polygon is always 9. A triangle has 3 sides and the sum of the angles is 180° (8 + 1 + 0 = 9). The sum of a quadrilateral is 360°, of a pentagon 540°, of a hexagon 720°, etc.

As we are talking about Pythagoras, I should mention that the letter that corresponds to the number 9 is Theta, initial of *Theos*, the Greek name of *God*. It is convenient for the Masonic tradition to use the pentalpha to represent the connection between nature, human creatures, and God. By the way, I cannot resist the temptation to close the circle by saying that the word *Theos* is composed of the letters Theta (9), Epsilon (5), Omicron (70), and Sigma (200). The sum of these letters is 284. By reduction, this number becomes 5 (2 + 8 +4 = 14 and 1 + 4 = 5).

According to the ancient Greeks, the pentalpha is created by adding the letter *Alpha* to each side of the pentagon. This is how you obtain the famous five-pointed star. The number becomes 5, and the number of segments 15. I will come back to these numbers when I explain a few things about Qabalah.

Around the sixth and fifth centuries BCE, Greek philosophers began to work on the structure and dynamics of living beings. Pythagoras believed that the world resulted from some mixture and combination of four primordial elements: earth, fire, air, and water, plus a fifth principle, aether. Philolaus, a Pythagorean initiate, very clearly synthesized this structure of four elements by saying that there are five bodies in the sphere: fire, water, earth, air, and the circle of the sphere, which is the fifth. Plato used these ancient representations and connected them to special geometric symbols. Earth was linked with the cube, air with the octahedron (three-dimensional figure with eight sides), water with the icosahedron (three-dimensional figure with twenty sides), and fire with the tetrahedron (three-dimensional figure with four sides). Plato put the dodecahedron (three-dimensional figure with twelve equal pentagonal faces) in correspondence with the whole, the world, because it is the solid that resembles a sphere most closely. In another passage of *Timeus*, Plato explained four important orders in nature, which are gods and the celestial orb (fire), winged animals (air), animals of the earth (earth), and aquatic animals (water).

The famous text of the *Corpus Hermeticum* (books of Hermes) develops this notion of the five elements. We will use it later in our practice.

Point 3: We saw that Qabalah has been used extensively in several parts of the Masonic tradition. I want to give you some examples associated with the pentalpha and its links to the notion of God. The name of God in the Torah is composed of four letters: *Yod, Hei, Vav,* and *Hei.* Very often the abbreviation of this word is composed of the two letters, *Yod* and *Hei.* The number of this word is 15 (Yod = 10, Hei = 5).

Christian Qabalah has been developed from this origin and has used the representation of the pentalpha as a basis of an extensive discussion about the name of the Savior *Jesus,* or, in Christian Qabalah, *Ieschouah.*

Amphitheater of Eternal Wisdom, first published in 1609, is a book well known to the followers of the Western tradition. It was written by Heinrich Khunrath, who was born in Leipzig in 1560. Khunrath was a medical doctor, an alchemist, a Qabalist, and, according to his book and engravings, probably a theurgist.

One of the allegories in this book represents the Qabalistic world: in the center is the image of Christ in the position of a cross, placed in the middle of a rose of light. The representation shows a fire around him, with five main extensions that create a pentalpha. Five Hebrew letters are placed around him, each one on a branch of the pentagram. The letter *Shin* is placed at the top, surrounded by the four Hebrew letters of the name of God, creating the new name of Ieschouah (*Yod, Hei, Shin, Vav, Hei*). There is considerable discussion about this new sacred name. The addition of the letter *Shin* to the symbol of the Eternal God is important and significant. It is also interesting to notice the connection between the shape of the letter and the Christian Trinity. Three small flames are at the top of this letter. Each of the letters of this name is associated with an element. Turning counterclockwise, we see *Yod* (fire, red, left foot), *Hei* (water, blue, left hand), *Shin* (ether, brilliant white light, forehead), *Vav* (air, yellow, right hand), and *Hei* (earth, deep brown, right foot).

The pentalpha is one of the main symbols of the second degree of Freemasonry. It is present in the tracing board and in the initiation itself. Consequently, this is an important symbol to integrate into spiritual practices.

Esoteric Freemasonry uses symbolism coming from the Hermetic tradition. In the first part of this practice, you will use a very interesting excerpt from the *Corpus Hermeticum*. It can be considered as a way to balance the five elements present in every human being. The four elements have already been activated during the first initiation in a specific sequence. Here the fifth element, the ether, is added. Then all five are organized and placed under the protection of the goddess Isis. You can stop after this first part and proceed to the closing ritual. You can also add the second part and proceed to the closing ritual just after. Feel free to choose whatever you feel is best for you that day.

When the opening ritual to the second degree has been completed, take time to relax and breathe. Let your mind observe the tools you prepared, the candles, the tracing board, etc. Do not try to interpret the symbols present in front of you. Just regard them as visible manifestations without any special meaning.

First Part: Revelation from Isis

After a few minutes and while relaxed, read the following text softly. In order to pronounce the words correctly, read so you can hear yourself saying them, but no more. Do not read the titles of the following parts. They are indicated in square brackets and are used only to indicate on which element the text is focused.

Isis said to her son Horus:

[The Balance of the Elements]

All things in this world are shaped by words and actions; the source of everything is in the ideal world, which emanates to us, through the principles of order and measure, all of manifest reality. Everything in existence came from above, and everything in existence will go down once again.

From this movement, the holiest nature places in the living being the following clear sign: the breath we take in from above, we take in from the air, then we send it back to what is above, and draw another breath in again. To accomplish this, we have a pair of bellows: when we have closed our mouths, which we used to receive the breath of air, then we are no longer in this domain. We have returned to what is above us. We have other abilities that derive from a specific dosage of these elements in a corporeal mixture.

Each human body is comprised of these four elements, from which a condensation is exhaled which surrounds the soul, and then spreads throughout the body, yielding something specific for that person. This is the way psychic and corporeal modifications occur.

[Fire]

If there is overmuch of the element of fire in the structure of the body, then the soul, which is naturally hot, and which became even more ferociously hot as a result of the increase of heat it received, is manifested in the living being by developing an enthusiastic nature with a strong and ardent body.

[Air]

If there is overmuch of the element of air, the living being becomes lightweight and more unbalanced in his body and soul.

[Water]

If there is overmuch of the element of water, then the soul of the living being vacillates, and is always ready to increase and enlarge its presence into the surrounding area. Water has the capacity for uniting with other elements; therefore, these living beings will tend to develop relationships with others. When water spreads out all around in large quantity, it dissolves everything, absorbing all these things into itself and becoming what it absorbed. Due to the water they contain, it is quite impossible for the body to keep its inner agglomeration. Consequently, when disease appears, it dissolves and loses its inner principle of cohesion.

[Earth]

If there is overmuch of earth, then the soul of the living being becomes rigid, because, as the organs of perception thicken, the pores are not large enough for it to get out so it stays inside the body, isolated by itself, hindered by the weight and the density of the mass of the body. The body is firm but inert and heavy. It moves unwillingly under the impulse of the will.

[Quintessence—Aether]

Eventually, if all the elements in the body are well balanced, then the living being has enough heat for action, light for movement, a temperate condition in the joints, and adequate firmness in their cohesiveness.

May the whole nature of the world hear now, because these are the words of the one who has mixed fire, air, water, and earth with order and moderation and who stands at the heart of the power of the breath and aether.

Powers that are within me, sing in concert with my Will!

Blessed Gnosis, by Thee illumined, with your assistance I can celebrate the Light of the Divine, and rejoice in Joy of Mind.

Ye, all Powers, sing the hymn with me!

While you have learned this from me, let us veil with silence what concerns this miraculous power, revealing to no one the mode of transmission of regeneration, so that we are not counted among the divulgers.

That's enough. Both of us were busy, us to talk, you to listen.

Now you know yourself in the light of the Intellect.

After a few moments, regain consciousness of your physical body, open your eyes, and possibly take some notes on what you felt or understood.

Stay silent for a few moments, breathing deeply and feeling relaxed. Let your feelings and ideas emerge. Then come back to the place you are, being aware of every part of your body. If you want to stop your practice after this first part, move slowly and take a few notes if you need to, and proceed to the closing ritual at this degree. If you want to continue with the second part, breathe and relax a little longer before proceeding.

Second Part: Incarnation of the Blazing Star

Note: As I explained about Christian Kabbalah, the blazing star has been associated with the five Hebrew letters by various initiatic orders such as the Kabbalistic Order of the Rose-Cross. In this practice, you will use the correspondences between these letters and the colors, and the elements we provided earlier. Here is a reminder of these equivalences: *Yod* (fire, red, left foot), *Hei* (water, blue, left hand), *Shin* (ether, brilliant white light, forehead), *Vav* (air, yellow, right hand), and *Hei* (earth, deep brown, right foot).

Practice: Once you are relaxed and your breathing appeased, stand up and take the pentagram position, with your legs spread and arms extended horizontally. Keep breathing quietly. Empty your mind as much as you can of any thoughts, noticing the air coming in and going out, feeling the air on your skin. Be aware of your muscles keeping your body in that position.

After a few moments, visualize in front of you the red Hebrew letter *Yod*. After a few moments of silence, pronounce the name of this letter: "Yod."

Continue to focus on this letter, and pronounce its name nine more times. While you pronounce its name, visualize that the letter is moving in the direction of your left foot. After the ten pronunciations have been achieved, the letter is just upon your foot.

Release your visualization and for a moment come back to your body, feeling your breathing and your muscles.

After a few moments, proceed in the same way for the other letters. You will adapt the color and the movement of the letter according to the list provided earlier.

When you have achieved the full process of the five letters, breathe for a few seconds.

Then pronounce the sacred name *Ieschouah* eleven times. Each time you pronounce this name, visualize a bright light turning clockwise and moving from one letter to another.

When this is done, breathe quietly again while you relax your position. Stand still for a few moments, with arms along the body. You can then sit down.

Take a few notes on what you felt or understood.

Proceed with the closing ritual of this degree.

The 24-Inch Gauge

This Masonic tool is often used in the first degree, but in esoteric and Egyptian Freemasonry we find it in the second degree. You need not be surprised by these inconstancies. As I noted previously, there is no universal rule about the attribution of the symbols. Even their names are sometimes similar but not identical.

. This is what is usually said in old Masonic monitors about this tool: "

> The Twenty-Four-Inch Gauge (also written Gauge) is an instrument used by operative Masons to measure and lay out their work; but we, as Free and Accepted Masons, are taught to use it for the more noble and glorious purpose of dividing our time. It being divided into twenty-four equal parts is emblematic of the twenty-four hours of the day, which we are taught to divide into three equal parts, whereby are found eight hours for the service of God and a distressed worthy Brother, eight for our usual vocations, and eight for refreshment and sleep.[21]

The large majority of the comments that come from this statement try to link the work on the stone and the division of the day. At first glance, the numbers are significant: 24 hours, 8, and 3. A few texts highlight the number 3 as the representation of the triangle, when the gauge is folded. Not much is said about the number 8. Without going too far, it is obvious that the evocation of God associated with the number 3 refers to the Christian idea of the Trinity: Father, Son, and Holy Spirit. Division of the day into several periods

---

21. Malcolm C. Duncan, *Duncan's Masonic Ritual and Monitor*, 1866.

has always been common in monasteries. The idea of Freemasonry as a secular spiritualistic initiatic movement places the initiate in this position, aiming to reconcile daily life and spirituality. We can also remember that on the east wall of the temples, a triangle with a central eye can often be seen representing the divine. The number 8 has always been associated in the Christian tradition with the meaning of resurrection. From the birth of Christian symbols, the most ancient baptisteries were built in the shape of an octagon. It is very likely that the architectural source can be found in Byzantine art and, more specifically for this octagonal shape of the fourth-century Church of the Nativity, located in Bethlehem, in the West Bank, Palestine. Another famous example of such Byzantine octagonal design can be found in the modern city of Pamukkale (ancient city of Hierapolis) in the martyrion of the Apostle Philip in Turkey. As shown in one of my previous books, *Hidden Mandalas,* octagons were frequently used in the Roman and Byzantine mosaics. This number and these designs are the manifestation of what is called the Hermetic tradition, born in Egypt in the priesthood of the god Djehuti (Thot). This is the right place to mention this paternity.

Mentioning that the division of this gauge is 24 and corresponds to the hours of the day is not enough if we want to unveil its mysteries. You should have realized by now that ancient initiates loved to play with symbols and numbers, spreading clues and dots to connect. This is the case here in a sense that should be obvious to anyone who is not working with the metric system, which is rooted in a different symbolism. It is said that this tool is a 24-inch gauge. As a matter of fact, the inch comes from the Latin *uncia,* meaning 12, and equal to $\frac{1}{12}$ of a Roman foot. The link between one inch and 12 is significant for us. Then the number 8 comes to mind, as the gauge and the day have been divided into 3 parts of 8 hours (or inches). As the inch is often divided into fractions of 8, we can multiply 8 by 24 to obtain a total of 192 ($1 + 9 + 2 = 12$ and $1 + 2 = 3$), which is convenient on a symbolic level. You can see now how symbols are intertwined to develop layers of meaning. For those who want to continue to play with this symbolism, I invite you to consider the number 192, which corresponds, according to Qabalah (Gematria technique), with the expression "man of Merodach," the son and successor of Nebuchadnezzar, King of Babylon.[22] If you want to consider that each inch of the gauge should be divided into 16 instead of 8, you will obtain the number 384 (16 x 24), which for the Gematria corresponds to the expression "The anointed one" or "messiah of Yahweh," which is even more significant.

---

22. See 2 Kings 25:27 and Jeremiah 52:31.

We should go further and ask why the day has been divided into 24: 12 hours of light and 12 hours of darkness. It is no surprise to discover that ancient Egyptian priests developed this principle and used it in their rituals. Several papyri have been discovered that explain these divisions and give countless descriptions for each hour, providing the names of the divinities, the wardens, symbols, and other fascinating representations.

But before filling out the days with these extensive mythological stories, ancient priests looked at the stars. What they saw was order and beauty. From the observations and needs, three calendars were developed. The first one was lunar. It was based on 12 months, each month beginning with the first day after the new moon. The second calendar was based on 365 days divided into 12 months of 30 days (plus 5 epagomenal days). The third calendar included 309 months to match the two other calendars. The 12 signs of the zodiac were each divided into three decans placed under the protection of specific divinities. From this division, it became important to divide the day into units. Egyptians were the first to divide the day into 24 hours. The 12 hours of the night are said to be stellar and have a duration that changes during the year according to the duration of the night between sunset and sunrise. This is the same thing for the 12 hours of the day.

Progressively, the need for stable units for astronomers gave rise to a division of hours that was not linked to the daily movements of the sun and the stars. However, the early variable division continued to be used by Egyptian priests in the divine world. Every day, the god Re crossed the sky on his bark, and the full world followed his path. Ancient rods (gauges) in the shape of squares were found in several tombs. These are associated with a plumb, and it was previously supposed that they were used to measure the hours with the shade of the sun. After verification, it has been revealed that these tools would have been symbolic, with their empiric divisions in 4, 5, or 6. Their shape is very evocative in the context of Freemasonry.

To complete this brief panorama of this tool, I should mention an amazing symbol that places the Masonic gauge together with the measurement of the visible and invisible world. This artifact is the Egyptian cubit rod. The cubit was a linear measure, and few of these rods have been found. Maybe one of the most famous belonged to an architect called Kha. This artifact exists today in the Museo Egizio in Turin (Italy). Full representations and details of this artifact can be found on my website (www.debiasi.org). This object is made of ebony and gold and would have been used as a symbol of the function. The part of this rod that is best known is the upper side, which provides various divisions and symbols expressing the measurements of space. The back of the rods give us measurements of astronomical proportions. The sky is now associated with the earth.

But the base of these ceremonial rods gives us a fascinating origin to our modern tradition. On one of these rods a dedication has been written: "Life, Prosperity, and Health." This is a unique opportunity to clearly see the symbolic meaning of such a ceremonial tool.

The base of the rod is divided into three horizontal sections. The inscriptions begin by this revealing declamation: "This is a communication for those who enter daily into Mendes. As Khnum lives, as the sun goes down and that which is in heaven arises." Egyptologists suggest that this rod would sometimes have been used vertically as a gnomon. With the inscriptions on the base, we can clearly see this connection between the material world, the stars, and the world of the gods. Can we be surprised that such a ceremonial tool would have been owned by an architect, who had completed the degree of a Master Mason and reached the highest initiation possible in this tradition?

Based on the complex and endless symbolism of the gauge, I had the opportunity to experiment in the past with a meditation that has always been fascinating. This is a good opportunity to realize how deep esoteric Freemasonry can be, and how limited is a canonic interpretation repeated endlessly.

Practice

When the opening ritual to the second degree has been completed, take a little time to relax and breathe. As you did in the previous practice, see the tools in front of you as if they were just visible manifestations without any special meanings.

After a few minutes, while relaxed, stand up and place the Egyptian rod (or the 24-inch gauge) in both hands. Place it on the palms of your hands and raise your arms to the sky, saying:

Life, Prosperity, and Health!

> *As Khnum lives, as the sun goes down and that which is in heaven arises.*
> *As initiate, I invoke the presence of Re to protect me during the crossing of the night.*
> *I invoke the presence of the serpent that guards the first double door of the night!*
> *Open for me these gates to your very realms to achieve my journey in peace!*
> *May the powers of all the divinities of the first hour give me their blessings and protection to come to rise at sunset as the sun does in its radiant glory!*

Hold the rod vertically in both hands in front of you.

Focus your mind at the level of your feet while you begin the declamation of the following twelve invocations. During the crossing of the twelve gates, using your visualization, ascend along your spinal column until you reach the top of your head for the twelfth gate.

I invoke the presence of the serpent Saa-Set that guards the second double door of the night!

May the second gate be open!

May the powers of all the divinities of the second hour give me their blessings and protection to pursue my journey in peace!

I invoke the presence of the serpent Aqebi that guards the third double door of the night!

May the third gate be open!

May the powers of all the divinities of the third hour give me their blessings and protection to pursue my journey in peace!

I invoke the presence of the serpent Tchetbi that guards the fourth double door of the night!

May the fourth gate be open!

May the powers of all the divinities of the fourth hour give me their blessings and protection to pursue my journey in peace!

I invoke the presence of the serpent Teka-Hra that guards the fifth double door of the night!

May the fifth gate be open!

May the powers of all the divinities of the fifth hour give me their blessings and protection to pursue my journey in peace!

I invoke the presence of the serpent Set-Em-Maat that guards the sixth double door of the night!

May the sixth gate be open!

May the powers of all the divinities of the sixth hour give me their blessings and protection to pursue my journey in peace!

I invoke the presence of the serpent Akha-en-Maat that guards the seventh double door of the night!

May the seventh gate be open!

May the powers of all the divinities of the seventh hour give me their blessings and protection to pursue my journey in peace!

I invoke the presence of the serpent Set-Hra that guards the eighth double door of the night!

May the eighth gate be open!

May the powers of all the divinities of the eighth hour give me their blessings and protection to pursue my journey in peace!

I invoke the presence of the serpent Abt that guards the ninth double door of the night!

May the ninth gate be open!

May the powers of all the divinities of the ninth hour give me their blessings and protection to pursue my journey in peace!

I invoke the presence of the serpent Sethu that guards the tenth double door of the night!

May the tenth gate be open!

May the powers of all the divinities of the tenth hour give me their blessings and protection to pursue my journey in peace!

I invoke the presence of the serpent Am-Netou-F that guards the eleventh double door of the night!

May the eleventh gate be open!

May the powers of all the divinities of the eleventh hour give me their blessings and protection to pursue my journey in peace!

I invoke the presence of the serpents Sebiand and Reri that guard the twelfth double door of the night!

May the twelfth gate be open!

May the powers of all the divinities of the twelfth hour give me their blessings and protection to pursue my journey in peace!

Visualize for a few seconds a shining light rising at the top of your head, surrounding it and growing until your full body is placed at the center of a golden sphere.

Still holding the rod vertically, press it upon the front of your body. Keeping this position, say:

May Life, Prosperity, and Health be with me now and forever!

So mote it be!

Breathe slowly, fully aware of the power of these words, and then return the rod to the altar.

Third Degree

The Founding Myths

At its beginning, Freemasonry had only two degrees: Apprentice and Fellowcraft. The equivalent of a Master was in fact called *Accomplished Fellowcraft*. Mastership was achieved by the realization of a masterpiece recognized by one's colleagues. This is still the case in Europe in groups of professionals such as masons, chefs, carpenters, etc. However, Freemasonry evolved in a direction different from a real professional work. It became what is sometimes called *speculative Freemasonry*. The esoteric aspect of this tradition began to pressure the organization to implement rituals that were more spiritual than social. The concept of death and rebirth, typically used by religions, appeared as an essential part of the initiatic process. Undoubtedly, this introduction was a big step, indicating a clear attempt to make Freemasonry a substitute for religion. Of course, this idea has been opposed by the Masonic establishment for years.

The point here must be crystal clear. The core belief of Christianity is that the sacrifice and rebirth of Jesus Christ saved humanity from original sin. There was a complicated debate over whether this salvation occurs with or without our knowledge and belief. There is no need here to address the complexity of this theological analysis, but we should understand the implications regarding Freemasonry. The thing to realize is that, according to Christian belief, the sacrifice of the son of God has the power to save us. The idea that an initiation will help you to find a spiritual light that would otherwise have been hidden is contrary to Christian dogma. The idea that a person could experience his death symbolically during a ritual to be reborn is ludicrous and even heretical. This is why Freemasonry has been condemned by the Vatican, even if other Christian organizations did not rule against it. I suspect this is also why the creation of the third-degree ritual based on birth and resurrection was developed by esotericists following pre-Christian traditions, especially the "religions of Mysteries." Since Egypt was seen as the origin of the Western tradition, it was logical to use the famous myth of Osiris to build this mysterious third degree. Mainstream Freemasonry followed the trend by duplicating the story. As was often the case since the beginning of Christianity, they created a kind of pseudepigrapha. It was called the *myth of Hiram*.

Let's now follow the structure of these two myths and then we will be able to go further in this degree by doing some experiments.

The myth of Osiris was recorded by Greek writers and especially by Plutarch in his book *Isis and Osiris*. Although the story's structure is easy to follow, it is obviously a late composition that organized preexisting fragments into a more coherent whole. The myth follows some precise events: murder (death) of Osiris by Seth, disappearance of the body, quest of Osiris by his wife-sister Isis, discovery of the sarcophagus, preservation of the dead body, dismemberment of Osiris by Seth, second quest of Isis, assembly of Osiris by Anubis, resurrection of Osiris by Isis, and birth of Horus, the son of Isis and Osiris.

It appears that two stories with two different murders have been combined to create this unique story. The first murder was motivated by jealousy. Seth invited his brother Osiris to try out a sarcophagus made to Osiris's exact measurements. After sealing Osiris inside, Seth threw the casket into the Nile, and the coffin containing Osiris eventually became tangled in the roots of a tree in Lebanon. Long story short, Isis found it, brought it back to Egypt, and hid Osiris. However, Seth found him and dismembered him into fourteen pieces. After a long journey, Isis found every part, except the penis, which had been eaten by a fish. Interestingly, sacred temples have been built on each place where Isis found a body part. Anubis, god of the afterlife and mummification, assembled the pieces, and Isis, goddess of magic, resurrected Osiris. Eventually their son Horus avenged his father by killing Seth.

To anyone familiar with shamanism, the core of this story describes the sequences that are followed by a shaman during his final initiation. The initiate must die before being reborn. The process most frequently described by shamans is that the flesh is removed and thrown away until only the bones remain. Then they also are dispersed. At this point, the spirit of the shaman must stay aware of who he is, to be able to survive and come back to life. If his training has been followed properly, he will successfully cross the threshold of the dead. His bones will be cleaned and reordered, his new flesh and skin will return, and with his new first breath, he will come back to life.

This process has existed since the beginning of humanity and is still practiced in faraway countries such as Mongolia and Russia. No doubt the Osirian mythology and the death rituals in ancient Egypt come from the same source. Remember that this shamanic process, followed by initiates and priests, is the same journey you and I will eventually undertake. As ancient philosophers said, even if we are not aware of it, death is the main fear of every human being. Only the shamans, who by their initiations have crossed the mysterious threshold, have let the fear vanish forever. So it cannot be a surprise that Western ancient initiations have always placed death and resurrection at the core of their system. This is true for the Eleusinian mysteries, Orphism, Mithraism, and of course Freemasonry. However, before summarizing the Masonic myth, I must emphasize an essential point. With the adaptation of this eternal story, mainstream Freemasonry kept only the symbols, without the occult and real process. Imagine a shaman without proper spiritual training, incapable of entering the world of the spirits, unable to create a mystical trance, symbolically portraying his death and resurrection. Even if the spectacle is well enacted, no real inner transformation will occur. Fear of death will still be there, hidden in the deepest part of his being. Of course, he may have learned a few teachings about the fragility and impermanence of life, but nothing would have really changed. This is what Freemasonry did and this is why esoteric Freemasonry tried desperately to rediscover this occult process by going to the source of the Western tradition. Saying whether esoteric Freemasonry succeeded is another story, but I can say that if some very small groups or lodges came close to the core of the tradition, there have been very few throughout the centuries.

We can ask why mainstream Freemasonry didn't keep the full process if it was so essential. The answers are many and complex, but some explanations can be inferred from the historical context in which the adaptation was effected. I should remind people interested in the past that the world was Christian. As I mentioned at the beginning of this section, the notion of death and salvation is very different in shamanism. Modern Freemasonry has always been obsessed with Solomon's Temple, and it is on this basis that the story of the third degree was built. Nevertheless, by highlighting the following main sequences, we can see that the core of the archetype remains: murder (death) of Master Hiram by three workers, disappearance of the body, quest to find the body, and resurrection of Hiram.

This story supposedly takes place in King Solomon's Temple. Of course, the same story is staged in the lodge room during the third degree. Hiram, leaving the temple by the east door, comes upon a worker who asks for the secrets of the Masters. Hiram refuses to tell the secrets, so the worker strikes him. Then Hiram tries to escape by the south door, but he is struck by a second worker and eventually killed at the west door by a third ruffian. Interestingly, the symbolic journey of the master being murdered follows the movement of the sun during the darkest time of the year: winter. At the autumnal (fall) equinox, the sun rises in the east. Then at the winter solstice, the sun rises from the southeast and goes down to the southwest. Remember what has been said about Mithraism and the connection between the symbolic cosmos recreated in the Mithraeum and the movement of the soul. Freemasonry has succeeded in keeping this ancient symbolism, which is also found in the sacred mysteries of Eleusis. The master's corpse is buried on the side of a mountain close to the city of Jerusalem. This is not just a random note about a mountain: the oldest tombs in ancient Egypt were circular holes, with mounds of sand at the top. These were reminders of the original mound that emerged from chaos at the beginning, when

Atoum created the whole universe. The mound is a solar symbol representing the first light coming from Re on the first day of creation. Sometimes even the light going through the clouds gives this vision of a mound or a pyramid made of luminous rays. Later, this mound became the pyramids we can still see today.

Burying Hiram under such a shape creates a striking similarity. One of the nine masters searching for Hiram discovered that the soil had been moved, and a small green tree had grown on it. In other stories, the masters placed a green branch on the tomb (instead of finding it) and came back to inform Solomon. After nine days passed, they returned to the tomb and dug to find the corpse almost rotted. They moved him out of the tomb by holding him on five precise points of his body. This image of raising the corpse to resurrect him was symbolized in Egypt by the raising of the pillar Djed. A significant difference at the end of the story had a huge impact on Freemasonry. In this version, the masters succeeded in moving the corpse out of its grave but failed to resurrect Hiram, as they did in every similar myth. Instead, they brought back the corpse of the master to bury him in a decent tomb with all the honors required.

Today, when the initiate Freemason experiences the initiation of Master, he listens to the story of the murder of Master Hiram and creates a mental identification with him. In other rituals, he plays the role of Hiram and the murder is reenacted on his person with a modification at the end of the story. In this case, when the new initiate is raised to a standing position, he is considered reborn or resurrected. I must emphasize that this difference, though essential, is rarely highlighted. The usual explanation is that the Master Hiram lives again through the new master. This poetic interpretation is interesting but represents a clear divergence from the original archetypes. We are talking here about a duty of memory, which is essential for a tradition but different from the initial purpose of such a near-death experience. The initial intent was to give the opportunity to a well-trained initiate to perform a real experiment. The founders of esoteric and Egyptian Freemasonry clearly saw this connection. For example, Marconis de Nègre, in his book *Masonic Pantheon* (1860), explains that "the Legend of Hiram, which most regard as the narrative of a simple historical fact, is a symbolic reminder. Hiram is evidently the Osiris of the Egyptians, the Mithra of the Persians, the Atys of the Phrygians, the Adonis of the Phoenicians, the Bacchus of the Greeks, and is, like them, the emblem of the sun, which, traversing the twelve signs of the zodiac, illuminates and fertilizes the northern hemisphere, then descending under the equator."[23] In a hymn attributed to Orpheus, the poet says that Adonis sometimes dwells

---

23. Marconis de Nègre, *Masonic Pantheon*, page #.

in the dark Tartarus, and that sometimes, ascending toward Olympus, he brings forth the greenery and ripens the fruits.

In Egyptian Freemasonry, the myth of Hiram includes some small nuances designed to root the myth in this symbolic black land of Egypt. Obviously, the poetry of these esoteric rituals manifests the intuition of those who wrote them. Thus, in the third degree of the Order of Memphis-Misraim, one of the officers says: "So perished Hiram, the righteous man, faithful to his duty unto death. From the fatal moment that deprived us of our Master, Egypt and our works are interrupted, but hope remains; let us not lose courage and strive to continue the unfinished work." Then raising the corpse of the master from the tomb, the master says: "You have your axis, your spine again. Your body is renewed, your heart has stopped beating. Then, you have come back to life. The golden pillar is set up and you may rejoice."

Eventually a beautiful hymn that could have been sung during an Orphic ceremony says: "Immortal man, I salute you! Never will my holy lyre dare to call you mortal. From heaven, in a solemn day, such as victorious, you must pass through the gate, shine in glory, and be with the Eternal God."

Opening Ceremony of the Third Degree

As with the second degree, it is sometimes interesting to change the energy of the work and practice esoteric techniques. When this is the case, you should add the following sequence to the first ceremony.

Before starting the sequence, you should add five extra candles, placed beside the three burning in the east. The total of candles in the east will be eight.

After placing these extra candles, breathe in silence for a moment and then say:

A Master Mason is symbolically seven years old and more.

   I learned the secrets of the letter G and the mysteries of the acacia are known to me.

Using your gavel, knock five times (2–1–1–1) as a Fellowcraft on your altar and return the gavel to its place.

I, (your name), stand in front of the mysterious door of the third degree of Freemasonry. I have meditated upon the teachings of the Fellowcraft and I have learned the nature of the real stone, which is my soul.

   Today I want to cross the threshold of this gate to reach the secret room where Master Masons meet, learn, and discuss.

I came here today to seek perfection, my hands showing the glorification of your name!

Open your arms, upper arms horizontal to each side of your body, forearms vertical, hands open, and palms facing east. Keeping this position, say:

I know the name of this door, which is "Khersek-Shu."
    I know the name of the upper leaf of this door, which is "Neb-Maat-heri-retiu-f."
    I know the name of the lower leaf of this door, which is "Neb-pehti-thesu-menment."
    Then thou Anubis, let me enter, as I know the secret names.

Breathe in silence for a few seconds, feeling the presence of the god, then release your hands and face west.

Extend your arms in front of you, hands open, palms up. Then say:

Great God, Master of the two Maat, I stand in front of you. My hands are pure. Let my heart be weighed on the scale of Truth, for it is pure. I never made dirty the clear water. I never blew out the flame of intelligence. I never veiled the light and hid the divine light. I never deteriorated beauty. I never protected my life at the expense of the lives of others. I never distorted the truth.
    I am pure! I am pure! I am pure! I am pure!
    My purity is the one of the great phoenix and I know the names of the divinities present in this place.

Release your arms and breathe in silence. Say:

I receive this symbol of purity and I am ready to work. I offer you this evidence of my sincerity and honesty.

Light the additional candles of this degree.

Light incense and arrange the tools placed on the sacred book according to the intertwining of the third degree.

Then knock nine times according to the following sequence: 2–1 (short pause) 2–1 (short pause) 2–1.

Still standing, put your right hand on your heart and say:

To the Glory of the Supreme Architect of the Worlds, to the glory of the gods and goddesses of the sacred land of Egypt, by the divine powers that are part of every human being, I declare open this ceremony working at the third degree of the Masonic order!

Then you can proceed to your work in the third degree.

Closing Ceremony of the Third Degree

If you have worked to the third degree, you should also close to this degree, prior to performing the full closing ceremony of the first degree. You should proceed as follows.

After a moment of silence, say:

I praise you, O Eternal Principle which no obstacle hinders! My soul and my heart desire to ascend to your realm!

Your benevolence and affection bless all living creatures and you bring to me the grace of Wisdom, Word, and Reason:

Wisdom for me to conceive you, the Word for me to speak about the Immortal Divinities, and Reason for me to know you.

I rejoice in having been enlightened by your wisdom!

I rejoice because you have shown me your Power!

I rejoice because you have deified me by the sanctified elements I received within me!

The prayer I offer you has only one goal: to learn to know you and to praise you!

Extinguish the five extra candles that are in the east.

Then knock nine times according to the following sequence: 2–1 (short pause) 2–1 (short pause) 2–1. Still standing, put your right hand upon your heart and say:

To the Glory of the Supreme Architect of the Worlds, to the glory of the gods and goddesses of the sacred land of Egypt, by the divine powers that are part of every human being, I declare closed this ceremony working at the third degree of the Masonic order!

Ceremony of Self-Initiation into the Third Degree
Preparation of the Ritual

As with the other self-initiations, I recommend performing this initiation during a quiet period.

Your Preparation

Remember that you are already a Fellowcraft, so you will wear your white apron during the first part of the ceremony according to what you learned in the second degree.

Preparation of the Room

Install the lodge room according to the instructions provided with the opening ceremony of the first and second degrees.

Entrance into the Room

When you are ready and all is in place, stand in front your altar (the representation of the lodge) and breathe in silence.

Using your gavel, knock 5 times (2–1–1–1) as a Fellowcraft on your altar and return the gavel to its place.

> I, (your name), stand in front of the mysterious door of the third degree of Freemasonry. I have meditated upon the teachings of the Fellowcraft and I have learned the nature of the real stone which is my soul.
>
> Today I want to cross the threshold of this gate to reach the secret room where Master Masons meet, learn, and discuss.
>
> I came here today to seek perfection, my hands showing the glorification of your name!

Open your arms, upper arms horizontal to each side of your body, forearms vertical, hands open, and palms facing east. Keeping this position, say:

> I know the name of this door, which is "Khersek-Shu."
> I know the name of the upper leaf of this door, which is "Neb-Maat-heri-retiu-f."
> I know the name of the lower leaf of this door, which is "Neb-pehti-thesu-menment."
> Then thou Anubis, let me enter, as I know the secret names.

Breathe in silence for a few seconds, feeling the presence of the god, then release your hands and face west.

Extend your arms in front of you, hands open, palms up. Then say:

> Great God, Master of the two Maat, I stand in front of you. My hands are pure. Let my heart be weighed by the scale of Truth, for it is pure. I never made dirty the clear water. I never blew

out the flame of intelligence. I never veiled the light nor hid the divine light. I never deteriorated beauty. I never protected my life at the expense of the lives of others. I never distorted the truth.

I am pure! I am pure! I am pure! I am pure!

My purity is the one of the great phoenix and I know the names of the divinities present in this place.

Release your arms and breathe in silence. Say:

I receive this symbol of purity and I am ready to work. I offer you this evidence of my sincerity and honesty.

Remove your apron, face east, and place the apron on the west side of the altar.

Now unveil the tracing board of the degree. Breathe in silence while looking at this powerful symbol. Kneel and place your hands on the altar, both palms touching it.

Read your oath for this third degree:

I, (your name), stand in the presence of this invisible respectable assembly of Masons, the wardens of this sacred temple, and in union with the egregore of Egyptian Freemasonry.

In front of me are the sacred symbols of the third degree, and I swear upon them to keep secret what the invisible masters will reveal to me in the process of this ceremony and during my individual practices.

I swear to work with zeal, constancy, and regularity to understand the Masonic tradition and apply its principles in my life.

I swear to continue the practice of the highest moral principles.

So mote it be!

Stay silent for a few seconds, then stand up. Open your hands wide in front of the east and say:

I am here to find perfection. My hands are pure and glorify the highest powers of the cosmos. The acacia is not yet revealed and the land of Egypt has been placed in darkness.

Sacred temples have been desecrated and destroyed. The divine presence has been veiled and the divinities have left their beloved land. I am here to find the truth and rebuild the visible and invisible temples.

The Masonic tradition tells an ancient story of plot and murder. This symbolic myth has been linked to the Bible and the figure of the architect Hiram-Abif killed by three Fel-

lowcrafts trying to extort from him the secret passwords and signs of the masters. As a matter of fact, this eternal story is not new and is the late adaptation of the murder of Osiris by Seth and his accomplices. Through it, the priests of ancient Egypt were describing in symbols the mysteries of death. They were presenting spiritual keys in order to directly experiment with this final episode of our life and relieve us from the fear of it. According to their beliefs, it was then possible to cross this threshold in full awareness, still living in the afterlife. But these are mysteries far higher than the degree on which I stand today.

I need now to commune with myself and follow the mysterious process taught a thousand years ago. My inner self will hear the sound of these ancient invocations. My soul will recognize the sacred words and will begin the process of building my inner temple. Then I will symbolically die as a Master Mason to come back to life as an architect.

Let the ancient mysteries be once again accomplished by the power of the symbols, the words, and the spirit.

So mote it be!

Cross your arms on your chest, the left over the right, and say:

I come forward and I tell my name to the invisible guardians of this sacred land.

"Dweller in the moringa" is my name.

I am come from the north city where I saw the leg and the thigh.

I said, "I saw the voices coming from the land of the Phoenicians," and they gave me a burning torch and a small column of earthenware. Then at night I buried them close to the coffin at the edge of the lake of Maat. This is the place where I found the scepter-ouas of flint. Its name is "Giver of Breath."

Then I lay back on the coffin and cried. I extinguished the flame and broke the small column. Then I threw them in the lake.

Open your arms wide while saying:

May the door of the two Maat be opened!

Release your arms and relax them on each side of your body. Continue by saying:

To pass this door I must know all its secret words. As I pronounce them, may the powerful guardians of this place allow me to enter in the room of the Righteousness, the two Maat.

"Pointer of truth" is the name of the front panel of the door.

"Scale pan to weigh fairness" is the name of the right jamb of the door.

"Scale pan of wine" is the name of the left jamb of the door.

"Ox of Seb" is the name of the threshold of the door.

"Toe of this mother" is the name of the strike of the door.

"Eye of Sobek, master of Bakhou" is the name of the bolt of the door.

"Chest of Shu, which he received as protection from Osiris" is the name of the leaf of the door.

"Young snake Uraeus" is the name of the lock rails of the door.

Extend your forearms horizontally in front of you, palms down, and say:

To walk in the room of the Righteousness, the two Maat, I must know the passwords. As I pronounce them, may the powerful guardians of this place allow me to walk in that sacred and hidden place.

I have been purified and I stand firm on both my legs.

"Creation of Ha" is the name of my right leg.

"Walking stick of Hathor" is the name of my left leg.

Close your hands in front of you, both palms of your hands vertical and in contact with each other. Say:

"The one who knows the hearts and looks into the stomachs" is the name of the guardian of the door.

Raise your forearms vertically in front of you, palms vertical, then open them toward the east and say:

I salute you with respect, Thot. I am pure from the bad actions that have been committed on the sacred land of Egypt. I was not among the murderers and criminals. Let Osiris know that I stand here today to cross your realms and be reborn.

My bread is the sacred eye. My beer is the sacred eye. My offering to the dead is the sacred eye.

Release your arms and bow forward, saying:

I salute you who is in the sacred western desert!

I know you and I know your name. May the one who is dead be freed of the worms who eat their flesh and drink their blood.

With a slow movement, kneel and lie down on the floor. Close your eyes and breathe in silence. You are Osiris, who died and is resting in the darkness. You are relaxed and you begin to descend into the deepest part of your being. Abandon any thoughts. It could be good not to exceed eight minutes here or, most importantly, not to fall asleep.

If you have memorized the short sequence that follows, say these words before opening your eyes:

I am Re. I am the creator who is under the sacred tree. I am the master of eternity. I am intact.

Open your eyes, still lying on the floor. You can use the text you previously placed close to you or speak it from memory.

My hairs are those from Noun.
My face is that from Re.
My eyes are those from Hathor.
My ears are those from Oupouaout.
My nose is that from Khent-Khas.
My lips are those from Anubis.
My teeth are those from Selkit.
My molars are those from the divine Isis.
My arms are those from Ba-neb-Ded.
My neck is that from Neith, lady of Sais.
My back is that from Seth.
My phallus is that from Osiris.
My flesh is that from the Masters of Kher-âha.
My chest is that from the Grand of prestige.
My belly and my spinal column are those from Sekhmet.
My buttocks are those from the Eye of Horus.
My thighs and my calves are those from Nout.
My legs are those from Ptah.
My toes are those of living falcons.
There is no part of me that is without a god, and Thoth protects my integrity.

I am the one who is unknown and who is reborn intact. I am yesterday, I am now, and I am tomorrow.

Slowly rise and kneel in front of your altar. Raise your arms in front of you and place the palms of your hands a few inches in front of your eyes. Say:

I am the one who was in the sacred eye. Nothing bad can affect me or oppose me. I am the one who opens the gates of the sky. I am the one who shines and rises from the dead.

Turn the palms of your hands toward the east and continue saying:

The gates of the sky have been opened for me. The gates of the earth have been opened for me. The bolts of Geb have been opened for me. The starry sky has been opened for me.
   I can again use my heart, my arms, my legs, my mouth, all my members.

Stand up, but not fully. Stay bent over and place the palms of your hands on your face, with the tips of your fingers upon your eyebrows. Keeping this position, say:

My right eye is the bark of the night. My left eye is the bark of the day. My eyebrows are those of Anubis. My fingers are those of Thoth, and my hairs are those of Ptah-Sokar.

Breathe in silence for a few seconds. Then in a single movement, stand up straight, saying:

I stand up as Osiris! Again, I have a back. Murderers have lost.

You are now standing up straight, both arms relaxed on each side of your body. Continue, saying:

I am the one who stands up straight and the Djed is behind me.
   I am Osiris, the reborn, the Eternal Architect who is raised from the dead.
   May the light continue to shine in the temple that has been rebuilt!

Breathe in silence and visualize around you an intense, bright golden light. You are in the light and the light surrounds you.

Then using your gavel, knock the shots of the degree on your altar in the following sequence: 2–1 (short pause) 2–1 (short pause) 2–1.

Open the sacred book as you usually do and arrange the tools on top of it according to the intertwining of the third degree.

Stand up, put your right hand on your heart, and say:

To the Glory of the Supreme Architect of the Worlds, by the divine powers that are part of every human being, I declare this temple fully open in the third degree of the Masonic order!

Solemn Declaration

Cross your arms on your chest, left over right, with the crossing point of your arms upon your heart. Bow your head and say:

To the Glory of the Sublime Architect of the Worlds, in the name of the Masters of the Egyptian Freemasonry, in the presence of this invisible respectable assembly of Masons, and by the power of the ritual I just performed, I solemnly stand in the room prepared for this third degree.

Release your arms and tie the apron of the masters around your waist. From now on, every time you perform a ritual practice at this degree, you will wear this apron instead of the white one.

You can sit if you want and take some notes about the ritual you just performed.

Take time at the end of this ceremony to take a few notes about what you felt, your thoughts, and whatever seems good and useful to you.

You can now proceed to the simplified closing ceremony.

Closing Ceremony

After a moment of relaxation, you should close this ceremony with the closing ritual in the second degree followed by the simplified closing of the second and first degrees, as you did in the self-initiation of Entered Apprentice.

Individual Practices of the Third Degree
The Amenti

As we discovered in a previous chapter, the third degree is related to the mysteries of death and, more particularly in Egyptian Freemasonry, to the myth of Osiris. There is no doubt that this inner experience can be fully performed only within an authentic initiatic order or during a specific shamanistic practice. Nevertheless, the individual esoteric practices you are about to discover allow you either to reactivate and deepen this experience already received or to approach these mysteries through a series of meditations.

In the ritual openings, the lodge in the third degree is said to meet in the *Sanctum Sanctorum*, the *Holy of Holies*. Egyptian Freemasonry, along with several Masonic groups, called this place the *Middle Room* (the central or secret room). This is where Master Masons meet in the third degree. This expression has existed since the beginning of Freemasonry and several interpretations have been given. It is not necessary here to repeat the many comments about this name. Obviously, these two names indicate a very sacred space located in the middle of the temple and accessible only to advanced Master Masons. Another way to talk about this place is to say that Master Masons meet somewhere between the square and the compass.

Even if all the lodges do not place the same carpet, altar, or tools in the center of the room, the occult access to the true Holy of Holies is the same and it uses the secret gate we already described. With serious training, you know now how to use this gate to enter into this sacred space of the temple. You know how to perform your inner work in this secret space. According to the hermetic teachings, we are part of the divine. A Mason works on himself as if he were sculpting a real stone, to reveal the divine part hidden inside him. Our soul descended from the highest planes and is moved by the desire to come back to its origin. As Plato said, the motor of this desire is a kind of nostalgia for our origins. The initiate will learn how to use this energy to free his soul and ascend to the real center of the lodge, the Holy of Holies. For the ancient Masters of the Schools of Mysteries such as Apuleius, the gateway has been called the *threshold of Proserpine*, and it is crossed during the initiation. Obviously Masonic initiation is symbolic, but esoteric Freemasonry can help us to understand a deeper reality and use it through inner practices. The practice of the Amenti will help you to approach this mystery. The "sacred room" will progressively become a secret space in which you can silently withdraw. In this sacred place, it will be easier for you to meditate on the essential points of your existence, such as your soul, your moral values, and your role on this earth and beyond. Your goal should be the path of return to your divine origins when the time comes.

Process

Before you begin, find a black veil wide enough to cover your head to the shoulders, and a representation of the Egyptian gods Anubis and Osiris that you can place in front of you. All other tools are the ones you usually use for this esoteric work.

Proceed to the opening ritual in the third degree. Sit and begin with a few minutes of relaxation.

After a few moments, enter your inner temple following the usual practice. The place should be organized according to the symbolism of the third degree. You can use the tracing board provided in the appendix to help you.

Imagine that you are standing in front of the coffin covered by a black veil. Between you and the coffin is Anubis. Osiris is standing behind the coffin and to the east. Imagine that the gods are facing you. Breathe quietly while their gaze is directed at you, both piercing and penetrating but benevolent. Open your eyes and say to Osiris, and to the other gods who are present in this room, the following words:

Everything belongs to me, everything has been given to me. I came as a falcon, I left as a phoenix. Morning Star, open the way for me to return in peace to the good west! I belong to the lake of Osiris, and I ask you to open the way for me so that I may return and adore Osiris, the master of life!

Breathe for a few seconds in silence and continue, saying:

I have come here to see your perfection, my hands being in glorification of your true name. I came here, while the fir tree did not yet exist, while the acacia had not yet been produced, and while a floor made of tamarisk wood had not yet been made. If I enter in the secret place, I will quarrel with Seth, I will be friendly to him who come to meet me and who veils his face, having fallen because of secret things.

Then put the black veil on your head and say:

I was in Busiris and silence was made for me. I was in the temple of the one-who-is-on-his-mountain and I saw the head of the temple. Having entered the temple of Osiris, I removed the veils of the one who was there. I hid the one that I found decomposed. Having gone to the sanctuary of Osiris, I dressed the one who was naked there and offered myrrh to women in the lake of men.

Salute Osiris, placing your right hand on your heart, and say:

Greetings to you, great god, Master of the two Maat! I came to you, O my master, having been brought to see your perfection. I came to you and brought you what is fair.

Extend your hands forward with palms down toward the coffin and say:

My mortal body remains under this dark veil such as our master Hiram. Like you before your resurrection, he was placed by fate under the acacia waiting for his resurrection. Today, present in spirit in this room, I witness the death of all beings and the survival of the righteous and the pure, all those who have been able to work and direct themselves toward the shining daylight. Anubis guides me on the way to the Amenti so that from the darkness of my body may emerge the light of my soul joining the land of the blessed.

Turn your hands so that your palms are now facing the sky. Continue reading the text:

Osiris, know that I am pure, I am pure, I am pure!

My purity is the purity of this great Phoenix who is at Heracleopolis, for I am indeed the very nose of the Master of the breaths who will make all men live on this day of the filling of the eye at Heliopolis on the last days of winter, in the presence of the master of that country. I am someone who has seen the filling of the eye at Heliopolis. It will not happen to me in this country because I know the names of the gods that are there.

Lift the black veil from your head and place it on your shoulders and neck. Keep your hands always turned toward the sky and continue by reading the following words:

I am a man whose mouth is pure, whose hands are pure, and to whom it is said, come in peace!

I am pure, my anterior limbs are purified, my hind limbs are purified, my torso has been in the fountain of equity, all my members are free from equity.

Sit down for a few moments and meditate on inner purity and what you can carry into your soul once the time comes to give up your physical body.

Then put your veil on your chair and stand up. Imagine that you are in the center of the temple facing east. Osiris is also standing and his light makes him difficult to see. An intense light also surrounds you. This light is the light of Osiris himself, and you now share his divine light. Declare solemnly:

I am the Undying, I am Re who came out of the Nun. My soul is a god. I am implored in the bull. I am invoked in the ennead in this name of Eternal. I came to the existence of myself with the Nun in my name of Khepri in which I come into existence every day. I am the master of the light. I woke up with Re, master of the east, and life was given to me during his eastern manifestations. I have come to heaven and have occupied my throne which is in the east.

Sit and keep that light all around you. You are the resurrected Master, Ra enthroned in the east. Stay a moment in this light that filled your physical and spiritual bodies.

Then after a moment, release your visualization and, if needed, take some notes about what you felt or understood.

Close the ritual as usual, using the text required.

The Prayer Beads

In my book *The Magical Use of Prayer Beads,* I show how they were used in various traditions. I cannot recall reading a single Masonic text talking about the use of prayer beads. Maybe Freemasons didn't use them because they were obviously too linked to a spiritual or religious practice. However, I have noticed in the past few years that some Egyptian lodges introduced the use of very simple prayer beads based on an ancient Egyptian symbolism. I should note that such mantric meditation is very useful to disconnect from the world around us and refocus on a sacred world the initiate is trying to reach.

The prayer beads used here are composed of three series of seven beads. One set of beads is white, the second red, and the third green. They are linked to three Egyptian divinities: Serapis, Horus, and Isis. Each series is separated by a turquoise bead. A cartouche is attached to it. These three sacred characters on the cartouche are Ankh, Wedja, and Seneb. They represent life, prosperity, and strength (health). This is a text formula that often appears after the names of Egyptian kings.

Once the set of prayer beads is in your hands, it can be blessed with specific Egyptian prayers. I suggest using the following one:

I invoke the divine names of Djehuti, Serapis, Horus, and Aset.

May your light and power fill these prayer beads and give me the blessings and protection I need every time I use them!

Place the index finger of your right hand on the cartouche and say:

I invoke here and now the presence of Serapis, Horus, and Isis.

O immortal divinities, make me alive forever, intact and in good health!

Then move your fingers to the first series of red beads.
On each red bead of the first series, say:

Serapis, give me health!

Once on the turquoise bead, say:

O immortal divinities, make me alive forever, intact and in good health!

On each green pearl of the second series, say:

Hor-Pa-Khered, give me strength!

Once on the turquoise bead, say:

O immortal divinities, make me alive forever, intact and in good health!

On each red bead of the third series, say:

Aset, give me life forever!

Once on the last turquoise bead, say:

O immortal divinities, make me alive forever, intact and in good health!

Stay silent for a few seconds. Then stand up and speak the following invocation:

The bright Eye of Horus comes. The bright Eye of Horus comes. Welcome in peace and resplendent as Re in the horizon. He chases away the power of Seth before the one who makes it manifest. It was he who had taken Horus away and he sent his blazing fire against him. His flame manifests his presence from Heaven before your two sisters. The Eye of Horus is alive within the Ouryt. The Eye of Horus is alive. He is Ioun-moutef.

Sit again and meditate for a few minutes.
Take a few minutes to write down your ideas, if needed, then close your work as usual.

The Crossing of the Seven Gates

As you may now know, there is a strong link between the symbolism of the third degree in Freemasonry and several sacred texts of the ancient Egyptian religion. In this regard, the geography of the afterlife has been described very precisely and associated with an endless number of divinities and invisible powers. The signs and sacred words are everywhere and must be mastered to cross this land in full security. There are no similar examples in the Bible of such use of dialogs and passwords. They unveil for us occult processes that can be used in meditation to activate very powerful archetypes. The latter are capable of enriching our understanding of these mysteries and revealing the hidden abilities of our soul.

One fragment of this very book can be used in such a way. It is also interesting to see that it can be linked to Greek and Roman symbolism of the seven planets and their power. I describe this heritage extensively, along with practices, in my book *Rediscover the Magick of the Gods and Goddesses*.

Place in front of you seven candles lined up on the west side of the black-and-white mosaic.

As you did for the previous practices, open the ritual in the third degree, sit, and begin with a few minutes of relaxation.

After a few moments, enter into your inner temple with the usual practice. The place should be organized according to the symbolism of the third degree.

Close your eyes and imagine that you stand in front of a golden door. Keeping this visualization, say:

> *I call upon the guardian of the first door by his name: Adjuster!*
> *May the one with a loud voice report my call.*

Light the candle on your left and hold it in front of you at the level of your sexual organs. Keeping this position and aware that you are working on a spiritual level, say:

> *I am the one who creates his own light. I come to you, Osiris, and I worship you. Pure are the perfumes that flow from you and make your name Ro-setaou. I salute you, Osiris, in your power and strength. Arise, almighty Osiris, in Abydos. Cross the sky as Re to see all humanity. I am a dignitary of Osiris and what is said is real. I walk in the light of Osiris.*

Return the candle to the altar and bow for a few seconds. Raise your head again, visualize that you cross this golden door, and say:

The first door has been opened and I cross the first room.

Close your eyes and imagine that you stand in front of the second golden door. Keeping this visualization, say:

I call upon the guardian of the second door by his name: the One with the Spinning Face!
   May the breaker report my call.

Light the second candle and hold it in front of you at the level of your lower belly. Keeping this position, say:

I am the one who sat beside the Eye of Horus as one of the three, weighing the words as a companion of Thoth. I am under the protection of Thoth. Mastiou are without power in front of me and I walk through the flames. I pass freely to see Re among those who give offerings.

Return the candle to the altar and bow for a few seconds. Raise your head again, visualize that you cross this golden door, and say:

The second door has been opened and I cross the second room.

Close your eyes and imagine that you stand in front of the third golden door. Keeping this visualization, say:

I call upon the guardian of the third door by his name: the One with the Watchful Face!
   May the wolf report my call.

Light the third candle on your left and hold it in front of you at the level of your navel. Keeping this position, say:

I am the one who judges the two companions. I come to banish all evil from Osiris.
   I am the one who comes with the white crown.
   I secured and opened the path in Ro-setaou. I relieved the pain of Osiris and I walk in the path of light in Ro-setaou.

Return the candle to the altar and bow for a few seconds. Raise your head again, visualize that you cross this golden door, and say:

The third door has been opened and I cross the third room.

Close your eyes and imagine that you stand in front of the fourth golden door. Keeping this visualization, say:

I call upon the guardian of the fourth door by his name: the Vigilant One!
  May the one who repels the furious report my call.

Light the fourth candle on your left and hold it in front of you at the level of your heart. Keeping this position, say:

I am the bull, son of the kite of Osiris. Behold, I am the one my father supported. I obtain justice for him and bring back life to him. I am the son of Osiris and I walk in the land of the dead.

Return the candle to the altar and bow for a few seconds. Raise your head again, visualize that you cross this golden door, and say:

The fourth door has been opened and I cross the fourth room.

Close your eyes and imagine that you stand in front of the fifth golden door. Keeping this visualization, say:

I call upon the guardian of the fifth door by his name: the Blazing One!
  May the impetuous one report my call.

Light the fifth candle on your left and hold it in front of you at the level of your throat. Keeping this position, say:

I have brought the two jaws from Ro-setaou. I have brought the spine from Heliopolis. I have gathered your followers and pushed back Apophis and healed the wounds he made on you. I am the great one among the gods. I purified Osiris. I restored him. I joined his bones and put together his limbs.

Return the candle to the altar and bow for a few seconds. Raise your head again, visualize that you cross this golden door, and say:

The fifth door has been opened and I cross the fifth room.

Close your eyes and imagine that you stand in front of the sixth golden door. Keeping this visualization, say:

> *I call upon the guardian of the sixth door by his name: the Shifting One!*
> *May the one with a sharp gaze report my call.*

Light the sixth candle on your left and hold it in front of you at the level of your forehead. Keeping this position, say:

> *I come today. Open for me the path, as I have been created by Anubis. I am the assistant of the magician, the owner of the white crown, and the protector of Maat. I protected the Eye of Osiris and brought it back to him. Let me cross this place with you as a living one.*

Return the candle to the altar and bow for a few seconds. Raise your head again, visualize that you cross this golden door, and say:

> *The sixth door has been opened and I cross the sixth room.*

Close your eyes and imagine that you stand in front of the seventh golden door. Keeping this visualization, say:

> *I call upon the guardian of the seventh door by his name: the One with a High Voice!*
> *May the one who repels the enemies report my call.*

Light the seventh candle on your left and hold it in front of you at the level of the top of your head. Keeping this position, say:

> *I come to you, Osiris, and I worship you. Pure are the perfumes that flow from you. Cross the sky as Re to see all humanity. I say to all, "For Osiris I ask worship. May Osiris be powerful!*
> *Open the path of light to me!"*

Return the candle to the altar and bow for a few seconds. Raise your head again, visualize that you cross this golden door, and say:

> *The seventh door has been opened and I cross the seventh room.*

Close your eyes, with your spine straight and extended from the floor to the sky. Visualize this column of golden light in your spine and the bright white pharaonic crown at the top of your head. A golden snake is shining on your forehead. The starry sky above you shines with countless lights. Keep this powerful visualization and say:

As Osiris, I stand straight in glory. Again, I have a back. Again, I have vertebrae. The golden pillar Djed keeps me straight and brings me life, prosperity, and health forever!

Breathe and relax as these powerful words seal your practice in the invisible world.
Then sit and meditate for a few minutes.
Then you can write down your thoughts and close your work as usual.

Chapter 15

The High Degrees of Egyptian Freemasonry

To start, it is important to say a few words about what is called *high degrees*, or sometimes *side degrees*. I have already explained that today the Masonic system is composed of the three first degrees. Their rituals can be different according to the countries and the history of each organization. Freemasonry per se is just that and nothing more. Almost all over the world, there is no obligation to do more or to join other degrees. This is the only common principle. Nevertheless, it is very common for Master Masons to join these high degrees. They are structured according to several degrees different for each system: Scottish rite, Royal Arch, Egyptians, etc.

Probably no one will ever know the exact origin of these high degrees. Most of them were certainly organized in the eighteenth century in the wake of speculative Freemasonry. They are obviously linked with much older traditions. Between the fifteenth and eighteenth centuries, several groups and guilds were organized. Some of them focused on Qabalah, and others on Hermeticism, Neoplatonism, Egyptian religion, or Pythagoreanism. In the fifteenth century, the Italian Renaissance saw the emergence of the first groups focusing on Hermeticism. During the seventeenth century, Hermeticism and pre-Christian theurgy became more secretive due to politics and religious intolerance. Maybe as a consequence, Christian Qabalah began to become the main influence of that time on occultists and esotericists. The Rose-Cross movement appeared in Germany and influenced various groups. This new symbolism spreading in Europe merged with the Masonic appetite to create new sets of degrees. These centuries spawned prolific creativity, as evidenced by the vast number of degrees generated. At that time, the nature of the Masonic system made it easy to receive new influences. Then the initial enthusiasm led to an apparent confusion between all these different rituals.

Thus, in the last third of the eighteenth century, a desire for clarification led to the organization of systems of high degrees more defined, structured, and controlled by the Masonic organizations. Their characteristics became more clearly visible. The best known in Europe were the *Rite de Perfection* in the late 1760s, the *Scottish Rite Rectified* in 1782, and the *French Rite* in 1784. In the United States, the Scottish Rite was formally established in Charleston in 1801. At the end of the eighteenth century, Cagliostro (Giuseppe Balsamo 1743–1795) organized an original Freemasonry in Europe, explicitly referring to ancient Egypt. This creation significantly impacted the esoteric world of that time and became a source of inspiration for several other creations, smaller or larger. Almost everyone back then seemed to be interested in ancient Egypt and its rituals. Who would not have been moved by Master Masons invoking angels in a lodge and receiving communications from a prophetess hidden in the eastern part of the room?

For a long time, small groups continued to manifest their creativity and the number of degrees started to increase, from 3 to 33, then to 90, and even 99! Others were less ambitious. The Rite of the Perfect Initiates of Egypt created in Lyon (France) in 1785, probably from the book *Crata Repoa*, had seven degrees in all. The four degrees following the third degree of Master are Perfect Master, Perfectly Elected, Little Architect, and Perfect Initiate of Egypt. The Sacred Order of the Sophisians probably had three or four degrees. It was not until 1811 that the Egyptian Masonic organization called *Misraim* appeared, followed in 1838 by *Memphis*. Until 1881, these two organizations continued their evolution side by side. Gradually, they began to attract members of mainstream Freemasonry interested in Masonic symbolism, gnosis, Qabalah, Hermeticism, esotericism, and occultism. With 90 degrees for Misraim and 95 for Memphis, we can assume that all of them were not ritually performed. Indeed, some existed only by name, signs, and passwords, but without any ritual or teaching. These degrees were given by "communication"—that is, conferred simply and solemnly by declamations, during a short ceremony. Then the candidate was invited to deepen his meditation on the name of the degree that had just been communicated to him and of which he had been given little information.

This lack of content can be explained in two ways. First, it is easy to imagine the time that would be necessary to practice these various degrees regularly and simultaneously while continuing the usual work in a Masonic lodge. Moreover, not all degrees were considered to have equal importance. It is interesting to note that the Ancient and Primitive Rite of England (1881) used the 33-degree system defined by Yarker in the *Constitution, Statues, Ceremonials & History of the Ancient & Primitive Rite of Masonry* published in London in 1875. The *Antico and Primitivo Rito Orientale di Memphis* created in Palermo (Italy) and founded in 1921 by MacBean also used this structure of 33 degrees. France, Spain, Germany, and other countries eventually followed the trend. But as with the 95-degree system, the 33 degrees were not all performed ritually. Only the 11th (Knight Rose-Croix), 18th (Knight Kadosch), 21st (Patriarch Grand Installer), 22nd (Patriarch Grand Consecrator), and 33rd (Sublime Master of the Great Work) were conferred. It was not until 1934 that the Masonic organization of Memphis-Misraim validated its structure of 90 degrees plus 9 administrative degrees, the 99th being the degree of Grand Invisible Hierophant.

The largest French Masonic organization, the Grand Orient of France, maintained its lineage and rights on the original Masonic system of Memphis-Misraim. Although this organization didn't practice the rituals during the nineteenth century, they were preserved in a section of Memphis-Misraim within the *Grand College des Rites* (Grand College of Rites), the inner structure of the Grand Orient de France. This Grand College of Rites is a kind of repository used in Masonic organizations to preserve rituals that were once practiced by only a few. In 2000, a very small number of Master Masons, having the necessary authority and lineage, met and decided to reactivate this part of the inheritance. I was one of the few that started this idea and pushed it. I received the honor to work and reorganize the texts of all the rituals of this system. I also created a magazine (*Arcana*) for this Egyptian structure, and its first website. We decided to use the traditional name of *Grand Egyptian Order—Sovereign Sanctuary of the Rite of Memphis-Misraim*.

I worked for several years on this project as Grand Officer. Then the Grand Orient de France officially validated the rituals I had presented, with the system restricted to the members of this organization. These rituals are still used today and I am sure will continue to be used for a very long time. Besides the work on the three first degrees, we chose to structure the system on 33 degrees instead of the 99 degrees of Memphis-Misraim. The reasons were simple. The 99 degrees always include the 33 degrees common to another system called the *Scottish Rite*. In the eighteenth century, a famous English Mason called John Yarker (1833–1913) reorganized the Egyptian system into 33 degrees, putting aside the rituals of the Scottish Rite and keeping the original rituals of Egyptian Freemasonry. This is what we did in the Grand Ordre Egyptian of the Grand Orient de France.

As you can see, the considerable number of degrees is at once attractive for its fascinating rituals and discouraging for the time spent, sometimes in vain. Some Masonic organizations use such a system to keep their members involved, as they always hope for greater mysteries. Yet this is not a game. These degrees are real opportunities to discover more about a tradition. Some of them contain real keys to use in individual practices. Of course, all the initiates are not fully aware of that, but a genuine esoteric process has been hidden in various degrees. That is why in this book I give an example of individual practice linked to one of these degrees.

Chapter 16

The Arcana Arcanorum

Esoteric Freemasonry loves to use a succession of veils to reveal its mysteries progressively. The high degrees are a perfect example of that. As the final degrees are administrative, the initiates of this tradition decided to add a final superstructure to the system: a golden pyramid placed at the top of an obelisk. It was impossible to achieve such initiatic organization administratively, so the initiates, aware of the occult process, decided to add three secret degrees focusing only on the most advanced esoteric process: Arcana Arcanorum.

These three final degrees are traditionally placed within, or above, the last degree of the Egyptian Masonic system. Very little is known about them. Historically, the name *Arcana Arcanorum* is found in Rosicrucian literature during the eighteenth century, for example in the book *Secret Symbols of Altona* published between 1785 and 1788. This was the first time this name was used in the esoteric tradition, although equivalents can be seen, for example in the work of Michael Maïer as *Arcana Arcanissima* or in Cagliostro's writings as *Secreto Secretorum*. Cagliostro traveled to Naples in 1783, and it is possible that he met Freemasons there, and also members of the Academy of Secrets (Accademia dei Segreti), which had existed in that city since 1560.

It is likely that what became the three degrees of the Arcana Arcanorum originated in Italy in the movement of the Academies. Let us go back in time to understand where and how this manifestation occurred. The first academy was the Platonic Academy, founded in Florence in 1462 during the reign of Laurent the Magnificent. Marsilio Ficino was in charge of translating old Greek philosophical and hermetic manuscripts. Ficino, Pic de la

Mirandole, and other famous figures of that time also practiced hermetic rituals in the Neoplatonic tradition. The founders of this group considered themselves to be parts of the golden chain of initiates. This chain supposedly went back to Hermes through the leaders of the Platonic Academy of Athens. These academies were developed according to an encyclopedic and humanistic model, distinct from the scholasticism of that period. This trend became important when 500 academies opened around 1530. Among them, some worked in the spirit of the academies of Athens and Florence, philosophically on the visible level and ritually in private. This was the case for the Accademia dei Segreti in Naples and the Accademia degli Uranici in Venice. The latter was founded in 1587 by Fabio Paolini, a professor of Greek, who continued the work of Marsilio Ficino. He was also one of the nine founders of the Seconda Accademia Veneziana, which took over in 1593. For these Masters, the work was not just speculative and intellectual. The practice of the *Religio Mentis* brought together art, philosophy, and spirituality in a balanced way. Moreover, it is likely that Neoplatonist theurgic practices were practiced as private activities.

The concept of the academies evolved rapidly. To the original humanistic Neoplatonist philosophy, specific subjects were added, such as theater, music, classical languages, theology, medicine, and so on. Progressively, these institutions became what today we call universities. Some of these academies continued to work discreetly on the philosophical and theurgic level.

An English "lineage" originated from the travels and teachings of Giordano Bruno and the contacts between Paris, Oxford, and Cambridge that followed the arrival in France of the Italian philosopher Tommaso Campanella (1568–1639). The Platonic circles present in various universities demonstrated the permanence of Hermeticism and the practices that had been linked to it since the Renaissance. Until the seventeenth century, various groups maintained this tradition. A small group of Freemasons initiated into this hermetic and theurgic tradition gradually organized part of what they knew in three (or four) grades. This organization and continuation with the inner hermetic lineage was called by the traditional name of *Aurea Catena*, or *Arcana Arcanorum*.

As for the Italian lineage, it was not until 1816 that two brothers named Joly discovered the Arcana Arcanorum in Italy and brought it back to France, where it seems to have been handed over to the Grand Orient of France, probably in the form of an abstract of the last four degrees of the Rite of Misraim. Several spiritual or occult groups have since claimed the possession and practice of a real and complete edition of these "secret" degrees.

The Arcana Arcanorum seems to have been maintained in very few theurgic orders in three forms: symbolic, philosophical, and ritual. Although these three parts of the Western tradition have followed different historical directions, their coherence indicates their common origin. The initiatic tradition taught by the Neoplatonists, inspired by the classical myths of Orpheus, Isis, and Osiris, could have offered useful teachings to Masons who achieved their Masonic curriculum. However, it was often the opposite. These mysterious Arcana Arcanorum texts exist in several versions; a few of them have been circulated as teachings and short rituals of the 87th, 88th, 89th, and 90th degrees for the lineage of Misraim. Sometimes they are shown as initiations related to the 97th, 98th, and 99th degrees.

For some authors, such as Jean Pierre Giudicelli de Cressac Bachelerie, the Arcana Arcanorum contains teachings related to theurgy; that is, a connection with eons-guides who will help the initiate in the process of inner transformation. The few texts that are available publicly are always short and often ridiculous from a historic point of view. An Egyptologist would have to laugh listening to some of the prayers and invocations associated with the rituals of these high degrees. Nevertheless, keep in mind that a few small groups have access to more advanced material, and the oral tradition has always been very important. So when we know how the Neoplatonist and theurgic traditions have been maintained, we cannot reject the idea of an inner process described in some versions of the real Arcana Arcanorum.

It is essential to understand the intent of the initiates who created these secret rituals, and theurgy is a key factor here. This is why it's important to look for authentic initiatic orders when someone desires a real inner transformation. A symbolic work is useful but remains limited in its effect on your inner being. Christian Qabalah played a role in the esoteric history by transposing the ancient Hermetic teachings in its theological doctrine. A good example is the Kabbalistic Order of the Rose-Cross (okrc.org), founded in 1888 and still active today.

The goal of any initiatic school should be to provide a theoretical and practical way to master one's life. Obviously, it should not be limited to our daily life but must involve our spiritual and divine nature as well. Rituals, symbols, and teachings are the tools that any initiate can use to progress toward his spiritual enlightenment. Thus, every step of this training must help us to cross the multiple veils of illusions and get closer to what could be called "reality." In this authentic spiritual process, the Master is the one who has himself accomplished the path. He should not be a dogmatic figure preaching trust, but only the one with more experience on the path. Just as someone who has visited a country knows more than someone who has only watched a documentary about it on TV, the Master can give good advice and share his expertise.

In Freemasonry, experience is what matters most. This is also true in other initiatic orders and in life in general! The initiator is a normal human being, although he has more experience in his field than the new candidate. Nevertheless, not even the Master can escort the candidate beyond a certain point. Some experiences are deeply personal, and silence must be respected. The esoteric tradition explains that the initiate must then be able to contact the source of knowledge; that is, to find another guide who is not a human being. In some traditions, such an encounter occurs in a ritual called *invocation of the Holy Guardian Angel*. In some Masonic rituals, there is an equivalent. For example, in the Masonic system of the Flamboyant Star of Tschoudi and in the rituals of the Gold Rose-Cross, the *evocation of the seven primordial angels* can be used for the same purpose. A complete description of a similar practice can be found in the *Book of Abramelin* preserved in the library of the Arsenal in Paris and published in English in 1898 by S. L. MacGregor Mathers (1854–1918).

According to this tradition, the invocation of the Holy Guardian Angel is intended to help the adept contact angelic entities. From the success of this contact, the practitioner will reach an understanding of the mysteries of the soul and the afterlife. This type of practice is extremely important, because without it, it is impossible to go beyond the teachings received from the visible initiator. Of course, you can learn by yourself, but the notion of a spiritual guide is fundamental. If the Arcana Arcanorum contains the most advanced Masonic teachings we can receive, they should be pointing in the same direction, with real theurgic practices that allow the initiate to cross this spiritual threshold. Otherwise, these highest initiations are useless.

The Egyptian ritual of Misraim refers to that idea in its 89th degree when it says: "In this degree we can call the last of the Masonry in the Rite of Misraim, where a developed explanation of the relationship of men with the divinity and the heavenly spirits is given. This degree, the most astonishing of all, requires the greatest strength of mind, the purest morals, and the most absolute faith." To achieve this goal on a practical level, theurgy is the tool. This process is also called *inner alchemy*. I should add that several sections of the teachings of the famous mystic Gurdjieff unveil some key aspects of this occult process.

As you should now realize, the authentic Arcana Arcanorum is rooted in ancient Egypt, Hermeticism, and Neoplatonism. Theurgy unites these origins and unlocks the mysterious inner process. According to the teachings of this tradition, we have two natures that are deeply linked: material and immaterial. Plato is clearly the first person who wrote extensively about this duality. According to his work and that of all the Neoplatonists who inherited this tradition, our soul is immaterial and immortal. Metempsychosis is another central element of this philosophy, as is the question of the individuality of the soul. Even if they come from ancient Egypt, the esoteric works of the Arcana Arcanorum are based on the same principles. I wrote extensively about these concepts in my book *Rediscover the Magick of the Gods and Goddesses*, but let us consider now the main aspects of them.

For Plato, the upper soul, called the *nous*, is both intelligence and knowledge, to be distinguished from lower levels of the soul, called *thumos* and *epithumia*. Both of these constitute a kind of "material soul" that disappears with the body after death. These lower levels can be compared with what the esoteric literature calls the *astral* (or *energetic*) body. Only the upper part of the soul, the nous, is immortal and imperishable. Knowing that your soul is immortal is helpful, but you also want to know if you will continue to be yourself after death. There is a big difference between saying that our soul continues to exist after our death and saying that we will keep everything we have learned and remain aware of who we are! This tradition was one of the first to teach the doctrine of reincarnation, also called *metempsychosis*. However, the inner teachings go further than the usual theories you can find around you. Although our soul can go from one body to another through multiple lives, a real initiate learns how to accomplish this without losing his own identity and knowledge. All the other souls continue their transmigrations, but each time they lose what they have just experienced or learned.

Plato explained that our soul is in our body as a prisoner would be chained in a dark cave. The path of the initiate is to free himself and leave the cave to reach the light of the sun, which is the spiritual world. It can be seen as the salvation of our soul and be manifested by a real state of awareness. The ones who stay in the cave are merely preoccupied with the desires and animal impulses of the lower soul, and once dead, they return to the earth without any consciousness of what happened before. Morals also play a role in this inner development and should be considered an essential part of this ascent to the spiritual light. Theurgy (and somehow alchemy) has this goal and provides very efficient keys in this regard. The Masons that composed the Masonic version of the Arcana Arcanorum undoubtedly inherited this doctrine, since it was taught among the Kabbalist magicians of the sixteenth and seventeenth centuries. However, the philosophical and occult background of Masonic groups of this period was very poor: famous figures usually gathered in lodges focusing on pure philosophy rather than esotericism.

Only vague memories of theurgical and philosophical principles were used to build these degrees; even so, their teachings highlighted the idea of the possible immortality of the soul. In order for an initiate to reach these high degrees, it was necessary to distinguish between reality and illusion, and discover the secret rituals that would help him acquire his immortal individuality. Such are the principles that motivated the founders of these mysterious degrees. They are simple, but they must be practiced and not simply read. They require an effort. As Socrates said: "It would be perfect if wisdom were such that we could make it flow from a very full spirit to a very empty soul, as we are doing from a very full vase to another very empty one." [24]

Rituals and initiations would be meaningless if the tools were not used for a real inner work. The supreme goal and secret is there, in plain sight. It is clearly explained by Socrates but cannot be reached by simply hoping or believing: "Having thus reached a wider view of beauty, the philosopher (or the initiate) will no longer attach himself to the beauty of a single object. He will stop to love with the narrow and petty feelings of a slave, a child, a man, an action. Facing now the Ocean of Beauty and contemplating its manifold aspects, he will give birth unceasingly to beautiful and magnificent speeches, and thoughts will sprout in abundance from his love of wisdom, until finally his fortified and enlarged spirit sees a unique science, which is that of Beauty. For the true way of love, whether one engages in oneself or is allowed to lead oneself, is to start from the visible beauties and to ascend ceaselessly toward this supernatural beauty, passing step by step from a beautiful body to two, from two to all, then from beautiful bodies to beautiful actions, then from beautiful actions to beautiful sciences, to end up from sciences to that science which is nothing but the science of absolute beauty and to finally know Beauty as it is in itself. If life is ever worth living, it is at this moment when man contemplates beauty in itself." [25]

Without excluding rituals and initiations, it is on love and friendship, called in Greek *agape*, that this ascent is founded. This is the moment when harmony is established in our inner being, when this emotion of beauty makes us discover and feel the intensity and richness of our humanity, in relation to others and to the world.

---

24. Plato, *Symposium*, 175e.

25. Ibid., 211b.

Chapter 17

Consecration of the Lodge

Any sacred temple is always consecrated. It can be with simple prayers or with complex rituals of consecration that take place before, during, or after the construction. We can find such rituals in Mesopotamia, Egypt, and Rome and in most religions around the globe. Freemasonry has followed this tradition and most of the time rooted its ritual in the Bible with the use of corn, wine, and oil. Historically, the rituals of Misraim and Memphis have extended this consecration with long invocations and comments. Other, more intimate Egyptian Masonic groups, some of them still based on the rituals of Memphis-Misraim—the Most Worshipful National Grand Lodge of Egyptian Freemasons and the Sacred Order of the Sophisians, for example—have used esoteric principles to give this ceremony a greater efficiency. The individual ritual provided here is rooted in these principles and traditions.

As you can imagine, the consecration of a lodge installed permanently in a room dedicated to it is different from a space used episodically. But even in this case, it is good to perform such a ceremony. You can simplify it. For example, you can use a stone of foundation in the way explained here and keep it somewhere in your room. The consecration of Egyptian temples included ten rituals: (1) stretching the cord, (2) purifying the area by sprinkling gypsum, (3) digging the first foundation trench, (4) filling the trench with sand, (5) molding the first brick, (6) burying the foundation deposits, (7) initiating the building work, (8) purifying the temple, (9) presenting the temple to the deities, and (10) offering sacrifices.

Several of these sequences will be used here.

To begin, you should install your lodge as described here in the first ritual. The cord will be placed on the floor in the center of the lodge and rolled together to form a small hill. You should wear the apron of your degree.

Prepare the following specially for this ceremony:

- Four cups filled with sand, salt, water, and milk, respectively
- Small bottle of olive oil
- Myrrh incense
- Offering table with grains of wheat, a pomegranate half-opened, and bread
- Carafe of wine
- Two empty cups
- Clay powder and a carafe of water
- Mold for the clay (Any rectangular container made of plastic or wood would be suitable. It will allow you to create a small brick about 8 inches long, 4 inches wide, and 4 inches high. These dimensions are not absolute.)
- Blazing sword (straight sword or dagger if you do not have a blazing sword)
- Staff of Anubis
- Four tesserae with the symbols of the cardinal directions (see figure 32)

Ritual

Your lodge is installed. The lights and the incense are not burning but are ready to be used. Only the sacred fire has been lit. Take time to meditate and relax.

Stand up facing east, take your blazing sword in your left hand, and point up with your staff in your right hand. Knock 24 times on the floor with your staff. Move closer to your altar and place the staff vertically on the southwest corner. Then place the sword on the altar and point to the north.

Place the palms of your hands on your altar and say:

I am here today to purify, protect, and consecrate this sacred place built to the glory of the Supreme Architect of the Worlds, to the glory of the gods and goddesses of the sacred land of Egypt.

The Cord

Take your staff and plant it in the center of the hill made of cord, and say:

Depths have been opened for the people of Noun. The inhabitants of the light may walk freely. I take the cordage of the bark of Re.

Go to the west. Then do a circumambulation around your lodge, knocking softly on the floor with your staff at each step.

Come back to the west side of the altar and return your staff to the southwest corner of it. Take the tip of the cord and begin to unwind it. Move toward the west door and then walk clockwise, placing the cord all around the lodge. As you progress, make twelve figure-eight knots, six on one side and six on the other side. As you turn clockwise from the west, you will begin in the north. Each time you tighten a knot, say:

May this lodge be protected by the power of Aries!

Then continue with the names of the other eleven astrological signs: Taurus, Gemini, Cancer, Leo, Virgo, Libra, Scorpio, Sagittarius, Capricorn, Aquarius, and Pisces. If you have twelve stones around your lodge, try to place each knot close to each one.

When you are back by the west door, tie each tip of the cord, saying:

May this lodge be protected in the visible and the invisible.

The Natron

Take the cup containing the salt.[26] Pitch salt in the four directions (north, south, west, and east) while visualizing that the place is cleansed and purified. At the same time, say:

May this lodge be purified.

Return the cup to the altar.

---

26. In Egypt, natron was used instead salt. Natron is very close to it, though chemically it is slightly different. Natron was used for purifications and in the process of mummification. For years, real natron has not been harvested. If you know a place that provides such natron, don't hesitate to send me an email.

The Trenches

Take your sword and go to the west door. With the point of your sword, follow the cord all around the lodge, moving clockwise. During this circumambulation, visualize a trench being dug.

Go back to the altar and return the sword.

The Sand

Take the cup of sand and proceed as you did with the sword. Spread tiny amounts of sand all around the lodge as you fill out the trench you dug previously. Support this visible action by visualizing that the walls of the room are rising around you as you walk.

When you have returned to the west, come back to the altar and return the cup.

Molding of the Brick and Foundation Deposits

Take the small carafe of water and humidify the clay powder you prepared in the rectangular mold. Stir together both water and clay.

Then bury inside the clay the deposits you chose, such as a scarab, the ankh, a small statue of a deity, and grains of perfume. Then take your trowel and level the surface. Using one of the points of the compass, draw on the surface the three Egyptian symbols Ankh, Wedja, and Seneb, which represent life, prosperity, and strength (health). You can see these symbols on the cartouche in figure 33. Beside these hieroglyphs, write the name chosen for your lodge, the date of this consecration, and your name.

Then raise your brick and say:

> The lodge, (name of the lodge), has been founded and the offerings have been buried.
>   May the Supreme Architect of the Worlds, the gods and goddesses of the sacred land of Egypt, bless this brick and the sacred temple built on it.

Bring the brick to the northeast corner of the lodge and place it on the floor.

Initiation of the Building Work

Go back to your central altar and return all the tools you used.

Take the first tessera depicting the pillar Djed you prepared. Face west, raise the tessera, and say:

I am the one who stands behind the Djed. I am the one who was there when I repelled the murderers. I am the protector of Osiris.

Place the tessera on the floor, close to the west side of your altar.

Take the second tessera, depicting the figure of Anubis. Still facing east, raise the tessera and say:

I watch you. The one on the mountain makes sure that your attack fails. I repel your attack. I am the protector of Osiris.

Place the tessera on the floor, close to the east side of the altar.

Take the third tessera, depicting the symbol of fire. Face south, raise the tessera, and say:

I am the one who keeps the sand from sealing the secret place and repels with the torch of the necropolis. I am the protector of Osiris.

Place the tessera on the floor, close to the south side of the altar.

Take the fourth tessera, depicting a human face. Face north, raise the tessera, and say:

The one who comes to catch you, I will not allow him to catch you. I will catch him. I am the protector of Osiris.

Place the tessera on the floor, close to the north side of the altar.

Purification of the Lodge

Take the natron and proceed as you did in the second sequence of this consecration.

When this is done, return the cup and take the one containing water.

With the tips of your right fingers, project water in the four directions, as you did with the natron. Each time and simultaneously with the projection of the water, say:

Procul este profani.

Return the cup of water.

Light the incense. When the smoke begins to rise, open your arms, palms up, and say:

Supreme Architect of the Worlds, who embrace all the cosmos with one of your glances, who keeps in a just balance all the globes suspended to the azure vault, and which move with

admirable harmony by a simple emanation of your will, receive my tribute. May wisdom be
upon me as the rays of light that you dispense so kindly. May I never depart from the path
of virtue into which you lead me.

May this sweet perfume purify my heart and this place.

Take the censer, and beginning from the east, do one circumambulation while visualizing the place being purified with this perfume. Come back to the altar and return the censer.

Presenting the Lodge to the Divinities

Kneel, open your arms, palms up, and glance up toward the east. Breathe for a few seconds in reverence of the divine powers present in this lodge. Then say:

Supreme Architect of the Worlds, soul of the universe, Father of the universe, eternal source
of light, science, virtue, and happiness, hear my voice as I kneel in front of you.

Receive the offering of my fidelity and love.

Hail to you, Re, the most powerful of the sky, the oldest one of the earth, Master of
everything that exists, who established everything forever.

O shining Sun who rises every day at the horizon, may you shine for me forever.

I worship you at dawn, when you are at the zenith, and at sunset.

I salute you, Horakhty, Khepri! I rejoice when you appear at the horizon and light up
this sacred place with your rays of light. All the goddesses and gods are exalted when they
see you as the king of the sky.

Djehuti is at the front of the bark.

I came to see you and your disk rising from the horizon.

I salute you, as you rise as Re and live in Maat. Even the shiniest gold cannot be com-
pared to your splendor.

Praise to you, who rise in gold and bring light.

To you and all the goddesses and gods of my tradition, I present this lodge I prepared to
welcome you. I recreated the beauty of the cosmos and placed the sacred symbols that will
help me to begin my spiritual work and walk on the path of the return. I prepared myself for
this moment to be pure in front of you.

Be always welcome in this lodge! Enlighten me with your divine light! Help me to stay
on the straight line pointing to the three stars, symbols of the triple luminous essence of the
divine world: wisdom, justice, and benevolence. May you bless my life!

After a few seconds, cross your arms on your chest, left over right. Meditate in silence for a few minutes, breathing deeply and regularly.

Then stand up. Open your sacred book and place the square and the compass on top of it, according to the Master degree instructions (that is, the compass upon the square).

Take the small bottle of oil. If your altar is independent of the walls, you must anoint it now. Start with the east side. On the vertical surface, trace with the oil an Egyptian eye, Oudjat. Then draw around it a compass and a square. While doing that, say:

May the power of resurrection be upon this altar.

Proceed in the same way, pronouncing the same declamation on the south, west, and north sides.

If you placed stones around your lodge, go clockwise to anoint them, pronouncing the same declamation but replacing the word *altar* with *stone*.

Put your right hand on your heart and say:

To the glory of the Supreme Architect of the Worlds, to the glory of the gods and goddesses of the sacred land of Egypt, by the divine powers that are part of every human being, I solemnly declare this lodge consecrated!

Release your arms and say:

I'm not in the profane world anymore. May my works and those of all Freemasons all over the earth who are working as I am remain consistent with the Universal Harmony. May my work proclaim only the glory of the Grand Architect, the gods and goddesses of the sacred land of Egypt, the permanence of True Freemasonry and the Happiness of all Beings.
So mote it be!

Release your arms.

The Offerings

Take your offering table and stand in front of your altar. Hold the offering table with both hands in front of you. Maintain this position and say:

Supreme Architect of the Worlds, gods and goddesses of the sacred land of Egypt, I present to you these offerings as a gesture of my dedication to the Great Work that will be accomplished

in this lodge and in my inner temple. May these offerings please you, as I have prepared them
as a demonstration of my gratitude and fidelity.

Place the offering table on your altar or on a small table in front of it.
Take some grains of wheat in your hand and say:

Receive this wheat and may it feed our body and soul.

Take some bread. Break it and place it back on the table, saying:

Receive this bread and may it feed our body and soul.

Take the pomegranate that has been slightly opened, separate it into two, and place it
back on the table, saying:

Receive this pomegranate and may it feed our body and soul.

Take the small cup of milk and pour a small amount of milk on the table (or in a small
empty cup), saying:

Receive this milk and may it feed our body and soul.

Take the small cup of wine and pour a small amount of wine on the table (or in a small
empty cup), saying:

Receive this wine and may it feed our body and soul.

Stay silent for a few minutes. Then say:

Supreme Architect of the Worlds, gods and goddesses of the sacred land of Egypt, I thank
you for your presence and blessings.
   This lodge has been duly consecrated and has become a sacred place in which I can work
in peace to raise my soul to the divine light.
   May my work continue to be blessed and protected!
   So mote it be!

You can sit for a few minutes meditating on the ritual you just accomplished. Let the
offering stay in its place for at least one hour.
   You can now proceed to the closing of your lodge with the ritual of the first degree.

Chapter 18
Cagliostro and the Mysteries of the Prophetess

Without question, the Egyptian Freemasonry of Cagliostro is a significant part of what later became the Masonic Rite of Memphis-Misraim. Cagliostro's rituals were published in 1948 by a French writer named Dr. Marc Haven, who used a copy of the original manuscript, called *The Perfect Silence*, written in 1845 by Mr. Guillermet, standard bearer of the lodge. This is a funny paradox that such a leak came from a place in such a way!

This is not the place to discuss this amazing figure who was half-initiate, half-adventurer. However, it is worth noting that the wonderful and unique bust of Cagliostro sculpted by Jean-Antoine Houdon (figure 32) can be seen in Washington, DC, in the National Gallery of Art!

Cagliostro was a controversial figure due to his occult activities. We should acknowledge that most of the controversy was created by the Catholic Church, who arrested and eventually imprisoned him until his death. The Catholic Inquisition never tolerated Freemasons and occultists eager to practice and spread esoteric traditions.

The Egyptian Masonic system created by Cagliostro is surprising. It is built as a magic system using invocations, divination, consecrations, and much more. All these magical practices are organized according to the usual Masonic structure: degrees, initiations, opening and closing ceremonies, etc. Even if it had not been the only Masonic system using such a magical approach in its rituals (see the *Order of the Elus-Cohen*), it was in opposition to the two main powers existing at the time: the religious establishment, mainly represented then by the Catholic Church, and mainstream Freemasonry.

An initial examination of its system reveals that the rites used are profoundly linked to the Bible. Psalms, prayers, names of angels, and prophets are central. Even so, from a theological point of view, there is no possibility of reconciling the practices for believers and initiates. Such Masonic rituals can only be seen by the Christian churches as the manifestation of heretics flouting and rejecting the authority and role of the Church. We must not forget that according to Christian theology, Christ, along with the Church, is the only path to God. There is no other way to have direct access to the Father. Even more, the claim that an initiate can invoke angels of God to ask for their advice or assistance is in opposition to the very notion of sacrament and salvation. Such an attitude has always been condemned by the religious establishment. It has also been the same for anyone trying to reenact ancient cults and practices, such as oracles or worshipping ancient divinities.

Consequently, we should not be surprised at what we find when closely analyzing these rituals. We should keep in mind that the Judeo-Christian tradition was the language used then to express ideas that were more ancient and magical than religious. Cagliostro consecrates the lodge and Masonic tools as if they were used in a magical ceremony.

It should not be forgotten that Cagliostro lived at the end of the eighteenth century and that Christian Qabalah was a mix of pre-Christian Paganism, Judaism, and Christianity. One of the authors who clearly expressed this double influence as early as the sixteenth century was Heinrich Cornelius Agrippa in his three books of occult philosophy. For him, prophecy is a gift that is exercised when the gods or daïmons bring down the oracles to the prophetess.[27] Platonists called these descents "penetrations" of the higher spirits into our minds. These divine intrusions do not manifest when our soul is turned toward some preoccupation. They come when the soul is free from all anxiety. Agrippa states that trance is an illumination of the soul by the gods or the daïmons. The poet Ovid defends the same idea when he declares, "God is in us along with the possibility of conversing with heaven. The spirit descends from its ethereal throne." Agrippa uses the authority of Plato to explain that the gift of prophecy is like a bond. Our soul is not part of the senses that excite the physical body, but is separate from the body. As a prisoner of the body, our soul is seeking to free itself through the practice of philosophy or mysticism to rejoin the intelligible world. Trance or divination is the means by which it communicates with the spiritual world.

Cagliostro tried to recreate in his rituals ancient techniques of divination that were used in ancient Greece, specifically in Delphi. By associating ancient texts with archaeo-

---

27. Book 3, chapters 45–51.

logical observations, we can unveil how the consultation with the oracle took place. Then we can use this knowledge and associate it with Cagliostro's ritual to give you the individual adaptation of this oracle practice. As this book focuses on an individual approach and practice of Freemasonry, I will adapt this ritual for you, retaining the spirit of the original ceremony written by Cagliostro and the Delphic oracle.

Plutarch explains that Pythia (the Oracle of Delphi) came from one of the most honest and respectable families but was brought up in a house of poor peasants. She had no knowledge, art, or talent when she performed her function. It was with the virgin soul of all knowledge that she purified herself at the fountain of Castalia, before descending to the prophetic place (chresterion), drinking water from the source (Cassotis) and chewing laurel. Then she sat on a tripod, from which she received the communication from God. This sacred place was a forbidden room called the *adyton*, located in the basement of the Temple of Apollo. The consultants would stand in a neighboring room. They were separated by a curtain that concealed the prophetess from the eyes of the consultants. The adyton contained some ritual objects, the tomb of Dionysus, the sacred laurel, the omphalos of the earth, and the prophetic tripod. We do not know precisely how the ceremony took place, but the testimonies tell us that the oracle received messages from God. The ancients told us that exhalations came from the ground and triggered the trances. It is quite possible that this odor and its agreeable breaths, comparable to the sweetest and most precious of perfumes, escaped from the sacred place as well as from a spring. The science of perfumes has been used for a very long time, and it is very likely that perfumes were used on this occasion. The oracle was consulted both on matters of political life and on more personal matters, and was therefore at the heart of Greek life.

We can see that in these practices, the prophetess used a ritual process to disconnect herself from passions and purify her mind and turn it entirely toward the spiritual planes.

In his book *Mysteries of Egypt*, translated by Marsilio Ficino in 1497, Iamblichus explains that the divination practiced at Delphi used what we can call "enthusiasm" or "theophoria."

The goal was not to use magical powers, but to implement a mystical process rooted in asceticism and aiming to increase balance and awareness. Cagliostro used young girls as prophetesses, as they represented purity and simplicity. These were the virtues required by the magus before invoking the divine powers.

When these invocations were completed, the theurgist would have seen the pneuma descending and entering the prophetess. Then she could describe the greatness and quality of this spiritual presence. She could even sometimes command and govern it through a mysterious process. The prophetess sometimes saw this manifestation as a blazing fire she welcomed with reverence. Later, Proclus, following the same tradition and relying on both Iamblichus and the Chaldean Oracles, would explain that the ultimate goal of the invocation was the coming of the divinity, sometimes in an incorporeal form.

It is always interesting to inquire whether these divine manifestations were a reality per se or only the prophetess's inner vision. According to the ancient masters such as Iamblichus, the ethereal and luminous vehicle (psychic pneuma) of the prophetess was illuminated by a divine light. Consequently, an image was created in her mind to reflect the message of the gods. However, in some cases, the gods manifest their presence on the visible plan, external to the subject. In these Masonic rituals, it seems that it is the Master who determines by his invocations the manner in which the manifestation must take place.

The Statement

As you can see, the figure of Cagliostro is fascinating. Stories written by people who hated him distorted his character. This is why I feel it's important to hear directly from him. The following statement may not be objective, but it clearly reflects this famous man:[28]

> I do not belong to an epoch, nor a time. Outside of time and space, my spiritual being lives its eternal existence, and if I plunge into my thoughts by going back along the years, if I extend my mind to a mode of existence far from the one you perceive, I become the one I desire.
>
> Participating consciously to the Absolute Being, I adjust my action according to the environment around me. My name is that of my responsibility, and I choose it, as well as my function, because I am free. My country is the one where I momentarily ground my steps.
>
> Give to yourself the date of yesterday, if you wish, by attributing to yourself the years lived by ancestors who were strangers to you. Give to yourself the date of tomorrow, by the illusory pride of a greatness that will perhaps never be yours. I am the one who is.
>
> I have but one father. Different circumstances of my life have made me wonder on this subject of great and moving truths; but the mysteries of this origin, and the relations that unite me to this unknown father, are and

---

28. Statement of Cagliostro presented to the French Parliament, 1786. Original English translation by the author.

remain my secrets. Those who will be called to figure out, to see then as I did, understand and approve of me.

As for the place and the hour when my material body, some forty years ago, was formed on this earth; as to the family I have chosen for it, I want to ignore it. I do not want to remember the past in order to not increase the already heavy responsibilities of those who knew me, for it is written: "You shall not bring down the blind."

I am not born from the flesh, nor of the will of man. I was born of the spirit. My name, the one that is mine and from me, the one I chose to appear among you, is the one I claim. The one I was called at my birth, that was given during my youth, under which, at other times and places, I was known, I left it, as I would have left outdated and now useless clothes.

Here I am: I am Noble and Traveler. I speak and your soul trembles in acknowledging old words. A voice that is in you and that has been silent for a long time answers my call. I take action and peace returns within your hearts, health in your bodies, hope and courage in your souls.

All men are my brothers. All countries are dear to me. I travel from one to the other so that everywhere, the Spirit can descend and find a path to you.

I ask of the kings, of whom I respect the power, only hospitality in their lands and, when it is granted to me, I pass, doing around me as much good as possible; but I'm just passing by. Am I a Noble Traveler?

Like the southern wind, like the brilliant light of the South that characterizes the full knowledge of things and the active communion with God, I come toward the north, toward the mist and the cold, abandoning everywhere in my passage some parcels of me, giving of myself, diminishing me at each stop, but leaving you brightness, a little warmth, a little strength, until I finally stop at the end of my career, at a time when the rose will bloom on the cross.

I'm Cagliostro. Why do you need something more?

If you were children of God, if your soul were not so vain and curious, you would have already understood! But you need details, signs, and parables.

Now listen! Let's go back a long way in the past, as you want it.

All light comes from the east; all initiation, from Egypt. Like you, I was three years old, then seven years, then the age of man, and from that age I stopped counting.

Three times seven years are twenty-one years old and are the fulfillment of human development. In my early childhood, under the law of rigor and justice, I suffered in exile, as Israel among foreign nations.

But as Israel had with him the presence of God, as Metatron kept Israel in his ways, so did a mighty angel, watching over me, directing my actions, enlightening my soul, developing the underlying powers within me.

He was my master and guide. My reason was formed and clarified. I wondered, I studied, and I became aware of all that surrounded me. I traveled a number of times, around the chamber of my reflections, in the temples, and the four parts of the world. But when I wanted to find the origin of my being and ascend to God in a desire of my soul, then my powerless reason was silent and left me to my conjectures.

A love that attracted me to every creature in an impulsive manner, an irresistible ambition, a profound feeling of my rights to everything from earth to heaven, pushed me and threw me to life. The gradual experience of my powers, their sphere of action, their limits, was the struggle I had to maintain against the powers of the world. I was abandoned and tempted in the desert. I have struggled with the angel like Jacob, with men and with demons. When I defeated them, they taught me the secrets that concern the empire of darkness so that I can never get lost in one of the roads from which nobody comes back.

One day, after many journeys and years, the heaven listened to my efforts. It remembered his servant and, dressed in nuptial garments, I received the grace to be admitted, like Moses, before the Eternal.

At that moment, I received a new name and a unique mission. Free and master of life, I lived only to accomplish the work of God.

I knew that he would confirm my deeds and words, as I would confirm his name and his kingdom on earth. There are beings who no longer have guardian angels. I was among them.

This is my childhood, my youth, as your mind, anxious and desirous of words, was requiring. But whether my life has lasted more or fewer years, whether it has been spent in the land of your fathers or in other countries, what does it matter to you?

I am a free man. Judge my morals, that is, my actions. Say if they are good. Say if you have seen more powerful ones and therefore do not bother about my nationality, my rank, and my religion.

If, following their happy journeys, someone, one day, will approach the lands of the east that have seen my birth, may he remember me, pronouncing my name and the servants of my father will open before him the gates of the Holy City. Then, let him come back and tell his brethren whether I have lied to you or if I have taken in your homes something that did not belong to me!

Practice of Divination

I recommend a simple diet twenty-four hours before this ceremony: do not eat or drink in excess. The goal is to not be disturbed by your body. Both fasting and overeating can cause disturbances. Balance is the best state of mind for such a practice. I also recommend not to look at your television, tablet, etc. Let your brain calm down.

It is usual to wear white clothes, with the apron placed upon them. In several Egyptian Masonic organizations, a kind of long robe is worn over the daily clothes. Sometimes the robe is white and sometimes black. If you have a white one, you can use it here.

Besides the usual tools for your ceremonies, you should prepare a veil that will be placed upon your head. It should be yellow with white-gold fringes. The seals and names of the Olympic spirits should be embroidered (or painted) in gold, along with the symbols of the planets.

This veil should cover the head by falling on both sides, like the veils Roman priests placed on their heads during their rituals. But in this case, the veil represents the heavens. In addition to this symbolism, the veil is empowered by the names and seals embroidered on it.

Instead of this specific veil, you can use the one you used for the third degree ritual. In addition, you should also prepare a censer and a specific incense that reminds you of the spiritual dimension.

In addition, prepare seven seals of the spirits printed or drawn on a green cardboard sheet according to the representations in figure 37. These seven seals will be placed around the black-and-white mosaic. Prepare seven candles that will be placed upon the green seals.

You should also prepare a cup of water and place it at the center of this surface. The interior (or the whole) of the cup must be of a dark color.

When all these tools have been prepared, begin your practice with the openings you are now accustomed to. Make sure to open your lodge to the third degree. If you have already learned the techniques of the inner room, place your mind in this sacred place.

Once this is done, momentarily move away the three columns around the black-and-white mosaic pavement, as well as the eastern candles. Place the seven seals printed on green card stock on the mosaic according to the pattern shown in figure 38. Place the cup of pure water in the center. Light the seven candles. Sit down and meditate for a few moments.

When you are relaxed and your breathing is regular, stand up.

Raise both hands toward the east and say:

I, (your name), stand in front of you, O Eternal God, and I ask for your assistance to receive understandable signs and answers to the questions I am about to ask.

After a few seconds, release your arms. Take the white veil and put it on your head with the side of it at the top of your forehead, as ancient Roman priests did. The other parts of the veil will cover your head, neck, and shoulders. Your face is unveiled.

Then kneel in front of the east.

Bow your head and say:

Almighty and Eternal God, I dedicate my work to you. You know my weakness and fragility and I ask for your forgiveness. From the bottom of my heart I ask for your protection and help to reach the truth. Unveil for me the sacred mysteries. Call your servants and send them to me. May your benevolence and mercy bless me as I am about to begin this spiritual work of divination.

Remain silent for a short while, then stand up.

Use your gavel to knock three times on your altar.

Light your incense and raise the censer three times toward the east.

Keeping the censer high in the direction of the sky in your left hand, put your right hand on your chest and say:

Almighty and Eternal God, hear my voice that is coming to you!
Receive this incense as the offering I am presenting to you!
Grant me the powers I need to accomplish this spiritual work of divination.

Place the censer in front of you, between your body and the black-and-white mosaic.

Raise your hands toward the sky and invoke each of the Olympic spirits with the following invocation repeated for each one.

Spirit of (name of planet), I invoke you and ask for your assistance.

O (name of Olympic spirit), hear my voice. Come to this place and grant me the powers I need to accomplish this spiritual work of divination.

I am asking today to receive information about (subject of your divination).

If needed, add some incense and sit on your chair. You want a light smoke rising between your gaze and the cup of water in the center of the black-and-white mosaic.

Your eyes are half-closed and gazing peacefully at the surface of the water through the smoke of the incense. Place your gaze as you did when learning the mosaic tile. If you feel the need, you can close your eyes to better receive impressions or messages that can appear at this time. Be attentive to any feeling. It can be an inner feeling, a psychic manifestation, or even in some cases a physical feeling. Once you have perceived what appears to you as a sign (or after a moment of relaxation and meditation), stand up and say:

Spirits of the seven planets, (say the names of each of them), I thank you for your assistance and your power.

May a part of your divine powers stay with me as I am about to close this ritual.

Go in peace!

You can now extinguish the seven candles.

When this is done, raise your hands toward the sky and say:

Almighty and Eternal God, I thank you for your assistance and blessings.

May I remain under your protection and may your blessings continue to illuminate my life forever.

So mote it be!

You can now sit, take some notes, and proceed to the closing ceremony of your lodge.

Conclusion

Your journey into Egyptian Freemasonry has just begun, whether you had already heard about esoteric Freemasonry before this book or not. I know that this is the first time you have had in your hands a book about these subjects that you can use immediately. My advice is to do it. Don't wait to have everything ready before you begin. The spiritual training and most of the practices can be done immediately. Then, progressively, you will be able to go further with the preparation of your tools and individual lodge.

Freemasonry is a fascinating tradition. For more than three hundred years, it has attracted those interested in the Western tradition. Based on a very simple structure, several branches have appeared. Some proudly practice Judeo-Christian rituals and others focus on pre-Christian traditions, while humanistic Masonic organizations promote a secular view of initiation. Each of them is rooted in the same principles of three initiations and similar symbols. Each considers the importance of working to improve the quality of humankind and make our world a better place for everyone. Of course, some organizations consider these noble causes more important than outdated racism or discriminatory rules. I can easily understand that. As the Catholic establishment has always done, other organizations are trying to oppose any esoteric work. Undoubtedly, the reason is that free thinking can scare conservatives. When someone experiences these rituals and practices firsthand, they become more aware of the efficiency of the tradition and consequently see more clearly which ones are more superficial.

Freemasonry has a noble goal. Preaching the improvement of our morals and practicing philanthropy are essential, but the Masonic tradition has never been limited to these purposes. Esoteric Freemasonry and, more precisely here, Egyptian Freemasonry has always considered that spirituality should be explored practically and discussed. The masters who created these rites, from Cagliostro and the Sophisians to the masters of today, have always experimented and prayed. They have used this beautiful tradition and its keys to decipher the mysteries of the cosmos and the afterlife. Unveiling these mysteries, making the fear of death disappear, is an essential goal for anyone involved in this spiritual journey. Then maybe a desire to meet others will grow within you. You could be willing to add something else to your individual experience.

There are countless groups in the world linked to this Egyptian Masonic tradition. Besides the classic organizations of Memphis and Misraim, you can go to the roots and discover more about these two Egyptian rites in the Most Worshipful National Grand Lodge of Egyptian Freemasons and its pyramid of the high degrees called the Sacred Order of the Sophisians. If you are a Master Mason, you might also be eager to explore multiple ancient and rare Masonic rituals. You will find a specific link on the website of the Grand Lodge of Egyptian Freemasons. These gates and others are open for you, no matter the color of your skin, your gender, or your beliefs.

This book was written in the twenty-first century. The roots of the Western tradition come from the dawn of humanity. Some details or rules are irrelevant today, while other myths and rites are timeless. As Cagliostro did at his epoch, it is time for free thinkers to take these tools and explore. Then Osiris will begin to live again.

Appendix A

Mozart and *The Magic Flute*
by Philippe Milgrom

It would be difficult to imagine writing about Egyptian Freemasonry without even mentioning the famous figure of Mozart and his masterpiece *The Magic Flute*.

A few months ago, I had the chance to meet a very experienced Mason, Philippe Milgrom, and our conversation led to esoteric Freemasonry. I mentioned this book and Egyptian Freemasonry. I was pleased to learn that my brother had presented a lecture on this subject. As you may know, Mozart was a Freemason and his opera is an amazing creation that unveils more mysteries than we can imagine. Philippe authorized me to include his text in this book, and I am sure that everyone will enjoy this presentation.

When you listen to Mozart, the silence that follows is still Mozart.
—Sacha Guitry

Much has been written and said about *The Magic Flute*. It is without a doubt the most well-known opera written by Wolfgang Amadeus Mozart, and with good reason. It is one of those special works of art that radiates brilliance to humanity. It is so rich in symbolism that numerous theories have developed to explain its significance. This is evident in the many different productions of the opera and the various interpretations by directors worldwide.

Yes, it really is magic, this *Magic Flute*, and for more than one reason, including:

• The music, which often travels beyond space and time

• The composer and all the artists he inspired

• And finally, in the message that each one of us can understand

We know very little of Mozart's spiritual life except that he was familiar with the universal and spiritual theories of his day. And we know he socialized with the circle of men that put those theories into practice.

Mozart's biographers have related the events of his everyday life, including his involvement with Freemasonry that began on December 14, 1784. It was in those circles of Vienna that all the important questions of his time were debated.

Mozart died in 1791, and the last decade of his life saw the crystallization of one of the largest groups of thinking men in Europe. The roots of this movement can be traced back to François de Lorraine, an alchemist and the husband of Maria Theresa of Austria. He joined the Freemasonry in Vienna in 1731.

Vienna subsequently became a Masonic capital and an asylum for foreign Masons persecuted by the Church for their opinions. Vienna attracted Florentine Masons who found a safe haven from the cruelty of the Inquisition. And Rosicrucian branches in Prussia, proliferating since the mid-seventeenth century, penetrated the high society of Vienna.

It was in the midst of the battle between the Reformists and Counter Reformists of 1614 to 1616 that three manuscripts were published in Cassel: *Fama Fraternitatis*, *Confessio Fraternitatis*, and the *Chymical Wedding of Christian Rosenkreutz*. These manuscripts were supposedly written by Johann Valentin Andreae in association with a mysterious fraternity of Rose-Croix philosophers and spiritualists.

I mention these dates, 1614 to 1616, to show that Mozart probably used numerology to discreetly show that he knew about these manuscripts. For example, if we count the number of measures in the first two scenes of the second act of *The Magic Flute*, there are 1387 and 1616, respectively. By comparing these numbers to dates, one finds 1378 as the birth of the Christian Rose-Croix (by switching the last two numbers, a typical secret practice in the eighteenth century), and 1616 was the year the *Chymical Wedding* was published.

The Old System Gold Rose-Croix order created by the Lodge of Three Globes in 1777 in Berlin claimed to be the only representative of authentic Freemasonry. Its eminent members included Prince Frederic-Guillaume, heir of the Prussian king Frederick the Great, and also Count Dietrichstein, the Grand Master of the Grand Lodge of Austria.

And we must not forget the alchemist groups of Bavaria, particularly the Illuminati of Bavaria founded in 1776 by Weishaupt and affiliated with Freemasonry since 1781. This secret organization had the sympathy of Goethe and French revolutionaries such as Mirabeau, Condorcet, Camille Desmoulins, Brissot, and many more who elevated the spirit of humanity along with spiritual ideals developed by the Rose-Croix for all humankind.

All these groups claimed Masonic affiliations but were of diverse interests.

But we should come back to Vienna, where Masonic lodges flourished. We can count seven, and an additional eighth hermetic and Rosicrucian lodge founded by Urban Hauer, father of the Melk monastery. This Benedictine monk was disillusioned by Church dogma and desired to explore a more universal spirituality.

These lodges, counting members of the nobility and diplomats in its numbers, reunited all of the Empire.

One of the seven existing lodges, the Real Harmony, was important even if it was not established until 1781. It was a powerful lodge and directed by an exceptional man: Ignaz von Born, an old Jesuit who had been a mineralogist by trade. This lodge's ambition was to reunite the elite of Vienna, like the Nine Sisters lodge had done in Paris. It is said that Born was Mozart's inspiration for *The Magic Flute*'s character Sarastro.

Mozart was initiated into the lodge called the Charity and become a Fellowcraft on January 7, 1785, in the Real Harmony lodge where Born was the worshipful Master. From what we know, Mozart practiced only blue Masonry (the first three degrees), but he was probably aware of the foundation and spiritual circles of the Viennese Masonry of the time.

Mozart joined another lodge, the New Crowned Hope, after the decree of Emperor Joseph II restricted Masonic activity in Vienna. This lodge included powerful people in the capital, including Count Johann Esterhazy, imperial and royal Chamberlain, as Acting Worshipful Master. The ritual was imprinted with religiosity and was respectful of the first article of the Anderson Constitution: "A Freemason cannot be a stupid atheist or an irreligious libertine."

Mozart, an enlightened spirit in this rich era, participated at all important meetings. It is his knowledge of the esoteric and of the basis of gnosticism (knowledge) that we find in *The Magic Flute*. He was so dedicated to his lodge that he introduced the two people closest to his heart: his father, Leopold (initiated on April 6, 1785), and his best friend, the composer Joseph Haydn (initiated on February 11, 1785).

Mozart lived surrounded by Masonic friends, including:

• Philippe Artaria, publisher of all his masterpieces

• Anton Stadler, his close friend

• Paul Wranitzky, composer of a successful opera based on a libretto by Gieseke, *Oberon, King of the Elves*. Gieseke came from Ratisbonne, where he knew Schikaneder, the official librettist of *The Magic Flute* and also a member of the Masonic lodge in that town. Gieseke, also a friend of Goethe, always claimed to be the librettist of *The Magic Flute*, saying that Schikaneder had only written the characters of Papageno and Papagena.

And now let's look at the masterpiece itself.

We observe in the characters and action of *The Magic Flute* the antagonism between opposing concepts: good and bad, man and woman, the ordinary world and the world of Masonry.

It is evident that Mozart desired to impart a message to the world. Within the depth of its themes, *The Magic Flute* shows us the link to the Masonic initiate's path that leads to internal battles during the search for truth in one's spiritual life.

Our existence is endowed with a personality totally adapted to this world.

When we are in distress, we may turn to some school of thought such as religion, science, or art that helps us make peace with the world, society, and humankind.

Between the corridors of life and death, we cannot live without asking some fundamental questions: Who am I? Where do I come from? Where am I going?

As we enter the spiritual realm, questions emerge such as these: What is real life? Is there life after death? Why do different religions oppose each other?

Then voila! An instructor appears: perhaps from an artist inspired to explain the process!

Up until the time of his own death, Mozart took great care that *The Magic Flute* transmitted such a message, as will be explained.

Various aspects of our internal microcosmic reality are symbolized by characters in *The Magic Flute*. Their names were chosen for specific reasons. According to American musicologist Paul Nettl, Tamino and Pamina mean "man and woman dedicated to Min"(Egyptian god of fertility), Papageno comes from the word *parrot* (one that repeats life's actions without learning from them), Sarastro reminds us of the initiate Zoroaster, and Monostatos is a contraction of *mono* (one) and *statos* (static), that is, one who does not move or change.

Every step of the path of initiation can be seen as an episode of the adventure that will be ours if we begin our spiritual search. And we will find that these ideas are often not well understood and need to be explained again and again.

There have always been scholars ready to teach us about the mystery of the universe and lead us along the way of initiation and knowledge. *The Magic Flute* shows us that Mozart possessed the knowledge of this philosophy.

As seekers of the truth, we are Tamino entering into this savage and chaotic world, dangerous and unknown as another of the opera's characters: the Queen of the Night.

This is our world, with all its contradictions, trials and errors, and total lack of harmony. We are helpless, attacked by the serpent that symbolizes our most blind but natural instincts, and we are helpless to defend ourselves. Like Tamino, we cry out for help.

We need to go beyond the elementary barriers of ordinary life to access the unconscious and accomplish our initiation work. We try to avoid the serpent of bad habits, base satisfaction, and temptation that pursues us along the way. How can we resist without losing all our strength and symbolically vanishing into this world of illusions?

Mozart represents these forces with the characters of the three Ladies who always appearing veiled. They announce themselves as messengers of the Queen of the Night. They show us that our worldly personalities possess three natural powers necessary for removal from the kingdom of darkness:

- The force of our hearts that desires to reverse the natural course of things

- The power of understanding that emanates from our brain

- The will to go forward on a spiritual adventure

After having slain the dragon, the three veiled Ladies act out a strange and amusing game of seduction with Tamino: each one wants to possess him for herself. And here too, while this new universe is opening up to us, three choices are offered as tempting opportunities:

- Mysticism that often leads to a blind religion

- The occult that pushes us to speculative research

- The temptation of power, with all its possible excess

But the danger recedes and Tamino is awakened by the babbling of a new character: Papageno, who symbolizes the natural facet of our being.

There is in each candidate of the soul's liberation a Tamino and a Papageno. But there is still more, because the candidate of mystery does not reduce his worldly existence on Earth to his character alone. He knows that he is a host animating a small world we call a *microcosm*.

Protected within the center of this microcosm is divine thought, symbolized by Pamina.

And in this microcosmic sphere, the superego and its karma—that is, the link between its past and future—totally dominates the emotions of our character. This aspect is symbolized by the Monostatos the Moor (African) and is an allusion to the long past of our earthly microcosm.

Our soul is held prisoner in a life of passion by a heavenly being that uses all the emotional forces of its body and mind. Monostatos wants Pamina too, but for himself, to enjoy her, and does not want to give her the chance to express the law of the Order of the Spirit. And as the heavenly being is clever and very subtle, Monostatos always conceals its most shameful acts beneath deceptive appearances. Thus he persuades Pamina that she is the prisoner of Sarastro.

But this is false.

Pamina, the divine soul asleep in each of us, belongs to the world of light, that is, the kingdom of Sarastro. But she is not in any way a prisoner. Besides, Pamina discovers the hoax and at the end of the first act throws herself at the feet of Sarastro, saying: "Master, I am guilty, I wanted to avoid your power. But this was not my fault. The bad Moor wanted to force his love on me. That was why, Master, I avoided you."

The Queen of the Night knows this story well too.

Her own story, which she describes to Tamino, of Sarastro's so-called abduction of Pamina is entirely false. Her hatred, expressed and exaggerated throughout the story, is emphasized by the music. But she understands that Tamino has fallen in love with her daughter and she begins a quest with the hope of retrieving her daughter.

It is the same for the seeker who is struck by a great desire for absolute truth. And the world will always try to recuperate a powerful love for its benefit.

The three Ladies quickly return, first to deliver Papageno.

During all this preparation for the initiation, silence is necessary, thus explaining the lock on Papageno's mouth. And the seeker looks for the truth and advises Papageno to never lie again. And now, with all the resources of a natural being, in the company of Papageno, Tamino can only succeed. Papageno and Tamino are always linked together.

And the next story demonstrates that.

Each one of them receives a magic instrument: a flute for Tamino and little bells for Papageno. The Magic Flute will allow Tamino to receive help from a divine source.

We later learn that the flute was created by the Master of the Spirit World, who is Pamina's father. This confirms that Pamina is a parcel of the divine. Pamina, daughter of God, is prisoner of her own character, and believes herself to be a part of the underworld and daughter of the Queen of the Night, until she meets Sarastro.

Tamino plays his flute four times:

- First, to call Pamina. But there is no answer, just as the candidate of mystery cannot penetrate the mystery on his own.
- Second, to show his joy. The libretto explains that Tamino discovers the sound of the instrument "charms" savage men. Here he alludes to the power of God blowing over animalistic Man, "animated" by the only forces of this world, receptive to something other than natural life.
- Third, after the beginning of the initiation, that is, after having received a spiritual gift. Calling Pamina again during the second act when she does go to him, his newly awakened spirit and soul must still remain silent when face to face with hers.
- Lastly, Tamino uses the power of his instrument to escape from the world of Hell. Papageno is given little bells, and every time he rings them, it is to resolve a problem linked to the natural aspects symbolizing the character of the seeker, including (1) to tame and avoid the anger of Monostatos during the first act, and (2) to call his Papagena, his feminine double. The seeker looking for his way does not have the obligation to use his natural possibilities represented by Papageno, but also possesses the qualities of the heart symbolized by Papagena, his real love.

And now everything is ready for the initiate's journey.

Tamino is aware of his mission. He has in his heart the flame of love, pushing him to desire divine accomplishment. He possesses the means to win, granted by Gnostic magic: the Magic Flute. But he does not know how to make use of it.

Papageno is the natural candidate for this great journey.

There is only one thing missing for the new seeker:

- Where to go?
- Where is the World of Spirit?
- How not to get lost?

Three young boys appear, as if descending from the sky. They symbolize three developing powers.

The key to this new situation is as follows:

The first fundamental initiation places the candidate in front of godly light in comparison with Man. Thus, he was presented at the beginning of *The Magic Flute* by the story of Tamino, the episode of the dragon, and the encounter with Papageno.

The second fundamental initiation gives him duty and also the possibility to undertake a regeneration process. And here Tamino receives his mission from the three Ladies and the Queen of the Night: to deliver Pamina. The instrument of this new link with the divine is the Magic Flute.

The candidate next thinks about the third initiation, the initiation of Mercury, the messenger of the gods who, from the old knowledge, was always linked to superior thought and included accordingly as a spirit of nature.

Thus, the great journey begins for Tamino and Papageno, guided by new forces that animate them.

The opera also shows Pamina escaping Monostatos, who covets her and wants her only for himself, by invoking the name of Sarastro. She takes refuge in a grove of palm trees, which in the language of mystery signifies the beginning of the end when the resurrection of the soul begins. And the Gnostic scriptures from early Christianity show Jesus revealing his secrets in a palm grove.

The following encounter allows Papageno to prepare Pamina for the arrival of Prince Tamino, who is coming to deliver her.

The story tells us Tamino is coming, led by three children, and we have previously learned what this symbol means. Each advises Tamino on his behavior: "Be firm, constant, and silent."

It is equally true that the candidate to mystery needs to be firmly told: "Be a man and you will win as a man." The road to initiation has the obligation to pass through real knowledge deep inside the body and soul. Remember what is inscribed on the front of the Temple of Delphi: "Man, know yourself and you will know the Universe and the Gods." And we are alone during this process.

Tamino must decide which temple to choose from. Will it be the temple of Nature, of Reason, or of Wisdom? But for him, there is only one possibility: that of the Heart. And to the priest welcoming and asking him what he is looking for in this saintly place, he answers, "Love and Virtue." And take note that he is not answering "Pamina"!

For the non-initiated spectator, this is right at this moment when the story of Mozart's opera becomes difficult to understand. We were comfortably involved in and enjoying a love story and suddenly there is a change of tone, and the music becomes more solemn. We are entering into a story with a highly spiritual theme.

We hope that the prior explanations have prepared you to follow Tamino, this most noble seeker of truth, on the path to mystery.

In this dialogue between Tamino and the priest (the Orator of the Lodge), on the threshold of the temple of Wisdom, a part of the truth is revealed to him. Yes, Sarastro (Born) reigns over the world of the spirit. No, Sarastro has not committed the rape of Pamina. Yes, the Queen of the Night abused Tamino.

Why this mystery? It is impossible to reveal this to the one that has not shown proof that he is worthy. This is to the despair of Tamino, candidate of mystery, who does not receive any reassurance on his search.

And the scene ends with these words:

• "When will this eternal night end?"
• "When will my eyes see light?"

Take note here, that we no longer pronounce the name of Pamina, but we invoke the force that she represents (Pamina = Light).

The candidate is now introduced to the mystery of the soul. Pamina, the soul, has been purposefully taken away from the natural world to be protected while waiting to be delivered by the love of a person dedicated to his search.

And the seeker, who asks for divine help, receives his first answer.

Tamino plays the Magic Flute, and it is Pamina who runs to him, but accompanied by Papageno. This occurs without counting with the eternal and internal enemy, Monostatos, who never wants change, seizes the two fugitives but is abruptly stopped by the sound of the little bells that Papageno happily had the idea to ring. And as it says in the dialogue, the bells symbolize Harmony.

Then Sarastro enters at the head of a solemn procession. This is his first appearance. Not only does he make excuses for Pamina fleeing, but he reveals only now that this was not only on purpose but for her own good, as he was keeping her far away from her mother.

Tamino, led by Monostatos, stands for the very first time in front of Pamina. There is mutual "recognition," and the first bond between them appears.

In other words, we find in this instant the link between the two centers of consciousness:

• From the mind: until now the search of Tamino was only theoretical;
• And from the heart: where the soul must reside.

The period of testing will now start, and Sarastro gives instructions to place a veil over the heads of the two characters, Tamino and Papageno, and take them to the temple.

End of the first act.

The décor of the second act of *The Magic Flute* is a palm grove. We are now at the starting point of the resurrection of the soul spirit.

Let us remember that Christian esoteric tradition is always symbolized by leafy trees. This is the world of eternal happiness. Even better, the palms here are made of gold, to show that they are a part of the universal spirit.

Eighteen chairs are placed, each one surmounted by a pyramid and a horn. The number eighteen, as you will later see, refers to the degree of Rose-Croix brother in the higher degrees of Freemasonry.

Also note that $1 + 8 = 9$, the number of man: the three centers renewed three times.

We are at this time in the heart of the mystery that will now unfold before us.

The action begins with a solemn procession of the priests, servants of Isis and Osiris. Next follows a deliberation of the initiated brothers and Sarastro, who is aware of the mystery that will give us the key to the opera: if Tamino succeeds in passing the initiating examination, he will be united with Pamina and they will reign and protect the Temple of Wisdom.

We cannot fail to see here the ultimate goal assigned by God to each human being: to realize in him or her the Chymical Wedding, devoted entirely to the soul, and thus being part of Wisdom that precedes the Saintly Spirit.

Tamino, judged worthy of initiation, now faces great dangers. It is true the candidate on his way needs to purify his mind, his heart, the seat of his profound psyche and goodwill, and that is not without risk.

The mind is first, and symbolically this is why: Tamino is left with Papageno in darkness that reminds him of the night of ignorance where he still remains. Papageno makes a significant observation: "This is strange, each time these men leave us, even if you try to open your eyes widely, you cannot see anything!"

And it is true the world burns with desire for natural perfection and thirsts for the ideal.

The Universal Teaching constantly repeats to us that this earth is a world of duality, of antagonism, of hot and cold, of love and hate, of good and bad.

Our world is, and will always be, foreign to the spiritual world.

The Queen of the Night knows this well, and this knowledge inspires her vengeance. She orders Pamina to kill Sarastro in order to still this famous solar circle whose foreign powers she covets.

Obviously, it is impossible for Pamina to commit such a horrible crime. She is of the kingdom where the Saintly Spirit reigns.

Sarastro, in the service of the Brotherhood, understands everything and reveals to Pamina the project the Brotherhood has for her and Tamino, if Tamino emerges victorious from his initiation journey, the Chymical Wedding of body and mind.

Then Tamino, who is still with Papageno, is introduced to the second examination: the Silence.

After the mental purification of the candidate to mystery, the next step of initiation concerns the emotion of man located deep in the heart's center. The light of mystery will never be able to penetrate within us if the turmoil of our senses, if our egocentric desire, still dominates our personality. To appease our emotional body, we must embrace the silence and respect it.

This is exactly what has been asked of Tamino, whose work is constantly disturbed by Papageno, who continuously chatters with other creatures. And Tamino, to respect his vows, even pretends to ignore Pamina when she appears before him, much to Pamina's great despair.

This shows that on the road, the candidate must be silent, even in front of the transformation of his soul, for as long as he has not been empowered to work with it.

And the examination continues because Tamino, even with Sarastro present, must ignore Pamina a second time before earning the right to proceed to the third initiation.

It still remains for the candidate to succeed in the renewal of his center of goodwill. The candidate now possesses the consciousness of the soul.

This is the reason why we see Pamina join again with Tamino, and they will experience the third examination together.

Pamina accompanies Tamino in crossing the flames that symbolize the ultimate initiation journey: the purification of the third center of the personality, the center of the unconscious, absolutely must be disentangled from its past and be purified by the flames.

This is the victory over the dragon, the guardian of the threshold.

Pamina, the new soul, will guide Tamino's steps.

"It is I who guides you, love will show me the way, and roses will pave the way."

Additional help comes in the form of two men dressed in black armor who serve as guides.

This seems to indicate that the candidate, facing great dangers, is protected by the double armor of his faith and his new determination.

The two men read an engraved inscription on a plaque, which it is said to be a reproduction of the engraving on the tomb of Hiram Abiff, the master builder of the Temple of Solomon. It ends with this advice to the candidate: "With a clear mind, he will then entirely dedicate himself to the mysteries of Isis."

In other words, having allowed internal penetration of the divine light, he can concentrate on the transfiguration of his body, soul, and mind.

It is possible to understand this like an allusion to the important role of the school of mystery, represented here by the college of priests, a body of teachers.

But there are many temptations in this first proof of the recognition of mystery.

These temptations are symbolized in the *The Magic Flute* by the three Ladies that reappear and try to distract Tamino and Papageno from their mission. But they fail and are chased away by the priests.

Meanwhile, the powerful heavenly soul of Monostatos tries to corrupt Pamina. He is interrupted by the Queen of the Night who has fomented the project to recuperate "the sun of seven halos" of which Sarastro has been guardian since the death of Pamina's father. For the Queen too burns with desire to possess the Saintly Spirit.

We now understand better why at the sound of the Magic Flute, the instrument of the Saintly Spirit on the road, the spiritual couple Tamino-Pamina penetrate first into the reality of the psyche, the domain of extremes, of opposites, of the struggle very well symbolized by water and fire, as so well described by Dante in the *Divine Comedy*.

At the same time, Papageno finds peace, and the forces of the natural world are set aside in favor of the power of the world of the mind.

A last appearance of Monostatos with his followers guiding the Queen of the Night and her three Ladies to the temple shows us that nature continually tries to object until the process of liberation is over.

But they disappear, crying, "Our power is crushed, we are plunged into eternal night."

The opera ends with a final note by the priests and the victory of the Chymical Wedding: "Glory to you, initiates! You have traversed the darkness."

Our intent was to bring to you tonight not another argument nor a new explanation, but a testimony of how a seeker of truth understands, feels, and sees this wonderful opera that is *The Magic Flute*.

And we did not even comment on the sublime music itself that Mozart linked to this story like a gift from God.

I cannot resist quoting these few words Goethe wrote about Mozart's *The Magic Flute*: "There is more to know in recognizing the value of this libretto than in denying it. It is enough that the audience enjoys the pleasures of this play while the initiates cannot escape from its ultimate significance."

If we were able to help you better understand that to travel a spiritual route is not to believe in some theology or to join in organized religion but to live for yourself during this great adventure of life, we will have accomplished a successful mission in showing you the way.

This quest, where we have discovered some points of view thanks to the symbolism of the characters, with their words and actions, and to the music of *The Magic Flute*, is the mission assigned to all humankind.

Appendix B

Allegory of the Cave

Philosophy is sometimes seen as complicated literature, disconnected from our daily lives. Ancient philosophy may even be seen as outdated. Having just read this book, you know that the Western tradition contains a very useful set of keys that can be used in our spiritual lives. Greek philosophers tried to decipher our real nature, with its fears, hopes, and desires, in order to help us understand the meaning of our lives and our destiny. Becoming more aware of who we really are could help us to live in peace and raise our consciousness. This kind of philosophy has the same pertinence today as it did hundreds of years ago.

In this long-standing tradition, Platonic philosophy has an essential place. Plato's work marks the birth of what is known today as philosophy. The Platonic philosophy associates two types of discourse: a mythical or allegorical and a rational. These two types are often connected.

The allegory of the cave can be found in an important book written by Plato, *The Republic,* book 7. [29] This allegory is surprisingly modern. It describes the situation of human beings in their lives, their illusions and their search for the truth. Since the latter is hidden, it is up to each one to discover it. This allegory of the cave reveals a process aiming to explain the real nature of human beings, their problems and anxieties (essentially related to death), and to help them understand their goal. Following this path, each of us will be able to build a happy and balanced life. The Platonist philosopher has solved this astonishing paradox: he knows how to live and enjoy life because he has learned what death really is. This search and its completion opens the doors of happiness, in the contemplation of the True, the Beautiful, and the Just.

---

29. The full excerpt can be found on my website at www.debiasi.org.

This allegory presents two different worlds: one outside the cave and a second subterranean one. They correspond to the immaterial and the material, the divine and the human. For now, let us consider the first of these distinctions. Within ourselves, two dimensions exist: material and immaterial. For Plato and the theurgic tradition, we are composed of a physical body and a spiritual soul. This soul is invisible to the physical eyes but is perceptible to anyone who prays or begins to practice spiritual rituals. Moreover, there is a connection between the soul and the spiritual world.

In Platonism, as for different schools of mysteries in antiquity, the soul is subject to transmigration. In Eastern religions, this process is called *reincarnation*. The soul belongs to the spiritual world, which is its natural environment and place of origin. When we were born, our soul descended into the physical body. When we die, the soul will come back to the spiritual world, then descend again into a physical body, and so on. This process is called *metempsychosis*.

It is easy to understand that in this theory, the soul exists before it is embodied. It stays in the spiritual world and is active, observing what is around it. As a matter of fact, this divine world is not empty. It contains the archetype of everything that exists in our physical world. During this period, our soul perceives the ideal of everything. Then it descends into the body and is locked up into it. This means that the spiritual soul, luminous and immaterial, descends into a body of flesh, obscure, thus losing access to a part of its memory. This obscurity, coming from the materiality of the body and the world, is represented by the cave. In Plato's allegory, the souls within their bodies are described as prisoners locked up in a cave.

Plato explains that this allegory represents our nature, although the situation varies slightly according to our spiritual evolution. We could say that our understanding will be more or less obscure, according to our inner awareness.

Plato describes the symbolic place in this way: "Imagine people in a subterranean place, in the shape of a cave, having in all its width an entrance opened to the light. These people have been there since childhood, their legs and their chains bound, so that they cannot move or see anywhere but in front of them, the chain preventing them from turning their heads. The light comes from a fire lighted on a height, far behind them. Between the fire and the prisoners passes a high road. Imagine that along this road is built a small wall, similar to the small walls used by puppeteers, above which they show their puppets."

This description provides important symbols. The prisoners have been there since childhood, their eyes looking only toward the bottom of the cave. They are chained side by side, but no one can see who is by their side. They hear well those who are close to them, and can speak to them but cannot see them. This symbol of sight is important, because they are not in a fully obscure cave. A fire burns behind them on the top of a small hill, projecting shadows on the wall. They are the shadows of puppets moving between the fire and the prisoners. Those who are chained from the beginning of their lives can see these shadows moving and talking. As the bottom of the cave reverberates the sounds. All think that these shadows speak to them and are real living beings.

Plato continues, saying: "Walking along this little wall, people carry objects of every kind, statuettes of men and animals made of stone, wood, and all kinds of material. Some of them speak and others remain silent." With this allegory, Plato wants to explain that all we perceive through our senses is only an appearance and has no more reality than the shadows on the bottom of the cave. However, as we live within this illusion from our birth, we believe what our senses perceive is real. We are in the same situation as the prisoners who are totally convinced that the shadows before them are real. We believe that the world around us is real because our eyes are looking outside, whereas to find reality, they should be turned inward. The allegory of the cave expresses the idea that what is external to us and appears to us evident from birth is false, while that which is interior is true. In this situation, prisoners in the cave should not trust their senses. For Plato, the first error comes from the senses.

There is an optimistic and a pessimistic way of looking at this condition.

The pessimistic view consists of considering that there is no way out, as everything is an illusion. Not being able to trust any of our senses or the judgment of other individuals makes us incapable of knowing anything as certain. In this case, birth is useless, except to be locked up, chained until death, with no possibility of deliverance. How could we possibly be freed when we do not even know we are chained?

The optimistic view supposes that someone can help us. The initiate knows that he cannot do anything alone. He needs someone who can help him get out of his torpor and his darkness by waking him up. But the senses need not be banished. It is only necessary to understand that they can be a source of error and illusion. We don't have to reject them; rather, we must learn to distinguish illusion from reality. The optimistic attitude is to say, "I am in darkness. My eyes do not perceive reality. Therefore, I must turn my gaze away from illusion to begin to see the light." We should continue to use our senses, but in a more cautious way.

Plato continued the text, saying: "This is a strange situation and strange prisoners. If they could talk together, do you think that they would take for real the shadows they see?" At this point, the discussion taking place in this allegory targets a kind of science based on illusions. Let us imagine, for example, that a pen falls on the floor. It is a material reality for you. If you ask someone "What will happen if I drop this pen?" no doubt the answer would be that this object will fall onto the floor. These assumptions come from our experience based on our senses. It is for us a material reality, whereas for Plato it is an illusory reality. The pen falls from our point of view. It is a vision related entirely to our perception and the world in which we live. This is a different reality if we consider the universe. This is why prisoners can create a science on which they all agree that, however, is not absolute.

But the allegory is not pessimistic. Something or someone can change our condition.

"Now consider," continues Plato, "what will happen to them naturally if they are delivered from their chains and cured of their ignorance." Here is the tipping point. Plato explains that a prisoner chained from birth cannot imagine freeing himself if he has no such example around him. Someone surrounded by materialists will rarely find different views of reality. He could stay in this situation and continue to consider the material world as the only reality. Our soul is so shadowed by our body that an external action is necessary to free us from the illusions. Therefore, philosophers or initiates must deliver prisoners from their chains.

As the prisoners are ignorant of their condition, the philosopher or initiator must break their chains, force them to stand up and turn around. The Greek word *metanoia* expresses this idea of modification of the gaze, of conversion. The word can be taken in the religious sense, but it is fundamentally a change of viewpoint. Prisoners must leave their lifelong beliefs. This can be perceived as a violent act, because seeing the light after being so long in the darkness is painful and difficult.

This conversion is accomplished in the Platonic philosophy through questioning. The philosopher will trigger a modification of the prisoner's gaze through a series of questions that are straightforward, simple, and lead to a better awareness of our contradictions. Eventually, they help us to unveil reality. At the beginning, we must accept the idea that something else exists beyond what was previously considered as real. Then we can accept turning away from the depths of the cave to begin the initiatic process of leaving it. Those who refuse will remain jailed and unconscious in this subterranean world. Perhaps their chains will even be thicker and heavier. Perhaps they will try to kill the philosopher or the initiator, as has happened several times in the past.

We should remember that here we are analyzing an allegory, a symbolic text. As such, it must be interpreted. The prisoner in the cave is the image of the soul imprisoned in the body. It must free itself to return to the spiritual world, to reconnect with its source and reach the truth. But, like the prisoners in the cave, this soul has forgotten its origin: it has lost all memory of the ideal world in which it lived before its birth. We can then ask ourselves how the idea of liberation might appear.

Metempsychosis is linked to reminiscence. In another myth, Plato explains that as we die, we symbolically cross an arid and hot plain. The souls who walk on this plain feel a great thirst. There is a river on the other side. All the souls who cannot control themselves rush and drink abundantly. Others drink moderately or not at all. This river of forgetfulness is called Lethe. The souls who have drunk abundantly will forget all about their past lives. Those who have not drunk a drop, like the soul of Pythagoras, will remember all their previous lives. When the souls come back in a new physical life, one of several situations will occur. Either the soul will retain all its memory, or it will only feel a diffuse, imprecise memory, like the desire for something noble. The soul will feel a kind of nostalgia for the ideal world. If the soul has lost all memories, no interest at all for spiritual ideas will exist.

Let us consider more precisely the first two cases. The first situation of full memory is that of an initiate, a philosopher such as Pythagoras, Socrates, or Plato. The soul is fully aware of what it has experienced in its past lives and in between. The initiate living in this material world is pushed by his memory to go back to his source, the ideal world. This is an individual initiative, carried out without external help.

In the second case, which most of us experience, we feel a certain nostalgia for this spiritual world, along with a lack in our lives, a desire to overcome our material condition. Awkwardly at times, we pass from one ideal to another, without finding satisfaction. Then one day we realize that the emptiness is the effect of this nostalgia of the spiritual world. Plato calls this *reminiscence*: the unconscious memory of the ideal world, in which we knew the Truth.

Anyone who begins an initiatic path, a spiritual quest, has been in such a situation at some point in their life. We are as prisoners in a cave, pushed by a desire to look for an initiator. A proverb says "The master arrives when the student is ready." The latter will open his eyes and recognize the master. At this moment only, when the desire is strong enough, the initiation can begin. Reminiscence and desire are the unconscious sources of our will to undertake the path of initiation. We can say that this desire comes from us, lying deep within our being. But we need the help of someone who knows the way, because our memory is incomplete. The remaining part was just enough to wake us up.

After turning our back to the darkness, we must discover the path that takes us out of the cave. For this, we need a guide. Imagine you want to climb a tall mountain and are inexperienced. It is much safer to follow a guide than to try to do it on your own. But a guide is not a guru. We need not agree blindly on everything as the only truth. In the Western tradition, reason is always present in this process. The initiator or philosopher works with the initiate's intelligence. He does not ask for blind faith. He asks him to open his mind, to be ready to challenge himself, to listen to his advice, to rely on his experience, but to keep his free will. With all this, the ascent can begin. Note that I said there is a need to use the candidate's intelligence: the initiator is the one who allows the initiate to find his center, but the way itself is internal. A true initiation transforms not only the inner being but also the outer being.

This process could be a psychological work, a therapy, or a psychoanalysis. However, this allegory suggests a more spiritual way: philosophy and initiation. It is not enough to say "know thyself and you will know the Universe and the Gods" and sit down. We must learn to know ourselves by using a particular technique based on three parts: theoretical study using philosophy, practice of initiatic rituals within a genuine tradition, and faith in the completion of this process.

We can now ask what happens when the initiator helps the prisoner to free himself. Here is what the text says: "Let one of these prisoners be detached, be forced to stand immediately, turn his neck, walk, and raise his eyes to the light. By doing all these movements he will suffer, and the dazzling light will prevent him from distinguishing those objects of which he saw the shadows." These injunctions seem to constrain the prisoner. As a matter of fact, when this kind of initiation takes place, the candidate is passive. He is not asked to look up, but the initiator forces him to look at this light. He may suffer temporarily. The brightness of the first light will blind him, and he may have a less clear perception than when he began his ascent. We should not be surprised by this. The first step following the discovery of light is confusion and darkness, but this situation will not last indefinitely. The remembrance of what was once perceptible in the cavern will be more vivid than the first glimmering that he is perceiving.

The mind is what allows the soul to be stable. Faith is present through the manifestation of desire, but stability comes from the use of our reason. This is why it is very important that the initiator also solicit the candidate's intellect.

The text continues: "If we force him to look at the light itself, will not his eyes be wounded? Would he not run away from it to return to the things he can look upon, and will he not believe that the latter are really more distinct than those which are shown to him?" We know that light can hurt the eyes, so there may be a great temptation to turn away from it and return to previous errors. It is more comfortable to spend your life in certainties rather than challenging yourself. If you want peace, it is probably better to choose faith or even materialism over initiation and philosophy. But if you want to seek the truth, then questioning is fundamental.

The text goes on to describe this initiatic path: "And if we remove him by force from his cave, make him climb the steep path, and bring him under the sunlight, do you think he will suffer and will complain about this violence? And when eventually he reaches the light, his eyes dazzled by this brightness, do you think he will be able to distinguish these things we now call true?"

Plato describes a progression that is necessary to accustom the soul to its new environment: "First, he will look at the shadows that are easier to distinguish, then the reflection in the water of men and other objects, and eventually the objects themselves. After this, during the night, he will be able to see the celestial bodies and the heavens more easily."

Let us recall the progression in this allegory. After his conversion, the prisoner saw the wall and the puppets moving above it. He understood that the shadows were merely illusions. Beyond, he distinguished the fire that burned on a small hill. This fire, which can be found in most of the initiatic temples, is the image of the sun, still inaccessible. It is the first step toward the perception of the real light, which can only be interior and intelligible. This is the light of the spirit.

The prisoner will rise and cross the first veil of illusion, recognizing light for the first time. This fire is the first appearance of truth. He will thus be able to continue his ascent and finally go outside the cave. But the initiator knows very well that the candidate cannot leave the cave without preparation. He could not bear the truth. Symbolically, he would become blind and go back into the darkness. Therefore, it is necessary to go out during the night and look at the starry sky only through its reflection on a lake. This progression is important. The order of the world is revealed during the night through its projection on the mirror of the lake.

Then the sun will appear. It will not be an image refracted like fire or the stars, but the sun itself. Gradually it will reveal itself in all its splendor to the initiate's consciousness. As Plato says: "In the end, I imagine, it will be the sun—not its vain images reflected in the waters or in some other place—but the sun itself in its true place, which he can see and contemplate as it is." The expression "see and contemplate" should be highlighted. These words express the overcoming of rationality and the attainment of contemplation. This is what we find in other Platonist texts, for example, the *Symposium*. This contemplation corresponds with the moment when the soul merges with the object of its quest. This experience gives birth to an inner understanding of the Cosmos and the One. With this distance removed, we can contemplate the sun as it is.

"After that he will conclude that this is the sun that makes the seasons and the years, governs everything in the visible world, and in a certain way was the cause of all he saw in the cave." This declaration should be considered symbolically. Indeed, the sun was not directly the cause of the shadows in the cave. The fire on the small hill was a symbolic image of the sun. This text describes something different from the real sun. It is the *nous*, the One, the All. This sun is the source of all things, the primary cause. Therefore, Truth is accessible to the initiate who wishes to rise toward it.

"Now," writes Plato, "remembering his first condition, the kind of wisdom that is taught there, and his companions in captivity, do you think that he will rejoice only of his own change or be sad for them?" Suddenly, he will realize the difference between his new situation and the previous one.

The initiate cannot fully enjoy having found the truth while thinking that there are still prisoners in the cave. He has a duty to them: even if it is difficult, he should go back to the cave. However, in the same way that he came out of the cave, his eyes will be obscured, as his knowledge is now different.

Trying to explain what he saw outside the cave could be almost impossible. The prisoners will laugh at him. To speak about an inner experience is something extremely delicate, and we should expect to be misunderstood. This is why Socrates, for the most part, abstained from teaching a doctrine. On the contrary, he preferred using questions to help others find the truth for themselves. But this process is risky. We know very well that for politics and religion, the risk is always present for those who encourage freedom and the exercise of critical thinking.

As Plato wrote, "And if anyone tries to free them and force them to leave this place, do you think they will try to kill him instead of suffering?" The answer is evident.

The initiatic path leading to the discovery of truth is hazardous. The allegory of the cave vividly explains our condition and goal: there is a real world, and reaching it is possible for those who have a real desire. While we must not believe that we will immediately find peace, the initiatic or philosophical path may help us to achieve this essential goal.

The progression may not be spectacular and will be marked by suffering. However, each step will bring us closer to this spiritual light. Then, when after our death we will cross this dry plain, perhaps we will better control our thirst and return to the cave, having kept our memory intact.

Bibliography

A bibliography can be interesting and useful. As you may imagine, since the beginning of Freemasonry until today, much has been written about this topic and the subjects related to esotericism. There are countless philosophers, Hermetists, and modern writers like myself.

Today, the internet gives us access to a lot of information and ancient texts. New translations of these texts are published from time to time, and it is a good idea to discover them. The *Corpus Hermeticum* (books of Hermes) is a good example of an improved translation.

Finally, I want to emphasize that with one exception, the books I mention here are not novels but tools. Don't feel you must read all the parts from beginning to end. Take the parts you like and carefully read the chapters you want to use. Leave the chapters that interest you less right now for another time.

Here are some authors and titles that can be helpful if you want to go further. Don't forget websites as well. They are good places to find information, even if it is sometimes more difficult to discern the true and the false, unlike with books, which are usually more reliable.

Books

All the books by E. A. Wallis Budge.

Crata Repoa: Initiation into the Ancient Mysteries of the Egyptian Priests, 1821.

The Constitutions of the Free-Masons by James Anderson A.M., 1734.

Duncan's Masonic Ritual and Monitor by Malcolm C. Duncan, 1866.

Egyptian Rite of Freemasonry Rituals by Cagliostro.

La Franche-Maçonnerie Rendue à sa Véritable Origine by Alexandre Lenoir, 1814.

Freemasonry in Olden Times by Robert Ambelain, 1985.

Literature of ancient Egypt (several editions are available): *Egyptian Book of the Dead, Book of Amduat, Book of Gates, Book of Breathing, Book of Hours.*

The Lost Keys of Freemasonry by Manly P. Hall, 1923.

Napoleon's Sorcerers: The Sophisians by Darius A. Spieth, 1970.

Ordre des Sophisiens by Jean-Marie Ragon.

Pour la Rose Rouge et la Croix d'Or by J. P. Giudicelli de Cressac Bachelerie, 1988.

Le Rameau d'Or d'Eleusis by Jacques-Etienne Marconis de Nègre, 1863.

The Secret Teachings of All Ages by Manly P. Hall, 1928.

Sethos by Abbé Terrasson, 1761.

Websites

I invite you to visit my Facebook page (www.facebook.com/jeanlouis.debiasi) and my website (www.debiasi.org). I regularly post original blogs and documents on topics related to this book. I also share updates from some of the following websites:

Aurum Solis: www.aurumsolis.org

Egyptian Book of the Dead: You can download this book from my website at www.debiasi.org.

Jeremy Norman's HistoryofInformation.com (general history and archaeology): www.historyofinformation.com

The Mason's Lady (women and Freemasonry): www.themasonslady.com

M. W. National Grand Lodge of Egyptian Freemasons: www.egyptianfreemasonry.org

Phoenixmasonry Masonic Museum and Library: www.phoenixmasonry.org

Pietre-Stones Review of Freemasonry: www.freemasons-freemasonry.com

Sacred Order of the Sophisians: www.sophisians.org

Figures

Chapter 5: From Esoteric Freemasonry to Egyptian Freemasonry

1: Scarab in lapis lazuli used in French Egyptian Freemasonry, circa 1780.
(Courtesy of the Château de Mongenan, France.)

2: Masonic plate showing a Masonic allegory in an
Egyptian setting, circa nineteenth century.
(Courtesy of the Museum of the Grand Orient de France, Paris.)

Chapter 8: The Sacred Order of the Sophisians

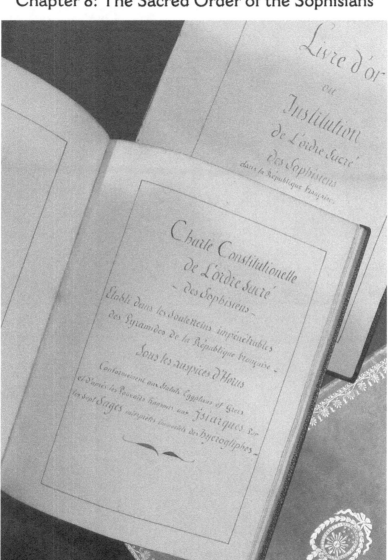

3: Book of the constitutions of the Sacred Order of the Sophisians, circa 1801.
(Courtesy of the Museum of the Grand Orient de France, Paris.)

4: The author beside the pyramid tomb of one of the founders of the Sacred Order
of the Sophisians, located in the famous Père Lachaise Cemetery in Paris.
(Courtesy of the author.)

5: The head of the Sacred Order of the Sophisians
after the interview about this Egyptian Masonic tradition.
(Courtesy of the author.)

Chapter 9: The Masonic Lodge

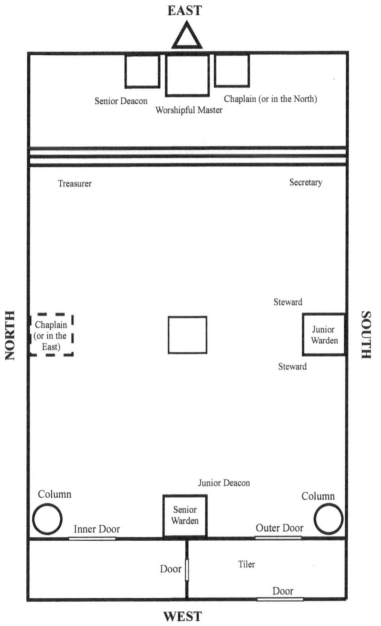

6: Blueprint of a Masonic lodge in mainstream Freemasonry.

7: Masonic lodge room in the Château de Mongenan (France).
All the tools, artifacts, and Masonic regalia are genuine
and date back to the eighteenth century.
(Courtesy of the Château de Mongenan, France.)

8: Symbols that can be used on the east wall of your Masonic lodge.

9: Masonic plate in the Egyptian style, circa nineteenth century.
The link to symbols used on the east wall is obvious.
(Courtesy of the Museum of the Grand Orient de France, Paris.)

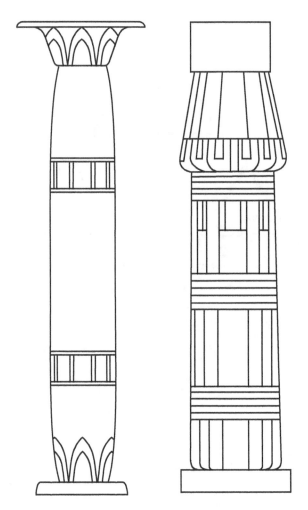

10: Two styles of Egyptian columns used in Egyptian Freemasonry.
They were painted, and you can find the colors in the section
dedicated to this book on my website (www.debiasi.org).

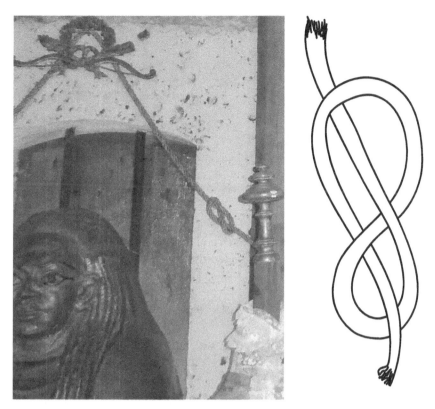

11: The cord that surrounds the lodge room has twelve figure-eight knots, also called *love knots*. (Courtesy of the author.)

Chapter 10: The Officers

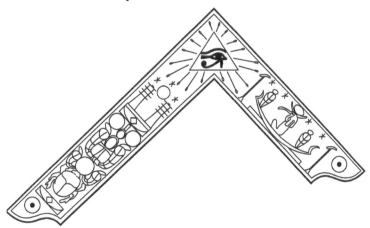

12: Example of a square worn by the Worshipful Master in Egyptian Freemasonry.

Chapter 11: The Tools

13: Interlacing of the square and the compass
in the first degree, Entered Apprentice.

14: Interlacing of the square and the compass
in the second degree, Fellowcraft.

15: Interlacing of the square and the compass
in the third degree, Master Mason.

16: Pentalpha

17: Sacred book. The sacred book used in Egyptian Freemasonry can be the famous *Egyptian Book of the Dead*. The square and the compass interlacing is shown at the first degree.

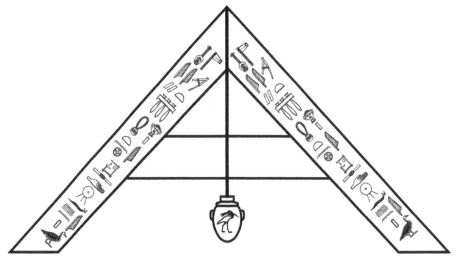

18: Level.

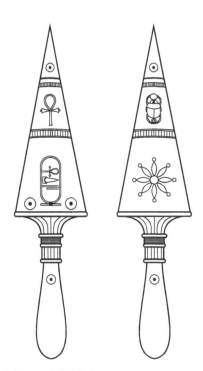

19: Trowel. This instrument was used
in the ceremonies linked to death and rebirth.

Rods, Staffs, and Scepters

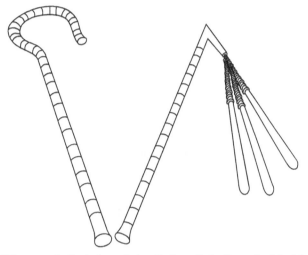

20: The crook (*heka*) and the flail or flabellum (*nekhakha*).
These were the two main items in the
royal regalia of a pharaoh in ancient Egypt.

21: Scepter.
This instrument was used in
various rituals of Egyptian Freemasonry.
(Courtesy of the author.)

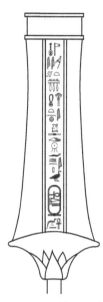

22: Sekhem. This scepter was used in ancient Egypt and is still used in rituals of the Sacred Order of the Sophisians.

23: Sword. Masonic blazing sword of the Marquis de Lafayette. (Courtesy of the Museum of the Grand Orient de France, Paris.)

24: Gavel.

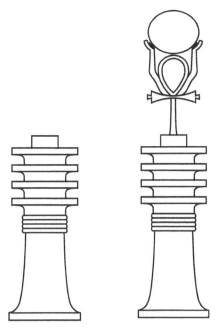

25: Djed pillar. Here are two examples of Djed pillars used in the
third initiation of some Egyptian Masonic groups.

26: Skirret.

Chapter 12: The Masonic Regalia

27: Masonic apron with Egyptian scenery, circa 1850.
(Courtesy of the Museum of the Grand Orient de France, Paris.)

Chapter 14: Rituals and Practices of the Three Degrees

28: Black-and-white mosaic. This design can be found in many lodge rooms and is used in the practice of the mystical gate.

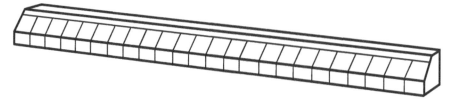

29: 24-inch gauge. This type of Egyptian rod has been found in several tombs of architects and is used in the practice of the 24-inch gauge.

30: Prayer beads. (Courtesy of the author.)

Chapter 15: The High Degrees of Egyptian Freemasonry

31: The great seal of the Rite of Misraim.
(Courtesy of the Museum of the Grand Orient de France, Paris.)

Chapter 17: Consecration of the Lodge

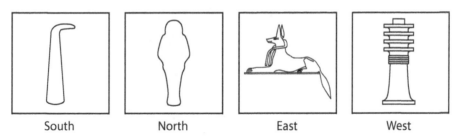

| South | North | East | West |

32: Four tesserae with the symbols of the cardinal directions.

33: Cartouche with Egyptian hieroglyphs meaning life, prosperity, and strength.
(Courtesy of the author.)

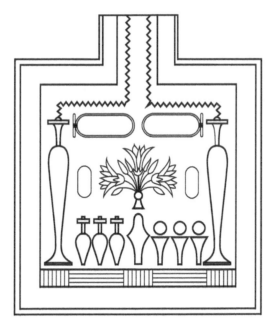

34: Offerings. This is an example of an Egyptian offering table.

Chapter 18: Cagliostro and the Mysteries of the Prophetess

35: Giuseppe Balsamo, Comte di Cagliostro, 1786.
(Courtesy of the National Gallery of Art, Washington, DC.)

36: Signature of the Comte di Cagliostro.

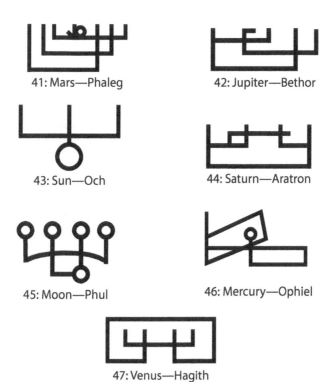

41: Mars—Phaleg

42: Jupiter—Bethor

43: Sun—Och

44: Saturn—Aratron

45: Moon—Phul

46: Mercury—Ophiel

47: Venus—Hagith

37: Seven seals of the spirits.

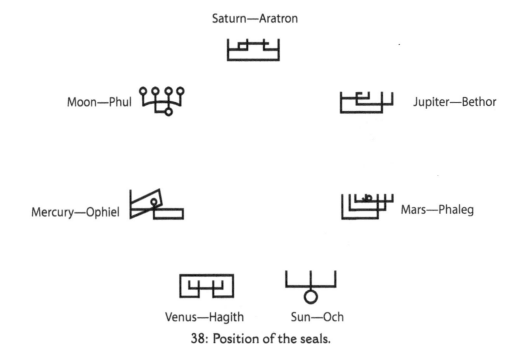

Saturn—Aratron

Moon—Phul

Jupiter—Bethor

Mercury—Ophiel

Mars—Phaleg

Venus—Hagith   Sun—Och

38: Position of the seals.

To Write to the Author

If you wish to contact the author or would like more information about this book, please write to the author in care of Llewellyn Worldwide Ltd. and we will forward your request. Both the author and the publisher appreciate hearing from you and learning of your enjoyment of this book and how it has helped you. Llewellyn Worldwide Ltd. cannot guarantee that every letter written to the author can be answered, but all will be forwarded. Please write to:

Jean-Louis de Biasi
℅ Llewellyn Worldwide
2143 Wooddale Drive
Woodbury, MN 55125-2989

Please enclose a self-addressed stamped envelope for reply,
or $1.00 to cover costs. If outside the U.S.A., enclose
an international postal reply coupon.

Many of Llewellyn's authors have websites with additional information and resources. For more information, please visit our website at www.llewellyn.com.